The Golden Fleece

Muriel Spark was born in Edinburgh in 1918 and was raised and educated there. After some married years living in Africa, she returned to England, where she edited *Poetry Review* from 1947 to 1949 and published her first volume of poems, *The Fanfarlo: and Other Verse*, in 1952. In the early 1960s she worked in New York, eventually making her home in Italy. Her many novels include *Memento Mori* (1959), *The Prime of Miss Jean Brodie* (1961), *The Girls of Slender Means* (1963), *The Abbess of Crewe* (1974), *A Far Cry from Kensington* (1988) and *The Finishing School* (2004). Her short stories were collected in 1967, 1985 and 2001, and her *Collected Poems I* appeared in 1967. Dame Muriel was made Commandeur des Arts et des Lettres (France) in 1996 and awarded her DBE in 1993. She died in Italy on 13th April 2006, at the age of 88.

Also by Muriel Spark from Carcanet Press

Curriculum Vitae
All the Poems
Mary Shelley

THE GOLDEN FLEECE

ESSAYS

MURIEL SPARK

Edited by Penelope Jardine

CARCANET

First published in Great Britain in 2014 by
Carcanet Press Limited
Alliance House
Cross Street
Manchester M2 7AQ

www.carcanet.co.uk

Selection and editorial matter copyright © Penelope Jardine 2014
Texts by Muriel Spark copyright © Copyright Administration Limited 2014

The right of Penelope Jardine to be identified as the editor of this work has been asserted by her in accordance with the Copyright, Designs and Patents Act of 1988
All rights reserved

A CIP catalogue record for this book is available from the British Library

ISBN 978 1 84777 251 0

The publisher acknowledges financial assistance from Arts Council England

Supported by
ARTS COUNCIL
ENGLAND

Typeset in Garamond by R. J. Footring Ltd, Derby
Printed and bound in England by SRP Ltd, Exeter

Contents

Preface ix

Part I. Art and Poetry
The Golden Fleece 3
The First Christmas Eve 6
Love 8
Ravenna: City of Mosaics 11
The Art of Verse 16
Ruskin and Read 18
Robert Burns 18
Andrew Young 22
Giacomo Manzù 23
The Desegregation of Art. The Blashfield Address to the American Academy and Institute of Arts and Letters, New York 26
The Wisdom of Mr T.S. Eliot 31
Ingersoll Foundation – T.S. Eliot Award 33
Pensée: T.S. Eliot 35
The Complete Frost 36
John Masefield 38
Decorative Art 44
Poetry and Politics 44
Emily Brontë 46

Part II. Autobiography and Travel
My Most Memorable New Year's Eve 57
When I Was Ten 57
Pensée: Scottish Education 58
My Book of Life 58
Note on My Story 'The Gentile Jewesses' 59

The Celestial Garden Party	60
What Images Return	63
Comment on 'The Poet's House'	66
The Poet's House	66
Footnote to 'The Poet's House'	70
My Madeleine	73
How I Became a Novelist	74
The Writing Life	77
Living in Rome	80
Venice	84
Istanbul	89
Tuscany By Chance	94
The Sitter's Tale	99
Italian Days	99
The David Cohen British Literature Prize, 1997	102

Part III. Literature

How to Write a Letter	107
Our Dearest Emma	110
Passionate Humbugs	110
Pensée: Biography	112
Fuzzy Young Person	113
The Brontës as Teachers	114
My Favourite Villain: Heathcliff	121
Mrs Gaskell	123
Mary Shelley. Proposal for a Critical Biography and Note	124
Mary Shelley: Wife to a Genius	126
Frankenstein and *The Last Man*	130
Shelley's Last House	137
The Essential Stevenson	140
Robert Louis Stevenson	142
Celebrating Scotland	143
The Books I Re-Read and Why	143
London Exotics	144
A Drink with Dame Edith	147
Pensée: *Miss Brodie* on the Stage	150
The Short Story	151
Daughter of the Soil	151
Heinrich Böll	155
Eyes and Noses	155
Simenon: A Phenomenal Writer	157

CONTENTS

The Book I Would Like to Have Written, and Why	160
Pensée: The Supernatural	161

Part IV. Religion, Politics and Philosophy

Testament of Faith	165
Ailourophilia	166
All God's Creatures	168
The Sermons of Newman	176
Newman's Journals	180
An Exile's Path	181
A Sleep of Prisoners	182
Psychic Searchlight	183
A Pardon for the Guy	184
The Religion of an Agnostic. A Sacramental View of the World in the Writings of Proust	186
The Only Problem	191
The Mystery of Job's Suffering	192
An Unknown Author	197
Man's Estate	199
Kierkegaard	201
Karl Heim: Two Important Works	201
Letter from Rome: The Elder Statesmen	203
Ritual and Recipe	211
The Next World and Back	212

Publishing History

Part I. Art and Poetry	213
Part II. Autobiography and Travel	215
Part III. Literature	218
Part IV. Religion, Politics and Philosophy	221

Index of Names	224

Preface

Good literary essays, in particular, have sustaining and stimulating qualities, like deep wells and clear rivers.*

Muriel Spark asked me to collect her essays, reviews, journalism, interviews, broadcasts, speeches, opinions – in other words, her prose writing – and make a selection for publication, while helping her with her other work: that is to say, keeping an eye on her books with publishers all over the world, business correspondence, card indexes and filing. (Her archive is extensive and mainly to be found in the National Library of Scotland, Edinburgh, and the McFarlin Library at the University of Tulsa.)

In the long-ago summer of 1991 Muriel rented a house for the month of July on the German island of Sylt in the North Sea, off Denmark. We drove up to North Schleswig and put the car on a double-decker open train, which raced out to the island on a causeway from Niebüll. Sylt is a popular holiday island, long and thin, with one side exposed to the elements with sand-dunes and cliffs; the other, landward side, faces a shallow inland water with a ribbon of sand inhabited by wading birds. Here, in Kampen, I spread out a lifetime of Muriel's essays and reviews.

Little did I know then how many years were to pass before I would have sorted these down to a selection for this volume. Soon after this almost idyllic holiday, Muriel decided she must have a hip operation and that was the beginning of years of pain for her, operations to put things right which didn't, and which took up all her days and nights and energy. What she did achieve in those following years was quite

---

*Muriel Spark, in her book choice, *Sunday Telegraph Review*, 30 November 2003 (Frank Kermode's collection of essays, *Pieces of My Mind*).

astonishing. She published her own volume of autobiography, *Curriculum Vitae*, in 1992 and, despite being in and out of hospital until 1995, she continued to publish and write. In 1996 she published a new novel, *Reality and Dreams*. She was to publish two more novels (*Aiding and Abetting* and *The Finishing School*) before she died in 2006.

Those latter years were, unfortunately, not as peaceful as they should have been: family problems and an unauthorised biography took away a lot of joy and undermined her courage. Her sense of adventure was not diminished, however, and we set off for long journeys by car to Spain, to Portugal, to Berlin, for congresses, British Council events and literary festivals.

In a 2003 interview, when she had just finished her last novel, Muriel said that she was going to concentrate on another volume of memoirs. She made notes and yes, she meant this then, but in fact her next book was to have been another novel, *Destiny*. I think she really was not inspired enough to write about herself and all the difficulties as well as all the joys of her life. She knew them all, they were past, they no longer interested her. Besides, she felt, as Graham Greene did, that as you went on your autobiography involved too many other living people. She really wanted to get on with the excitements of creation and the idea for a new novel nearly always crept into her dreams and devoured her attention.

Journalists demand to know 'What is your favourite book?', 'Who is your favourite author?', 'What book would you like to have written?', 'Which writer do you admire most?', 'Who has influenced your writing?' and so on. By nature, a writer's journalism must contain a certain amount of autobiography. Some of Muriel Spark's answers provided here to such questions reveal, I think, huge areas of her experience and idiosyncrasies, which are not to be found in essays on Cardinal Newman or reviews of C. Day Lewis's poems. I hope that some of the short pieces and *pensées* in this volume will therefore, in some measure, fill the gap of Muriel's unwritten memoirs.

So, after many interruptions, I sorted these prose pieces down to a selection of her thoughts on art and poetry, her autobiographical pieces and travel, her writings on literature and finally some mixed religious, political and philosophical essays and reviews. The outcome is a book which, I believe, tells many things, mainly about the author Muriel Spark, and I hope throws light on how she felt when young, in tune with the solitary sadness of the Brontës; how she was inspired as a writer and became a Roman Catholic from reading Cardinal Newman; how amused she was by some of the curiosities that came her way to review, such as *Our Dearest Emma*, the crazy Abbot Aelred (who is not included here) and the fashionable tattooist Professor Burchardt; her empathy with Mary Shelley waiting for Shelley's boat to return to San Terenzo and her later struggle in London to support her son, Percy, so like Muriel's own hard times, as, virtually, a widow or a single mother she fought to support her own son.

I would like to say here that the essay, often quoted by scholars, entitled 'My Conversion', published in *Twentieth Century*, CLXX, autumn 1961, was not an essay of Muriel Spark's but an interview she gave to a priest, who wrote his own version of what she said in reply to his questions. They were not her own expressions: it was his essay, and it was his title. In fact she had nothing to 'convert' from. She embraced Christianity of her own free choice, first Anglicanism and then Roman Catholicism. Her family were mixed Jewish and Protestant and they didn't object. Her father rarely went to the synagogue because, as a working man, he was working on the Sabbath. Her mother seems to have hedged her bets and had menorah, crosses and Buddhas, as well as a statue of the Venus de Milo for good measure. For them, what was good for Muriel was good.

I am struck, on reading the many essays and reviews of half a century ago, by the extent to which God and religion have now gone out of our daily lives. In the 1950s and 1960s it was natural that in any article, book or radio talk on the arts, literature, music, painting, and also science, these subjects would almost always be viewed or reviewed in relation to our inner spiritual values, with references to God, some deity at least, and religion in general.

I found that most of the pieces I selected fell into some sort of category, such as 'Art' or 'History' or 'Travel'. Inevitably, there is a preponderance of writing which could be defined as 'Literature': essays on other writers, reviews of books, opinions on the classics. Muriel reviewed weekly for the London *Observer* for approximately ten years; consequently there are many short commentaries on books of the time with interesting titles that have entered the language, such as *Not Waving but Drowning* or *The Loneliness of the Long-distance Runner*. It was tempting to include these here for their charm, like credits in early films which 'introduce' Shirley Temple, Marilyn Monroe or James Dean. But they didn't in the end quite merit selection.

I have begun this book with the essay titled 'The Golden Fleece', since it was one of Muriel's earliest essays, published in 1948. The story of this ancient Greek myth must have appealed to Muriel's early passion for the savagery of the Border Ballads and as a story it lacks none of the many dramas of life: love, adventure, adversity, betrayal, success, triumph, cruelty and loss. It is all there.

For the sake of avoiding repetition, I have had to omit a paragraph or two in some of the pieces, indicated by ellipses. Very occasionally I have added a missing word, indicating this with square brackets. In the case of certain essays where history has altered the truth of some statements, I have left the original text and provided footnotes. Some of the early essays probably do not incorporate recent scholarship, but I have included them for what they say historically.

Titles have been chosen according to my instinct. Muriel Spark's own titles for her pieces were frequently changed by newspaper editors. Sometimes Muriel's original title has prevailed, but not always, since the newspaper's published title can be more appropriate. Occasionally I have given a simplified version in preference to either, such as just 'Venice' for 'Venice out of Season' or 'Venice in Fall and Winter'. Even Venice has changed since those far-off days of 1981: every season is in season and you may no longer visit Venice without tourists.

It has been difficult to trace some of the many reviews from earlier days, their titles, publishers and dates. There are also some existing typescripts without provenance, telling nothing of whether they were ever published and if so when and by whom. And in one or two cases even Muriel herself was not sure whether she had written something or not and whether it was published. The information online is not entirely reliable either.

Fortunately Muriel kept her mind until the last day of her life and was always lucid. I asked her to look at most of the articles that have been included here and tell me whether she would like them published or not. She read them again, rejecting several and lightly touching up others for spelling, punctuation and meaning. I have tried to follow her instructions, which included 'tick', 'OK', 'maybe' or 'perhaps', 'to be revised', 'omit', 'touch up', 'hold', 'combine'. These were quite easy to agree with, but of course I could not 'touch up' or 'revise'. Some of these pieces are in the present book, un-touched-up and not revised. Others have been dropped.

Although I have sought to include a wide selection, I have eliminated many essays, and reviews in particular, on books or subjects which I suspect are no longer of general interest. I have here and there chosen a piece of writing which I think shows Muriel Spark's thoughts on a subject of curiosity, such as 'Cannibalism' or 'Tattooing', or a reply to a question which shows an aspect of her life, such as 'My Most Memorable New Year's Eve'. Tattooing was at the time of writing less fashionable than it is today and a rarity outside of sailors' dockside bars.

There arose the difficulty of placing an essay in a suitable category. Essays on subjects such as 'Cats' I feel instinctively belong to 'Art and Poetry', but are also suitable to be placed here under 'Autobiography and Travel'. They might even be at home in 'Religion' or 'Philosophy'. There is no end to where cats might not pop up.

Many of the early reviews mention 'Mr' or 'Miss' So-and-So, which now feels old-fashioned. In most cases I have changed this by omitting the titles and inserting first names.

Like her character Mrs Hawkins in her novel *A Far Cry from Kensington*, Muriel was always ready to help a friend with sensible and good advice. She was not over-influenced by other writers, but some certainly encouraged and inspired her: the Poet Laureate John Masefield for his narrative talent and charm; Cardinal Newman for his clarity of vision and exquisite prose; Max Beerbohm for his style and wit; Henry James for his wonderful stories and perspicacity.

Muriel Spark was a natural-born communicator: few people who saw her on stage at a reading or public event will have forgotten her wit and sense of irreverent fun. In 2003 she answered a journalist from *Il Messaggero* newspaper in Rome by saying, 'It is my first aim always to give pleasure.' In this she was similar to Nabokov, who also wrote with brevity and wit. In his Introduction to Nabokov's *Lectures on Russian Literature*, Fredson Bowers specified that 'the magic Nabokov felt so keenly in literature should be aimed at pleasure'. Even the literary critic Frank Kermode, in his Preface to *Pieces of My Mind*, wrote of criticism that 'in paying tribute, or even when cavilling, ... [it] must also give pleasure, like the other arts'.

Many students and fans have testified over the years to the way in which Muriel Spark's books changed their lives. As a writer she was enormously hard-working and utterly dedicated, to the exclusion, often, of many passing distractions. This did not mean that she did not enjoy life greatly when it came her way, but that first and foremost came her work and she fought like a tiger to get this out to the world to read. Her work was truly a vocation for her. She took literature in a sense as a religion. She believed in her talent for writing and had plenty to say, so that she devoted herself to it as to a calling. In her essay 'What Images Return' she wrote: 'Myself, I have had to put up a psychological fight for my spiritual joy.'

Muriel did not actually think of herself as 'exiled' from anywhere. The *OED* defines 'exile' as 'penal banishment, long absence from one's country, also figuratively, and a banished person (lit. & fig.)'. She was not banished literally or figuratively, and returned to Scotland to visit throughout her long life, but she did not live there again or feel exiled from the life there. It was more a place of memory, where you have lived but no longer live, like visiting the past to which you are unable to return. She had a difficult life and her sharp wit, what John Updike once called her 'sweet sting', which she used to amuse and brighten people up, was her own courageous way of overcoming difficulties. None of her several biographers seems to have picked this up – neither her brave and generous spirit nor the optimism and joy of her personality, which I hope show in the autobiographical pieces.

Muriel Spark's novels are fundamentally story-telling and, like the student in Vladimir Nabokov's class at Cornell who was asked his reason for taking the course, I too join the course here 'because I like stories'. So I start with a story, not a new one but an old, a very old one: the exciting story of Jason and the Golden Fleece.

Penelope Jardine
2014

Part I

Art and Poetry

Art is an act of daring
The Finishing School

The Golden Fleece

One of the most interesting commissions ever entrusted to a goldsmith was that given to Jehan Peut of Bruges, in 1432, by the Duke of Burgundy, for twenty-five collars of the Order of the Golden Fleece. In the archives of Lille there still exists a record of 1080 *livres* received by Peut for his work. We can imagine with what pride he applied his skill to every feature and lineament of the insignia, which was to become the symbol of one of the most coveted Orders of Chivalry in Europe.

'The golden fleece' has had a mystical significance in the literature of the world since the third century BC. The story, although a familiar one, loses none of its charm in the re-telling. According to the old Greek legends, two young relatives of the King of Thessaly named Helle and Phrixus had so incurred the displeasure of their stepmother that she decided to kill them. She was prevented from doing so, however, by a golden ram with wings, sent by the gods to carry the boy and girl away. Helle fell off the ram's back into the sea, now called the Hellespont after her. Phrixus came safely to land at Colchis, where he immediately sacrificed the ram as a thanksgiving to Zeus. The ram's marvellous golden fleece he hung upon the branch of a tree, in a garden guarded by a fierce dragon.

Legend tells us further how the King of Thessaly, desiring to dispose of his nephew Jason, the rightful heir to the throne, claimed that the golden fleece belonged to his household. Believing that the recovery of the fleece was an impossibility, the King commanded Jason to fetch it, hoping that he would be lost through the perils of the journey. Jason was undaunted. Runners were dispatched to all parts of Greece, calling on the heroes of mythology to join the young prince on his dangerous mission. Hercules the giant, Orpheus the singer, Canthus the soothsayer, the twins, Castor and Pollux, and many others came flocking to take part in the adventure. In high spirits the gallant company set sail in the *Argo*, unconcerned that the way to the golden fleece was fraught with direst peril.

However, after many trials, the fleece was finally won with the help of Princess Medea of Colchis, who afterwards married Jason. We are told with what joy and expectations Jason brought the golden fleece back to Thessaly. Instead, however, of regaining his place as heir to the kingdom, Jason fell foul of his uncle, who dispossessed and banished him. Such is the legend.

It was Philip the Good, Duke of Burgundy, who founded the Order of the Golden Fleece on the day of his marriage (January 10) to Princess Isabella of Portugal in 1429–30. History does not record the year with exactitude, nor is it known whether or not Philip was inspired by the ancient legend or whether he chose the name from some other motive. We know, however, that the House of Burgundy had become so powerful during the fourteenth and fifteenth centuries as to rival the Crown itself.

Philip the Good was himself a man who lived a life of high purpose – he devoted himself to the development of culture and learning, and became an enthusiastic protector of the arts. He had records made of Burgundian customs, and the commerce and industry of France thrived under his encouragement. It would seem reasonable to conjecture that, having decided to install a new European Order of Chivalry, Philip turned to the Golden Fleece because of its significance as a symbol of spiritual intervention.

Whatever be the true reason, it is clear that in its design the insignia was in no sense a rich ornament lavishly set with precious gems as one might have expected in those days of rich embellishment and ornamentation. The collar was made of steel, the pattern in the form of an arrangement of the letter B (Burgundy), alternating with firestones. From this simple collar hung the symbolical Golden Fleece forming the badge. The enamelled ring from which the badge hung bore the legend 'Pretium laborum no vile' – 'Not an unworthy reward for our labours'. The Knights were encouraged to wear their insignia constantly, which they did with dignity and pride.

The ceremony of conferring the Order of the Golden Fleece was an elaborate one. A Knight of the Order in a capacity of 'godfather' presented the new member, and a Secretary of high rank delivered a speech of presentation in French. The collar and emblem of the Order were the Knight's property throughout his lifetime, but at his death they reverted to the Order.

At first the Knights of the Golden Fleece were limited to thirty-one, including the Sovereign, who was the Grand Master, but it was later declared that any number might be created from among Catholics;

in the case of Protestants, Papal sanction was required. The Knights' primary duty was to aid the Sovereign in times of war and danger. Periodic meetings or Chapters of the Order were held at which all disputes between Knights were settled.

Who, then, were these Knights of the Golden Fleece who fire our imagination by their chivalry and valour? At first they were chosen from the distinguished houses of Burgundy, the Netherlands and France – men who conformed to the founder's ideal of knightly honour and noble birth. Not all the subsequent Grand Masters of the Order, however, possessed such lofty principles as its founder. As time went on the dispensation of the Order sometimes became a matter of diplomatic expediency.

Although the Order of the Golden Fleece was bestowed for the most part on royalty and men of noble rank, it has not been exclusively so, for in 1898 the Crown of Spain conferred this honour on the President of France, Felix Faure, in recognition of the mediation of France at the termination of the Spanish-American war.

As the dukedom passed from Philip to his son Charles the Bold, so did the Order of the Golden Fleece continue under the aegis of the House of Burgundy. However, when Charles' daughter Mary married Maximilian, Archduke of Austria, a gallant but unreliable gentleman, the Grand Mastership of the Fleece came into the possession of the royal House of Hapsburg. Maximilian's son, on his accession to Castile in 1504, brought the Grand Mastership of the Order to Spain, where it remained until the Hapsburg dynasty became extinct on the death of Charles II.

The Order of the Golden Fleece then reverted to Austria, having been claimed by the Emperor, Charles VI, who installed the Order in Vienna with great pageantry, in 1713. This action was bitterly contested by Philip V of Anjou, inheritor of the Crown of Spain by the will of Charles II. Philip V maintained that the Grand Mastership of the Fleece was irrevocably bound to the throne of Spain, and at the Congress of Cambray he formally protested against the Emperor of Austria's claim. The dispute was settled temporarily by the intervention of England, France and Holland, but a state of ferment still existed, and it was not long before Spain and Austria were again involved in heated argument. No definite solution was ever found. It came to be tacitly accepted that the Order existed in both countries, becoming known either as the Spanish or the Austrian Order of the Golden Fleece.

The Austrian branch of the Order permitted a red ribbon to be substituted, except on occasions of ceremony, when a Knight of the

Golden Fleece must have presented a magnificent appearance. On such occasions he wore a surcoat of deep red velvet lined with white, over which was thrown a purple velvet mantle, white-bordered and lined with white satin. Gold embroidery encrusted with firestones further adorned this splendid attire. His cap was of purple velvet, gold-embroidered, with a small hood attached, and his shoes and stockings were Burgundian red.

Edward IV of England, a kinsman through marriage of the House of Burgundy, was the first English monarch to receive the Order of the Golden Fleece.

Henry VII was invested with the Order in 1491, the year of his signing of the Treaty of Medina del Campo with Maximilian of Austria – a security against their mutual enemy, France.

By his betrothal to Catherine of Aragon, in 1502, Henry VIII was elected to the Order at the 77th Chapter, and his contemporary, James V of Scotland, also became a Knight of the Order. A wardrobe Inventory of James V, dated 1539, records 'The ordure of the Empriour with the golden fleis'.

The history of this romantic Order of Knighthood is recorded for us in the tapestries and embroideries at Berne, embellished with the arms of Burgundy and the insignia of the Golden Fleece, in the banners at Saint Gall, bearing the Fleece device, and in the paintings which remain to us of those men who attained the honour. Notable among these is the Duke of Wellington – one of the few Englishmen to receive the Order – and whose portrait wearing the Golden Fleece is to be seen at the National Portrait Gallery.

[1948]

The First Christmas Eve

It is always good to see a painting in the very surroundings in which it was conceived and made. Frescoes have a greater chance of resting in their original home than other forms of pictorial art, and this is especially fortunate in the case of the fifteenth-century Tuscan artist Piero della Francesca. His mural sequence, *La Leggenda della Vera Croce* (The Legend of the True Cross), for instance, is in perpetual harmony with the interior of the Church of Saint Francis, in Arezzo, whose walls it enlivens. His *Madonna del Parto* (Madonna of Childbirth), although it has been shifted, remains in its native pastoral and fertile environment near the spot where Piero painted it, some time after 1450, on the wall of a church later demolished.* Originally, the fresco was the only adornment of a tiny cemetery chapel which replaced the church, situated below the quiet Tuscan hill town of Monterchi. The picture (which has been moved again to a spot nearby) is easily accessible from the road between Arezzo and Sansepolcro, birthplace of Piero della Francesca and repository of many of his richest works.

Piero's mother came from Monterchi, which is probably why, at the height of his maturity, he accepted the commission to depict the Madonna in so quiet and unimportant a place. Everything about this painting is dramatic. The Madonna is in the last stage of her pregnancy. The Nativity is imminent.

Piero della Francesca was a humanist with a deep sense of the sublime. His Madonna (Our Lady of Childbirth) is a substantial country woman and at the same time a majestic, archetypal figure. In no way is she the sort of Italian girl whom anyone might want to help with her problem: this lady has no problem, she has a purpose. She stands in an ermine-lined tent, a tabernacle.† She is larger than the angels who, like theatre functionaries, draw back the curtains for the audience, the entire human race, to witness Mary's marvellous condition at this hour. She is wearing a practical maternity dress, which unlaces at the side and in the front to accommodate her splendid bigness with child. Her right hand loosens the lacing of her dress, her left hand rests on her hip, palm upward, in a peasant-like gesture of pride, almost defiance. She wears a halo of burnished gold which mysteriously mirrors the pavements of the original church, but not her own head, so that she, like the angels, seems to be transparent in the light of eternity. She bears this halo with the dignity of a local woman of Tuscany balancing a basket of fruit on her head. The curtains of the womb-like tent part to reveal her – as if, about to deliver her child, she is herself about to be delivered from a vaster, cosmic womb.

---

*According to my local telephone directory, which features the fresco on its cover, the *Madonna del Parto* was probably painted in 1445 and discovered at Monterchi in 1888. It has been moved to a local school-house in Monterchi, where it is exhibited in a greatly reduced form with much photographic analysis and information to justify its partial obliteration. Parts of the painting which were not done by Piero della Francesca were removed. When consulted earlier as to whether the fresco should be moved for exhibition in America, the eminent art historian Sir John Pope-Hennessy emphatically said, 'No, on no account should it be moved.'
†This 'ermine-lined tent or tabernacle' has been removed.

It is a Christian devotional picture, that of the first Christmas Eve. But the *Madonna del Parto*, with her radiant and aloof regard, her eyes focused somewhere beyond the ages, seems equally to belong to the ancient reaches of mythology and to our human destiny.

In Piero's time there was great theological controversy. The Renaissance questioned everything. What was the nature of the Virgin? Was she just an ordinary woman or was she of the divine essence? Questions about spirit and substance were argued endlessly. What is spirit? What is substance? To-day we know more about substance than ever before, but the more we know the more it is recognised that we know nothing. Five hundred years have taught us nothing new about the life of the spirit. Piero della Francesca, like all great artists, did not accept any dichotomy between spirit and matter. There is no spirit without substance; the whole of nature is impregnated with spiritual life. His *Madonna del Parto*, one of the few pregnant Madonnas, is both human and touched with divine revelation. It is a work that reposes in its own mystery: Life emerging into the life of the world, Light into its light.

[1984]

Love

There are many types of love. In ancient Greece from whence all ideas flow, there were seven main words for love. Maternal love is like, but not the same as, love of country or love between friends. And love of fellow men and women which the old Bibles called charity is also something akin to these, but different.

What I'm writing about here is exclusively the love we mean when we are 'in love'; and it includes a certain amount of passion and desire, a certain amount of madness while it lasts. Its main feature is that you cannot argue about it. The most unlikely people may fall in love with each other; their friends, amazed, look for the reason. This is useless; there is no reason. The lovers themselves may try to explain it: 'her beautiful eyes', 'his lovely manners, his brains', and so on. But these claims never fit the case comprehensively. For love is inexplicable. It is something like poetry Certainly, you can analyse it and expound its various senses and intentions, but there is always something left over, mysteriously hovering between music and meaning.

It is said that love is blind. I don't agree. I think that, on the contrary, love sharpens the perceptions. The lovers see especially clearly, but often irrationally; they like what they perceive even if, in anyone else, they wouldn't. They see the reality and something extra. Proust, one of the greatest writers on the subject of love, shows, in his love-story of Swann and Odette, how Swann, civilised, well-bred and artistic, saw perfectly clearly that Odette was vulgar, promiscuous and not at all a suitable partner for him in the Parisian world of his time. Right at the end of a section of the book Swann even resigned himself to the loss of Odette: 'After all, she was not my style'; nevertheless, at the beginning of the next chapter Swann is already married to Odette, because he adored her, and couldn't resist her, even while unhappily knowing and loving the worst about her.

Falling in love is by nature an unforeseen and chance affair, but it is limited by the factor of opportunity. The number of people in the world any one person can meet is comparatively few, and this is usually further limited by occasions of meeting. In *The Tempest*, Miranda exclaims when she first sees Ferdinand:

>   I might call him
> a thing divine, for nothing natural
> I ever saw so noble.

But if she had never seen Ferdinand — if there had been no storm, no shipwreck, to bring him into her life? Undoubtedly this nubile maiden would eventually have become infatuated with Caliban. Even though she has said of him,

>   'Tis a villain, sir,
> I do not love to look on.

— Miranda would inevitably have become enamoured of the monster, knowing him, by comparison with her father, who was taboo, to be hideous; because Caliban was the only available male within her range of opportunity. Prospero, of course, was aware of this danger.

To-day there is an English aristocratic family, of which the four daughters have all married dukes and earls; and, goes the apocryphal story, when the mother is asked how she managed to marry her daughters 'so well', she replies, 'They never got to meet anyone else but dukes and earls.' If the story isn't true, it's to the point.

Love is not blind and it is also not deaf. It is possible to fall in love with a voice, a timbre, a certain way of talking, a charming accent. Many inexplicable love affairs, especially those of the long past where we only have photographs or paintings to go by, would probably be better understood if we could hear the lovers speak. Many a warped-looking and ill-favoured Caliban has been endowed with a winning, mellow and irresistible voice. Many a shapely and gorgeous Ferdinand caws like an adenoidal crow. And the same with women – one often sees how a husky, sexy voice takes a raddled face further in love than does a little-girl twang issuing from a smooth-cheeked nymph.

The first time I was aware of two people in love was when an English master and an art-mistress at my school got engaged. They observed the utmost discretion in front of the girls, but we registered their every move and glance when they happened to meet in the corridors. We exchanged endless information on this subject. These two teachers were not at all lover-like. Both were already middle-aged, and alas must now be dead. He was tall and gawky with a long horse-like face, and eyes, too, not unhorselike. She was dumpy, with the same shape over and under her waist, which was more or less tied-in round the middle. They were both pleasant characters. I liked him better, because he was fond of English literature; she, on the other hand, was inclined to stick her forefinger on to my painting and say, 'What does it mean? It doesn't mean anything.' Which of course was true, and I didn't take it amiss. The only puzzling thing about this love-affair was what he, or anybody, could see in her. What she could see in him was also difficult to place, but still, he had something you could call 'personality'. She, none. We pondered on this at the same time as we noted how he followed her with his eyes – they were dark, and vertically long – and how she, apparently oblivious of his enamoured long-eyed look, would stump off upon her stodgy way, on her little peg-like legs, with never a smile nor a light in her eyes. One thing we learned: love is incomprehensible. He saw the same person as we saw, but he saw something extra. It never occurred to us to think that perhaps she was an excellent cook, which might very likely have been the magic element in the love-affair. It might also have been the case that neither of them had really had time to meet anybody else.

Observing people in love has a certain charm and sometimes, entertainment value. But to my mind watching them actually making love is something different. I find it most unappealing to walk through a London park on a mild spring day and find the grass littered with couples making love. It turns me up, it turns me off. I don't understand how voyeurism turns people on.

With animals, strangely enough I feel the opposite. I live most of the time in the Italian countryside, and nothing is more attractive and moving than to look out of the window on a sunny morning, as I did recently, and see a couple of young hares making love. He hopped towards her, she hopped away. He hopped and she hopped through the long grass, till at last he hopped on. Then, too, not long ago, driving with a friend down a country road we had to stop while a horse mated with a mare. There were a number of cars but we all lined up respectfully and with deep interest for it was known that the owner of the horses, who was standing by, depended for his living on events like this, and was delighted that the horse had at last arrived at his decision, even in the middle of the road. The horse mounted the mare slowly, laid his nose dreamily along her flank, entered her precisely, and performed without bungle. The horse-coper radiated joy and success. The horse and mare moved off casually into a field and the caravan of cars went its way.

The aspects of love that one could discuss are endless. But certainly, as the old songs say, love is the sweetest thing, and it makes the world go round.

[1984]

Ravenna: City of Mosaics

Ravenna is a pleasant northern Italian town practically on the Adriatic coast. The city and its surroundings are flat, which makes for easy walking and accounts for the city's bicycle-cult. Bicycles are parked thickly, leaving the streets comparatively free of standing cars. I live in Tuscany and Rome and am used to the southern and central Italian cities which teem with expansive human life and self-conscious beauty. But Ravenna gives a clean, rational, hard-working impression. There are arcades and shopping-malls. Its modern industries of oil-refining and fertiliser production are outside the city, along the coast. Since Ravenna was bombarded during World War II, most of the buildings are modern or reconstructed, but fortunately still not tall enough to dwarf such landmarks of antiquity, as a leaning tower (preserved under the tutelage of the local Lions Club), the churches, baptisteries, the Cathedral.

In Ravenna is the tomb of the exiled Dante Alighieri who finished the *Divina Commedia* there shortly before his death in 1321. The tomb is a quaint edifice of the eighteenth century, altogether inadequate to the grandeur of its purpose. Byron lodged in Ravenna during his courtship of the Countess Teresa Guiccioli and was involved in the city's violent politics; the site of his lodgings is commemorated by a plaque.

But Ravenna is not essentially a city of exteriors. Its truly great marvels are the mosaics on the interior walls of its early medieval (sixth- to seventh-century) monuments – what Byron called '...her pyramid of precious stones.../Of porphyry, jasper, agate, and all hues/Of gem and marble...' (*Childe Harold's Pilgrimage*).

Ravenna was from the earliest times on the Eastern trade route. The important period of its history began in the fifth century. Rome was on the wane, her troops were evacuating Britain and Gaul to defend Italy. Ravenna, now a few miles inland, was then on the sea coast, a famous Roman port that had been built by the Emperor Augustus. It was always busy with exotic traffic. One can imagine the poet John Masefield's 'Quinquireme of Nineveh from distant Ophir' coming into port with its 'cargo of ivory/And apes and peacocks/Sandalwood, cedarwood, and sweet white wine'.

The art of mosaic mural designs and representations constructed of small coloured stones and glass, often on gold foundations and imbedded with mother of pearl, had already appeared in Italy by the end of the Roman Empire. By the classic process of invasions, battles, murders and usurpations, Ravenna fell within the power of the Visigothic emperor, Theodoric, largely to whom and to whose Byzantine successor we owe the marvels of cultural heritage preserved in Ravenna to-day. No photography can really convey the effect of these mosaics. The nature of mosaics is based on prismatic reflections. Picture postcards and photographs are very good for depicting the close-up details, but the total impression can only be got by being there, inside those buildings, and walking around. From every point of contemplation a new aspect emerges from each picture.

Mosaics are more durable than other pictorial arts; they are less likely to be badly restored or faked. The work of restoration and preservation of Ravenna's mosaic treasures in recent times has been particularly fine and diligent, involving centimetre by centimetre attention and minute toothpick treatment of the original cementing.

It helps to know that in those early days, and to those artists and their patrons, theology was politics, and that many of these mosaic murals were inspired by the Arians, a heretical, powerful and, in many ways, noble branch of Christianity. The Arians acknowledged the human supremacy of Christ but denied his Godhead. It is also useful to know that the monuments belong to three periods: the imperial,

PART I. ART AND POETRY

fifth century, influenced by the adventurous Catholic Roman Galla Placidia and her brother Honorius; the period of the Arian Theodoric, in the fifth and sixth centuries; and the Catholic Byzantine period dominated by the Emperor Justinian and his wife, Theodora, who was attached to the Monophysite heresy which held that in Christ there existed the divine nature alone.

There is always a connection between an art form and the thought process of the people to whom it spoke. Just as Renaissance art, with its defiant portraiture, its flowing robes and hair, its fluid religious figurations, addressed itself to a new humanistic spirit, bursting with adventure and bold concepts of good and evil, so do the mosaics of the early Middle Ages, still and tranquil, gleaming in their own spiritual light, reflect the encroaching oriental sensibility.

To know something of the history of these records of faith, triumph and civilisation, adds to their appreciation. But if the nuances of Western history between the late fifth and seventh centuries are not your vital passion, you can, with equal and marvellous profit, simply plunge into the glory of colour and light that liven the walls and domed ceilings of Ravenna's monuments, as did Henry James, lamenting 'the thinness of [his] saturation with Gibbon and the other sources of legend'.

The sites of interest fall within a rectangle and are of easy access. Most of the interiors are lit by means of a coin machine, so it is advisable to take a supply of small coins.* Any itinerary is equally dramatic in its effect, but it is perhaps more logical to start with one of the oldest examples. This is the small but sumptuous Mausoleum of Galla Placidia, built in the form of a cross, an oratory bejewelled with symbols. A semi-circular cupola represents a deep blue, gold-starred sky surrounded by the Lion of St Mark, the Bull of St Luke, the Eagle of St John and the Angel of St Matthew. Each alcove is decorated with lively animal symbols mingled with more stylised abstract designs. The predominant colour is greenish blue. Above the entrance shines a picture of the Good Shepherd and six mystic yet realistic sheep. Here, too, are the famous drinking doves, symbols of souls quenching their thirst for peace, perched on the edge of their vase.

In all the mosaics of Ravenna, bird, flower and animal symbols abound. One can only marvel at the patience of the artists who executed them, grading the stones from dark to light with the fidelity

---

*No longer necessary.

of mural painting and the added dimension produced by the cut of each tiny stone.

Not far from this mausoleum is the Basilica and Presbytery of San Vitale, one of Ravenna's patron saints. Its exterior is a geometrical arrangement of octagons, rectangles and curves unique in Europe, combining the genius of Rome and Byzantium. The interior is vast and harmonious. The dazzling mosaics here are both Roman and Byzantine, clearly distinguishable in the cursive scenes in the choir and the more stylised and rigid pictures in the apse. Here again colourful wild life abounds among biblical narrative episodes. And the stern, patrician, Empress Theodora attended by her ladies faces her husband, the Emperor Justinian, flanked by his men. Theodora, reputed to have begun her career as a dancer and prostitute, had a formidable influence over her husband, his army and politics. She instituted strict laws against the prevalent traffic in young women, and for the protection of divorced women. She was violently ruthless with rebels. But here, she is dignified and serene, and, as always with oriental mosaics, I have the impression of deep silence.

The Arian Baptistery belongs to the end of the fifth century. In 561 it was reconsecrated to Catholic use. The octagonal chapel stands near the Church of Spirito Santo, formerly an Arian cathedral. The picture in the centre of the domed ceiling shows Christ being baptised, his nude body half submerged in transparent water. This miracle of mosaic portraiture conveys an unusual youth-Christ, patient, fully human and somewhat astonished.

The Neone Baptistery near the Cathedral (early fifth century) has a similar medallion-type depiction of Christ's baptism, with an older Jesus, among water motifs, and, as in the Arian baptistery, the central medallion is surrounded by a spoke-like design formed by the Twelve Apostles. Looking up, one receives the impression of a vividly patterned, iridescent bowl. The baptismal font, the adult immersion, is octagonal, faced with marble and porphyry and inset with a pulpit of Greek marble. This is a wonderful point from which to look up and around the richly decorated interior, whirling as it seems to do, both towards and away from the gazer. The Cathedral itself holds many features of sculptural interest, especially a marble pulpit, decorated with carved lambs, fish, peacocks, deer, doves and ducks – an ecological sermon in itself. Whatever the symbolic import of the animal motifs, plainly those Christians valued their wildlife and household beasts.

Another jewel-box is to be found in a small oratory inside the Archbishop's Palace, adjacent to the Cathedral. This is remarkable for its portraiture. Particularly fascinating is a representation of Christ as a soldier in a short kilt and cloak.

The famous Basilica of Sant'Apollinare Nuovo was built by the Arian Theodoric and later reconsecrated to the Catholic church. Its immediate effect is of total majestic harmony. The architecture and the mural decorations, although not all of the same period, blend together in one conception. On each side of the long central nave three levels of friezes surmount the pillars. The lowest level bears, on one side, a formal procession of Martyrs, and on the other, a corresponding procession of stately Virgins, the latter culminating in a breakthrough of eager movement as the Three Kings, almost running, approach an enthroned Madonna.

In this church the transition between the heresy of the Arians and the restored Catholic religion can be clearly seen. Near the door is a mosaic picture of the Palace of Theodoric, whose Arian saints were originally shown there. These heretics were later replaced, but not by orthodox saints: their places were tactfully 'covered' by a series of quaint mosaic curtains. Sant' Apollinare Nuovo is such a pleasing place, such an immaculately detailed, wide, serene, statement of faith and art, one should spend as long as possible walking around. It deserves at least two visits.

The Basilica of Sant' Apollinare in Classe (Classe is a fraction of Ravenna, now about four miles from the present city) owes its survival from Allied shelling to the intervention of 'Popski' (Vladimir Peniakoff), the celebrated World War II commander. His 'private army' of twenty-two men was an independent demolition squad. In his book *Popski's Private Army* he tells how he prevailed on his gunners to postpone an attack on Sant' Apollinare in Classe for twenty-four hours while he sent a party to visit the bell-tower where Germans were believed to be posted. The rumour proved untrue and the church was saved. He is commemorated by a grateful plaque in the cloister. This monument now enjoys the support of the Rotary Club. Sant' Apollinare in Classe has an apse of breathtaking loveliness. The mosaic picture on the arched ceiling portrays a glorious jewel-encrusted cross symbolising Christ in a still, sublime, pastoral surrounding. Marble columns of great dignity line the wide central nave. Groupings of columns are one of the most effective features of the church.

All this being said, there is still everything left unsaid about the treasures of Ravenna. In the National Museum are fine collections of carved marbles dating from early Roman times, ancient woven materials, ivories, ceramics. The Church of Saint John the Evangelist was founded by Galla Placidia as a votive offering for her survival from a storm at sea during her return to Ravenna from Constantinople in the year 424. This is the oldest church in Ravenna and was seriously war-damaged. It has a wall display of salvaged mosaic pavements, the most attractive of which are naïf representations of scenes from the thirteenth-century Fourth Crusade. The Church of St Francis is striking for its crypt constantly under water, but observable from the upper church; it is partly paved with its original fifth-century abstract mosaics. Outside Ravenna, along the Adriatic coast, are the pine woods beloved of Dante in his latter days, and of Boccaccio and of Byron. These woods are not, by their nature, very dense. But, menaced by the modern environment, they are thinning out.

[1987]

The Art of Verse

Verse is often considered an inferior form of poetry. Not so. It is a literary form by itself, a craft verging on art. At its best the practice of verse emerges as poetry. We talk of the nonsense verses of Edward Lear and of Lewis Carroll although they do draw strength from the poetic imagination.

Poets who practise 'free verse' are seldom aware of what they are freed from: the study of verse is a sadly forgotten one. In my view poets cannot work freely unless they are fully experienced in the makings of verse. There are verse forms to be considered, lengths of lines, rhymes internal and external; rhythms regular and sprung, the use of alliterations; in short, the raw materials which are the musical basics of poetry.

I know of no great poet who has not been fully acquainted with the study of verse; and I am convinced that any poet or indeed anyone who writes prose, would benefit from a knowledge of what verse is, and from the actual practice of villanelles, triolets, rondeaux, Shakespearean sonnets, Petrarchan sonnets, kyrielles, chants royal, to mention some. Each has a distinct function in the conveyance of meaning and artistic pleasure. The various forms of metre were themselves the subject of a verse written by the nineteenth-century poet Samuel Taylor Coleridge:

> Trochee trips from long to short;
> From long to long in solemn sort,

> Slow Spondee stalks, strong foot! yet ill able
> Ever to come up with Dactyl trisyllable.
> Iambics march from short to long:
> With a leap and a bound the swift Anapaests throng –
> One syllable long, with one short at each side,
> Amphibrachys hasten with a stately stride:-
> First and last being long; middle short, Amphimacer
> Strikes his thundering hoofs like a proud high-bred racer.

From this example can flow an infinity of inspired irregularities.

There is far more to creative writing than just to sit down to write and simply vent your feelings. Shakespeare, our Mozart of literature, knew well the emotive and aesthetic power of metrical variation:

> Our revels now are ended. These our actors,
> As I foretold you, were all spirits, and
> Are melted into the air, into thin air;

And how well suited to the conversational form were the measured Alexandrine metres of the nineteenth-century poet Arthur Hugh Clough in his narrative poem, 'Amours de Voyage':

> Am I prepared to lay down my life for the British female?
> Really, who knows? One has bowed and talked, till, little by little,
> All the natural heat has escaped of the chivalrous spirit.

Rhyme is no longer popular, except for comic verse, although some poets have told me that the search for an adequate rhyme-ending has sometimes been the fruitful source of a new image and even meaning. It is a mnemonic, and in this way a rhymed poem is easier to remember. It can also hypnotise. W.H. Auden's rhymed poetry is wonderfully thought-inspiring. In the hands of Dylan Thomas a rhyming word is always in the right place. As a mere excuse for the line ending, though, rhyme is indeed boring. No technique can really make a poet.

In my youth I practised and studied all verse-forms. I believe I owe to this activity a sense of how to manipulate language and organise sentences and paragraphs (the stanzas of prose) to procure an effect. I have always claimed that I write as a poet, that my novels come under the category of poetics rather than fiction. If this is even partly so, I owe it to my early apprenticeship with verse forms.

[1999]

Ruskin and Read

'I am, and my father was before me, a violent Tory of the old school,' Ruskin said of himself. In marked contrast with this nineteenth-century arbiter of taste, Herbert Read is a pacifist and an anarchist, particularly sympathetic to new ideas.

Yet to take another statement of Ruskin's: 'If we were to be asked abruptly, and required to answer briefly, what qualities chiefly distinguish great artists from feeble artists, we should answer, I suppose, first, their sensibility and tenderness; secondly, their imagination; and thirdly, their industry' – to take this statement and apply to Herbert Read's writings for a comment, we should find the two philosophers of art in substantial agreement, with the exception that Read would hardly be likely to use the word 'tenderness' in this context.

And there lies the difference between the two men and between two epochs. Ruskin was slightly soft in the middle; Read is a little too hard. Ruskin's influence spread out to inspire the whole literate community; Read's influence makes no such missionary move; he addresses the sensibility of an artistic elite; and it is his regret that the deeper ranges of aesthetic sensibility are lost to the majority of people.

Herbert Read's selection of essays, chosen to represent a 'philosophy' of art, are of special relevance to this question, which is closely bound up with that of education in art. Teachers will be especially impressed by the essay 'The Fate of Modern Painting'; and indeed, the whole book shows Read as a fundamental thinker who understands how far artistic expression has been separated from normal life. Peter Quennell's selection from John Ruskin's writings is a useful guide to the strongest current in nineteenth-century aesthetics.

[1952]

Robert Burns

The most appealing thing about Robert Burns is that he was innately free of the Calvinistic and puritanical constraints which blighted the mind of some of his contemporaries of the eighteenth century and hovered well into and beyond the nineteenth. At the bi-centenary of his death his songs and narrative verses can speak to our age directly and without inhibitions. To mark this anniversary two biographies appeared: *Dirt and Deity* by Ian McIntyre, which places Burns in his historical context, while in *The Tinder Heart* Hugh Douglas marvellously outlined Burns' life in the light of his chief enthusiasms: women and song. The accent of either book is so entirely different that neither stands in the way of the other.

Robert Burns was born in 1759 of a poor farming family at Alloway in Ayrshire, the eldest of seven children. Although he became in the public mind the legendary Son of the Soil, Burns was not the untutored genius that he was reported to be. His schooldays were short in years but his extraordinary intelligence made up for that. He preferred his verses to be in the Scots dialect but he could still write and speak good plain English. He studied even while helping arduously on the various farms that his father rented.

Burns adored women. Whenever he had sex, which was often, he wrote a song about it. There was a touch of the rooster about him. He had numerous children born out of wedlock, and never denied paternity. On the contrary he loved them and did what he could to comfort the mothers. One illegitimate child was brought up by his own mother and another by his wife, Jean Armour.

Burns made love all his adult life, joyfully, and all over the place. Any woman whom he slept with was in his eyes a jewel, a beauty. 'My heart,' he wrote, 'was completely (sic) tinder, and was eternally lighted up by some Goddess or other.' These Goddesses were all of his own peasant origin. He could not adapt his nature to what he called the 'boarding-school' expectations of fine young ladies. He preferred bonnie barmaids, servant girls, milkmaids and sturdy countrywomen. He advised his brother, 'Try for intimacy as soon as you feel the first symptoms of passion.' Eventually he married one of his first loves, Jean Armour, whose parents had once forbidden their union despite her pregnancy, only changing their minds after he was famous. By Jean he had nine children.

After the successful publication of his *Poems, Chiefly in the Scottish Dialect* in 1785, Burns withdrew from a plan he had formed of emigration to the West Indies. His first collection of verse was an immediate success. His fame grew. He went to Edinburgh where he was duly lionised. This did, and did not, go to his head. He formed friendships with titled men, scholars and benefactresses; he fell in love all over the place, but he knew it would not last. He was made much of in the grand houses, especially fêted by two older women, Agnes McLehose who was separated from her husband, and a widow, Frances Dunlop.

His relations with Agnes McLehose were not sexual due to her moral scruples, but they were very deep, and besides, it was a literary friendship since Mrs McLehose was an educated woman. With Mrs Dunlop, who was very much his senior, there grew a mother–son relationship which lasted many years until she discovered that Burns' sympathies were with the French revolutionaries.

It is difficult to realise that it is over 200 years since the death of Robert Burns, he was so 'modern' a genius, so uninhibited, full of virility, a hard drinker, bawdy, garrulous, at times self-contradictory to the point of hypocrisy, at others, too sincere for his own best interests. He could be tender and lyrical.

In conversation Burns was said to speak clear, succinct English. In his verse and poetry he spoke mainly as a child of the soil. Much of it was unprintable in his lifetime but he distributed his merry obscenities liberally among his friends.

You can admire Robert Burns or not as a poet, but there is really something compelling about his life. He is related fictionally to Tom Jones and is a spiritual forebear of Dylan Thomas. He was, for most of his life, a professional noble savage and peasant-genius.

His few years reached from 1759 to 1796. He worked on his father's tenant-farm in Ayrshire dutifully and hardily all the days of his youth. Though his schooling was haphazard and scrappy he was an ambitious and bookish young man, even while he pushed the plough.

He praised life exceedingly, even while he cursed and swore. He fornicated freely all his life, never failing in tender feelings towards the resultant pregnant girls and illegitimate children. He went back to farming, regularised his union with Jean Armour and finally obtained a less precarious job as an exciseman, which enabled him to concentrate some of his time on his literary concerns.

To his first child by a housemaid he addressed an ode:

> Welcome! My bonnie,
> sweet wee Dochter!
> Though ye've come
> here a wee unsought for…

By the time he was twenty-three Burns seemed to think in verse. Many aspects of his personal life are recorded in those Scots vernacular rhymes which were soon to enchant the reading population of Scotland and beyond.

PART I. ART AND POETRY   21

Like Sir Walter Scott after him, Burns collected old Scottish airs to which he set his verses, preserving a vocal cottage cultural tradition.[*] One realises on hearing these songs, the difference between the merely adequate poetry of the printed versions and their loveliness when set to their music. Burns' songs could be full of happiness or imbued with sadness. He wrote in many moods from many points of view other than his own. Some of his most successful love-songs present the girl's point of view:

> O wha'll mow me now, my jo,
> An wha'll mow me now:
> The sodger with his bandoleers
> Has bang'd my belly fu.

If this is difficult to decipher, a little imagination will serve the purpose.

Burns had no apparent difficulty in squaring his erotic productions with his more respectable life-style. After his last visits to Edinburgh and tours of the Highlands and the Scottish Borders, he took a civil service job as befitted a steady married man. But even as an excise-inspector he never ceased to fall in love and sing love's praises. He died at the age of 37 at his home in Dumfries in a wasted condition of an unspecified rheumatic illness; it seems that the very force and intensity of his feelings had consumed him.

One question is left outstanding. Why did Burns set such real and earnest store by his job? One sees that he felt the need for a settled income, but why that of an exciseman whose job it was to go snooping and tax-levying throughout his district? Fascinating as this may have been to a man who liked to ride about the countryside and socialise, the job certainly does not fit in with the exultant lilt of one of Burns' best songs, in which the exciseman is carried off by the devil. Is there not a dichotomy here between the desire for this particular occupation and Burns' free, anarchical soul?

[1995 & 1996]

---

[*]To celebrate the 200th anniversary of his death, the complete songs of Robert Burns were produced on compact discs by Linn Records in association with the Burns Federation. A twelve-volume set was planned. The first of these is exquisite, the result of patient and knowledgeable research into the instruments and music to which Burns set his songs. [Muriel Spark's note]

Andrew Young

Andrew Young is one of the most interesting independents of our time. As a pastoral miniaturist he resembles Robert Frost: his thrifty diction and the way he looks at domestic things recall John Crowe Ransom; Walter de la Mare comes to mind through his light and occasional archaic diction; Clare too seems represented in his Nature themes – a chastened Clare though; and the French symbolists are present at times. But for all this, Andrew Young does not write quite like anyone else, probably because he is a born artist. An artist, I mean, in the way that Chekhov is an artist, whose prose is to me the most forcible counterpart of Andrew Young's poetry. And an artist whose uniqueness and 'secret' is partly founded on good taste. There must be volumes of poetry left unwritten in the whole of Young's experience of Nature. But from this experience he has chosen to record very little, very briefly. And this little is as much and no more than his power of expression will cope with. That is, I think, his first asset – it is an asset to any poet to know that poetry is not only what you say, but how you say it, and to discover just what you are capable of saying.

What Andrew Young has to say is that he has seen the multifarious worlds of Nature from their side of experience. Unlike Wordsworth, of whom Nature was a projection, Andrew Young seems to know what it is like to be a mole, a hill, a thunderstorm. He does not speak as one identified with them – his poetry is not pantheistic – but as one who has been their guest. The way in which he conveys this attitude is very skilful. He speaks of Nature's otherness, in terms of its own reckonings, as a traveller might of the strange customs and conceptions of an alien people. This is how time appears in the world of an ancient tree, as Andrew Young sees it:

> One elbow on the sloping earth it leans,
> That steeply falls beneath,
> As though resting a century it means
> To take a moment's breath.

And on a dead mole, the poet reflects:

> For you to raise a mound
> Was as for us to make a hole,
> What wonder now that being dead
> Your body lies here stout and square
> Buried within the blue vault of the air?

Examining Young's method more closely, one finds repeatedly a kind of riddle-imagery which makes its impact a fraction later than the literal meaning. The missel thrush, looking down into a pool of water, sees the poet 'Crawl at the bottom of the air'. The poet revisits a scene after many years, and as he stares into the water each reflection, even his own, seems unchanged, until he remarks his hair touched with white. But he does not say it like that. He says it from the point of view of the water, in this riddle-language of his:

> Although I notice that my hair
> Now stirs a little foam in the smooth bay.

This type of imagery shows the freshness of the poet's vision. We are familiar with the fact that dandelions are orange-coloured, but the statement:

> ... dandelions flood
> The orchard as though apple-trees
> Dropped in the grass ripe oranges

invests the fact with strangeness and beauty. Because such a technique is so personal a part of Young's vision, he is not to be imitated.

[1950/51]

Giacomo Manzù

The Italian sculptor Giacomo Manzù was born at Bergamo, north-east of Milan, in 1908. Like all great artists, somehow he was born with a past, and he will die with a future.

Manzù's destiny touched on that of another man from Bergamo: Pope John XXIII, one of the two men with whom Manzù has been profoundly impressed (the other was Pablo Picasso). Manzù, like Pope John Roncalli twenty-seven years previously, was born into a poor and numerous family. Square-built and solid, he bears a resemblance to John XXIII whose portrait he was later to do in bronze, and under whose care he finally achieved the splendid Doors of St Peter's in Rome.

At the age of eleven, already with a passion for plastic art, Manzù was apprenticed to a wood-carver. From there he proceeded to work with a gilder, then a plaster-decorator. He modelled and drew in his spare time. He had an undeniable calling. At the age of thirteen Manzù attended an evening school of the decorative arts. His life as a sculptor, at first untaught, and with little experience of sculptural traditions, began when he was twenty. His great advantage was to be born of a nation endowed with a sense of its own immense artistic patrimony.

Manzù's work weathered the political furies of the 'twenties and 'thirties under Mussolini's fascist regime. One can well believe that, as he claims, neither the church nor the state had any influence on his work. Those were days when the social realism of the dictatorship stamped its hideous heroic rhetoric on sculpture particularly, grandiosely bewildering the masses.

Manzù's work gradually reflects an artist's experimental acceptance, rejection and assimilation of current movements, but in the late 1930s his unique potency with materials and his vitality began to be nationally recognised. The sculptor who impressed him most was, he said, Brancusi.

One feels, with Manzù, that the art has chosen the artist. He troubles definition. He has certain recurrent themes. Although he seldom makes more than one example from a cast, and never a series, he works back on ever-more interesting, and in most cases simplified, versions of figures and designs he made in his early years, even his boyhood.

The main recurrent themes are: a girl on a chair; still-life compositions on a chair; female busts and forms; the cardinals and religious figures interpreted humanistically, as in the bronze doors of the Basilica of St Peter's in Rome, Salzburg Cathedral, and the Church of St Laurenz, Rotterdam.

The girl on a chair: In Manzù's house there is a small, slightly frayed straw-seated cottage chair attached to the wall; it obviously had a near-mystical significance for the artist. In 1930 he began his first drawings of a girl on the verge of adolescence seated on the chair, and made his first sculpture in 1934. He returned to the theme, with other versions, after the war, when he began to gain an international reputation. 'By an uncontrollable impulse of emotion I united the two things', he has said, 'the chair, – the sole inheritance I received from my father – and the young girl. It was the first time I had seen a young girl naked, and I wanted to place her on a throne, like the most precious thing I had, in this way uniting my two treasures in one. I was convinced at that time that for the rest of my life I would never make anything else but that girl on that chair.'

When Manzù was asked if he thought the girl on the chair series was his best, he thought awhile, then said, 'Yes, I think so.' They are indeed wonderful and spare compositions of spatial form, in the mature versions gaining certitude and sincerity. (The critic Cesare Brandi has made the point that Manzù progresses not from naturalness but towards it.) The chair features in another series of bronzes completed in the mid-sixties and seventies. Fruit, draperies and crayfish, branches of vine and pear tree, are deposited like harvest offerings on the sublime rough-hewn chair, with its felicitous cubic effects of cross-bars and legs.

'The theme of women,' said Manzù, 'is what I always return to. Women are most important to me.' It is true that his female forms greatly outnumber the male figures. In 1954 he first encountered his life-companion Inge Schabel. The portraits of Inge recur in impressive variety, egg-shaped, majestic, serene. They are an achievement of stillness and light, eliminating everything around them. (Inge is beautiful, more tender and mobile in real life than in her timeless portraits.)

Manzù has said very little about his own work. 'To write would be arrogance', he said. But his brief comments are always pertinent. He was struck, as a child, by the shape of a Bishop rather than by the Bishop himself. 'My parents were religious and we were often in church. I remember the shape…' Later, as he pursued this theme to its culmination in the Cardinal series, he felt he could go on repeating variants of those standing cardinals and seated cardinals, confined in their copes, with all their geometric and restrained grandeur; but he stopped: 'I didn't want to academise myself'.

Manzù's innate and poetic psychological sense always informs both the conception of his themes and the actual composition. Among the variants of the David series, going back to 1938, David is depicted crouched on a stupendous mill-stone, like a street-boy with a foetus-like face, reaching for his defiant missile, the King of Israel in embryo.

The great bronze doors of St Peter's, so well-known to visitors from all over the world, were first suggested in 1947. A sculpture competition was set up. It was not till 1952 that Manzù received the official commission. The theme first required by the Curia was 'Triumph of the Saints and the Martyrs of the Church'. It is thanks to the supreme intelligence of John XXIII who, perceiving that Manzù could not live with these theological and iconographical set themes, accepted those natural to Manzù's genius. Manzù had by this time lost his faith in the Church, but the Pope had faith in Manzù and the spirituality he brought to the harmonious bas-reliefs. They depict death in a variety of legendary forms, but they rejoice even while they despair.

Manzù died in 1991. Spirituality was one of Manzù's most-valued qualities; to him it signified fervour, love, energy, and the inward life-force. But he was also extremely concrete in the execution of his ideas. His cardinals tell us something about cardinals, his children about children, his lovers about lovers. The variant bronze *Lovers* of 1966, 1977 and 1978 are almost mobile in their rhythm and exuberant baroque swirl. The orgiastic expression of the lovers brings to mind Bernini's *The Ecstasy of Saint Teresa* in the church of Santa Maria della Vittoria in Rome. They are spirit and matter combined.

Manzù has done important scenography, paintings in watercolour and oils, drawings, book illustrations, jewellery. He worked long hours. He said without hesitation that he dominated his material. Mention the word ebony, and his face lit up: '…it has like blood in its veins'. His only boast was, 'Conosco mio mestiere' (I know my trade).

[1988]

The Desegregation of Art

The Blashfield Address to the American Academy and Institute of Arts and Letters, New York

You know that I speak as a writer. And when I claim, also, to speak from the point of view of an artist, this is not to attach value or quality to what I write but because, rightly or wrongly, I think as an artist, I live as one, I have never from my earliest memories known any other life or way of seeing things but that of an artist, a changer of actuality into something else. You must know that I am not a thinker by profession but that, for me, ideas are inseparable from words or from any other material that the artist works with. This fact is my only qualification for addressing you at all and it is only right to declare myself for what I am, so that you will know more or less the limitations as well as the scope of my point of view.

And here is my point of view:

Literature, of all the arts, is the most penetrable into the human life of the world, for the simple reason that words are our common currency. We don't instinctively, from morning to night, paint pictures to each other, or play music to each other, in order to communicate; we talk, we write to each other.

And so, when I speak of the desegregation of art I begin with the art of letters. But I mean also the other arts, drama, music, painting – to-day, more than ever in process of abstracting themselves from the confines of separate faculties, already tending to become part and parcel of society, where they belong. We are living in times when there are fewer great artists, fewer great writers, but more and better art, better and more lively and a greater volume of writing. It is easy to say that poetry and the novel are on the decline compared with the great masterpieces of the past. But it seems to me that the art of speech itself has improved, standards of journalism and reportage have improved, speech has become sharper and more ready on everyone's tongue. We express ourselves more freely and with less clutter than ever before. It's true that in some parts of the world people are not permitted to say what they think; but even so, no-one can deny that they are very eloquent and very occupied to say what perhaps they don't exactly think. In Italy, where I live, when the millions of Americans flood in to enliven the summer months, we find them ready and able and eager to discuss everything and anything. And we ask ourselves where this great silent majority is that we hear about. Those quiet Americans certainly don't come to visit us.

Now leaving aside the other arts for the moment, I concentrate on the art of literature for the very reason that a distinction has to be made between the verbal communications going on every day, every moment of the day, and what we call literature.

I think that the art of literature is a personal expression of ideas which come to influence the minds of people even at second, third and fourth hand. Literature infiltrates and should fertilise our minds. It is not a special department set aside for the entertainment and delight of the sophisticated minority. And if this is true, then ineffective literature must go.

We all know that there is a lot of inferior literature about as there are inferior and boring examples of any other art. It is easy to say bad things must go. The critics, in every field of art, are never done denouncing what they feel to be bad art. They rightly prune and cultivate, they attempt to practise good husbandry. And as we become more articulate, itinerant, knowledgeable, we are more and more agreed on what is bad. And everyone knows we have to give up what is bad – it is a banal moral precept. What is wrong, what is bad, must go.

But I suggest now that we have to give up some of the good manifestations of art. Good things, when they begin no longer to apply, also must go. They must go before they turn bad on us. There is no more beautiful action than the sacrifice of good things at the intelligent season and by intelligent methods.

I'm sure you would like me to be more specific. And so I will be.

We have in this century a marvellous tradition of socially conscious art. And especially now in the arts of drama and the novel we see and hear everywhere the representation of the victim against the oppressor, we have a literature and an artistic culture, one might almost say a civilisation, of depicted suffering, whether in social life or in family life. We have representations of the victim-oppressor complex, for instance, in the dramatic portrayal of the gross racial injustices of our world, or in the exposure of the tyrannies of family life on the individual. As art this can be badly done, it can be brilliantly done. But I am going to suggest that it isn't achieving its end or illuminating our lives any more, and that a more effective technique can and should be cultivated. And then I shall offer my own idea of precisely what that method might be.

For what happens when, for example, the sympathies and the indignation of a modern audience are aroused by a play or a novel of the kind to which I have referred? I don't know for certain, but I suspect that a great number of the audience or of the readers feel that their moral responsibilities are sufficiently fulfilled by the emotions they have been induced to feel. A man may go to bed feeling less guilty after seeing such a play. He has undergone the experience of pity for the underdog. Salt tears have gone bowling down his cheeks. He has had a good dinner. He is absolved, he sleeps well. He rises refreshed, more determined than ever to be the overdog. And there is always, too, the man who finds the heroic role of the victim so appealing that he'll never depart from it. I suggest that wherever there is a cult of the victim, such being human nature, there will be an obliging cult of twenty equivalent victimisers.

I'm sure you all remember the silly old saying 'The pen is mightier than the sword'. Perhaps when swords were the weapons in current use, there was some point in the proverb. Anyway, in our time, the least of our problems is swords.

But the power and influence of the creative arts is not to be belittled. I only say that the art and literature of sentiment and emotion, however beautiful in itself, however stirring in its depiction of actuality, has to go. It cheats us into a sense of involvement with life and society, but in reality it is a segregated activity. In its place I advocate the arts of satire and of ridicule. And I see no other living art form for the future.

Ridicule is the only honourable weapon we have left.

We have all seen on the television those documentaries of the 'thirties and of the second World War, where Hitler and his goose-stepping troops advance in their course of liberating, as they called it, some city, some country or other; we have seen the strutting and posturing of Mussolini. It looks like something out of comic opera to us. If the massed populations of those times and in those countries had been moved to break up into helpless laughter at the sight, those tyrants wouldn't have had a chance. And I say we should all be conditioned and educated to regard violence in any form as something to be ruthlessly mocked.

If someone derides me, I don't like it. But at least I can begin to understand the mentality of the mocker. And I can mock back in such a way that he might understand mine. And so there may be room for a mutual understanding. But if he slides a knife between my ribs I'm unlikely to understand anything at all any more.

I would like to see in all forms of art and letters, ranging from the most sophisticated and high achievements to the placards that the students carry about the street, a less impulsive generosity, a less indignant representation of social injustice, and a more deliberate cunning, a more derisive undermining of what is wrong. I would like to see less emotion and more intelligence in these efforts to impress our minds and hearts.

Crude invective can rouse us for a time, and perhaps only end in physical violence. Solemn appeals to our sentiments of indignation and pity are likely to succeed only for the duration of the show, of the demonstration, or the prayer meeting, or the hours of reading. Then the mood passes, it goes to the four winds and love's labour's lost. But the art of ridicule, if it is on the mark – and if it is not true on the mark it is not art at all – can penetrate to the marrow. It can leave a salutary scar. It is unnerving. It can paralyse its object.

Does this sound as if I thought of the purpose of art as propaganda? Perhaps it does sound so, and perhaps I partly do. In a sense all art is propaganda since it propagates a point of view and provokes a response. But that isn't entirely my meaning.

I have often been asked to give an opinion as to what is the purpose of art. And I've thought of it a great deal. I've thought of this question for most of my life. And, so far, I've reached a generalised conclusion that the purpose of art is to give pleasure. Whether the form of art is tragic, comic, dramatic, lyrical, ironic, aggressive, it contains that element of pleasure which restores the proportions of the human spirit, opens windows in the mind. By means of art and literature our wits are sharpened, our intellect is refined, we can learn to know ourselves, how to appraise life with that pleasure which is the opposite and the enemy of boredom and of pain.

This is what I mean by canvassing as I do the idea that the only effective art of our particular time is the satirical, the harsh and witty, the ironic and derisive. Because we have come to a moment in history when we are surrounded on all sides and oppressed by the absurd. And I think that even the simplest, the least sophisticated and uneducated mind is aware of this fact. I should think there is hardly an illiterate peasant in the world who doesn't know it. The art of ridicule is an art that everyone can share in some degree, given the world that we have.

The cult of the victim is the cult of pathos, not tragedy. The art of pathos is pathetic, simply; and it has reached a point of exhaustion, a point where not the subject-matter but the art-form itself is crying to heaven for vengeance. The art of protest, the art which condemns violence and suffering by pathetic depiction is becoming a cult separated from the actions of our life. Our noble aspirations, our sympathies, our elevated feelings should not be inspired merely by visits to an art gallery, a theatre, or by reading a book, but rather the rhetoric of our times should persuade us to contemplate the ridiculous nature of the reality before us, and teach us to mock it. We should know ourselves better by now than to be under the illusion that we are all essentially aspiring, affectionate and loving creatures. We do have these qualities, but we are aggressive, too.

And so when I speak of the desegregation of art I mean by this the liberation of our minds from the comfortable cells of lofty sentiment in which they are confined and never really satisfied.

To bring about a mental environment of honesty and self-knowledge, a sense of the absurd and a general looking-lively to defend ourselves from the ridiculous oppressions of our time, and above all to entertain us in the process, has become the special calling of arts and of letters.

Ladies and Gentlemen of the Academy of Arts and Letters, you have been good to ask me here and to listen to my point of view, as I am, an artist, a sort of writing animal.

[1970]

The Wisdom of Mr T.S. Eliot

For the past few weeks, since *The Confidential Clerk* was first performed at the Edinburgh Festival, the daily Press has plugged the line that T.S. Eliot's new play, unlike the rest of his work, is not to be probed into for meaning; critics are to understand that this is witty West End entertainment, no mysteries. We are to treat it light and gay, or we shall make fools of ourselves.

We shall do that in any case (see *Wisdom* ix.14). I saw the play and found it meaningful. It has to do with faithfulness and idolatry, security and rootlessness, vague desires and precise fulfilments, parents and children, art and craft, success and failure. These themes increase the entertainment qualities of the play, they add to the gaiety and the pathos, and intensify the wit and propriety of the dialogue in all moods. There seems to be no reason why the most obvious serious themes in the play should not be discussed.

I will not tell you much about the plot; it is Greek in type, employing the principle of peripeteia or the reversal of circumstances; and this might be spoiled in the telling, for future audiences. But I will tell you what I can of the main themes, as I understood them, and this means, something about the characters, too.

The play has a talented cast. It is a Christian play; it contains Christian teaching and elaborates Christian ideas, some of which are to be found in the *Book of Wisdom*. Mr Eliot reaches a point in his dramatic enterprise, at which he conceives all his characters in the light of sympathy and compassion; these are lacking in his past dramatic work.

***

I would like to call *The Confidential Clerk* a Catholic play, meaning that it presents situations which are wholly true, and they are everywhere and always true. In his new sympathetic treatment of a character like Sir Claude Mulhammer (played by Paul Rogers), Eliot has had to risk blinding the audience to his fearful moral flaw. But this is progressively suggested, and in the last act, our pity undiminished, his life is forced upon us as the life of one, like the potter in *Wisdom*, whose 'heart is ashes'.

Mulhammer had wanted to be a potter in his youth; he had entered the city in reluctant obedience to his father. Now he is the merely successful surviving son of a wiser financier, persuaded that he had done the right thing, on the grounds that he would never have been a successful potter. He keeps a roomful of pottery for his secret aesthetic appreciation, or, as we might say, worship. He is in Chapter xv of *Wisdom*, but this is no guarantee that the author got him from that source.

However, Mulhammer is there all right. He has a supposed illegitimate son, Colby Simpkins (played by Denholm Elliott), for whom his love takes the form of persuading him to follow his footsteps. Colby had wanted to be a church organist, a successful one. Was he justified in abandoning his art to become his father's confidential clerk, on the grounds that he could have been only a minor artist? Colby is not sure, at first. The father gives him a sumptuous piano, a sort of counterpart to his own roomful of unserviceable clay.

***

This is a play in which everyone's longings are fulfilled, as the prayers of faithful people are answered, in a way in which they would never have had the courage to foresee.

The author appoints his characters to this end. Colby's supposed sister, Lucasta Angel (played by Margaret Leighton), 'who is rather flighty', and whose wings are desperately invisible, tenders, unaware, to their destinies, and herself emerges from darkness.

Eggerson, the old retired confidential clerk, is in many ways the most intriguing character. He is seen at the beginning, an old man preparing for the 'end of winter'; this ageing family servant is shown in a context of fruitfulness and fertility. In his retirement, Eggerson is the cultivator of a garden. He also cultivates the family up to their final deliberations. He seems appointed to conduct Colby, especially, into his promised land. Colby becomes a church organist.

When his parentage was in doubt Colby had wished for a father who had died before he was born, one whom he could know only by hearsay, and through documents. Colby's earthly parentage is accordingly revealed, but Eggerson has perceived a vocation for the priesthood, in Colby's aspirations.

Lucasta's need was for roots; she becomes engaged to a man of her father, Mulhammer's choice, but not for his reasons. Lady Elizabeth finds her real son, and he his mother to their mutual shock. Eggerson's desires seem fulfilled through Colby.

The play gives a renewed life to some points of Christian teaching which seem irrelevant to the modern world, such as our calling to a specific station in life, the need of parents for the security of children as much as the other way round, our need for roots in God. *The Confidential Clerk* has much wisdom.

[1953]

Ingersoll Foundation – T.S. Eliot Award

One of the best things in life for a writer who sets out to be an artist is to be appreciated by people whose opinions are generally respected and valued. That is the happy condition in which I find myself this evening and I thank the directors of the Ingersoll Foundation and the Rockford Institute. I thank all of you, for this expression of support for me.

I am particularly happy to be here on the spot tonight at this celebration. I want to tell you what happened the last time I received an award of comparable importance, many years ago, in Italy. The Italia Prize was awarded for a musical adaptation on radio of one of my novels. I shared the prize with the adaptor and the composer. Together we travelled from London to Verona where, in the magnificent castle, the prizes were handed out. The audience was composed of prominent townspeople, and personalities from the international community of arts and letters, all dressed in formality and grandeur. A banquet was to follow in our honour.

So, after the prize-giving everybody left, but we three prize-winners stood looking at each other in the empty castle hall while slowly the lights went out. A guardian came and told us to go away. Finally, we three went to a restaurant for our supper, which was a very merry one. Obviously the organisers of the banquet had completely forgotten about us. It was not till next morning that our invitations arrived at our hotels. Plainly there had been a hitch, but the amazing thing was that we, the guests of honour, were never missed – not that evening, nor ever.

Well, this time, here I am. Here, I am proud and relieved to add, we both are.[*]

As a recipient of the award which takes its name from T.S. Eliot and which, in the hands of the Rockford Institute, seeks an ethical consensus rooted in the fundamental ideas of Western Culture, I was prompted to look back on Eliot's writings on ethical and social questions, and in particular his book *Notes towards the Definition of Culture*, first published in 1948. It was strange and haunting to look back on Eliot's work almost forty years after I had studied him so closely.

---

[*]Referring to the prize-winning Swiss scientist who was to receive the Science Award from the Ingersoll Foundation.

It was haunting in the aspect of his continued relevance, the immediacy of his thought. Eliot was a prophet. What he had to say about the decline of Western Culture in 1948 is valid to-day in an even sharper sense than he could have intended for his time.

By culture Eliot meant not only our art, music and literature. He meant everything we do as a community, our customs and habits, our national events, 'the way of life of a particular people living together in one place'. He wrote that culture is not merely the sum of several activities but a way of life. He defined culture as the development of every activity of the human race. He contended that our culture arose specifically from religion.

Whether we can accept its perpetuation in religion or not, there is no doubt a strong spiritual element in what we call culture to-day. Again, in Eliot's words, 'Culture is something that must grow; you cannot build a tree, you can only plant it, and care for it, and wait for it to mature in its due time…'.

And yet, over forty years later, there would be no way of accepting, far less realising, Eliot's formula for the transmission of a civilised culture. Eliot's Utopia called for a spiritual elite, an aristocracy of taste, learning, manners and morals. Nothing of that kind can now occupy the mind of any reasonable, educated and full-blooded human being. Eliot's analysis of the decline in ethical and aesthetic standards which he observed in the world around him was brilliant. But no-one who fully loves life could possibly, now, accept his solution.

An American critic, the late Dwight Macdonald whose writings on the subject of mass culture were respected by Eliot, also treated of the deterioration of cultural standards. In his book of 1952 *Against the American Grain*, what Dwight Macdonald called Masscult and Midcult, he equally deprecated. He objected to the pressures on our spiritual lives of Hollywood and the disintegrating effects of popular literature and television on what he called High Culture.

But Macdonald offered a solution which Eliot himself described as an alternative to his own. 'The mass audience,' Macdonald wrote, 'is divisible, we have discovered – and the more it is divided, the better. Even television, the most senseless and routinized expression of Masscult (except for the movie newsreels), might be improved by this approach.'

Dwight Macdonald, in fact, finally refused to accept the masses as anything but an abstract. In his support he cited Kierkegaard's rejection of 'the public' as a concrete reality. Our cultural activities and our messages are addressed to groups of people. He foresaw the possibility that, in his own words, '...our new public for High Culture becomes conscious of itself and begins to show some esprit de corps, insisting on higher standards and setting itself out – joyously, implacably – from most of its fellow citizens, not only from the Masscult depths but also from the agreeable ooze of the Midcult swamp.'

As you see, I have only been able to skim the surface of a vast subject to which the nature of the Ingersoll Award gives rise; it concerns the protection of our human standards, the spiritual lives of our societies.

Speaking for myself I find that both high culture and moral philosophy are too often in the hands of people, who, while they have excellent judgment, have a limited sense of humour. The arts of ridicule and satire can be employed to demolish vulgarity, stupidity, crude and cruel behaviour. Ridicule is a strong and effective weapon. It should, I think, be studied as a means of expressing an honest literature in the world to-day.

For myself, moreover, I cannot dismiss any manifestation of mass culture *en bloc*. We should always observe; we should find what is preservable and precious among the welter of cultural phenomena with which we are constantly bombarded. This needs self-discipline, it needs self-training on the part of those gifted with ingenuity of approach, and with comprehension. Culture, after all, concerns the human spirit. A too narrow and severe discrimination can tend to annihilate ourselves, everything around us. And all to no effect.

Once in one of my novels I was drawn into writing a sermon. Into the mouth of the preacher I naturally put what he might be expected to say. But I added one strong conviction of my own which I find it relevant to repeat here: '...in whatever touches the human spirit, it is better to believe everything than nothing.'

[1992]

Pensée: T.S. Eliot

[...]

The influence of a poet like T.S. Eliot on younger poets is a good thing if it is received in a liberating sense; the release of language from a cramped and narrow range of poetic possibility was one of T.S. Eliot's services to English literature. His best influence on younger poets resides in the possibilities he does not himself develop. Obscure though he is often called, he made it possible for other poets to write more lucidly.

[...]

[1953]

The Complete Frost

Robert Frost is the first traditional American poet. Having begun with this apparently contradictory statement (if he is traditional how can he be the first?) as well as a vague one (what is the American tradition?), I had better say what I mean.

Tradition begins somewhere, but it begins as something other than tradition. It does not become tradition until it is well under way; it exists only in retrospect. The American tradition of poetry might have descended from Poe or Whitman. But it began with Emerson. Emily Dickinson wrote in the American tradition, and we can only say so now – and only because this tradition has found a durable repository in Robert Frost.

I know that in America, what I have called the American tradition is looked upon by some as a regional one, as a New England tradition. But that would not explain why John Crowe Ransom, a southern poet, shares with Robert Frost those very elements which make up the tradition (however widely Ransom departs from Frost in other ways).

The most notable elements of this American tradition, which are concentrated in Robert Frost, are: emotional and intellectual austerity; naturalness of expression; objectivity (true of Emily Dickinson who must not be considered a subjective poet merely because she wrote in the first person); domestic imagery. None of these elements are present in Poe; nor in Whitman – unless you believe his mode of expression was natural. But they are present in Ransom; while they are not present, for example, in Marianne Moore, an interesting poet who is outside the American tradition. These distinctions between American traditionals and untraditionals are only possible because the tradition has been confirmed, a basis for the definition provided, by Robert Frost.

Evidence of his contact with English Georgian poets appears in his first book, *A Boy's Will*; but between the publication of this, and his next work *North of Boston*, Robert Frost found his native genius. It was a transition from the poet of anonymously cultivated Georgian scenery, the poet of

> Out through the fields and the woods
>   And over the walls I have wended;
> I have climbed the hills of view
>   And looked at the world, and descended;
> I have come by the highway home
>   And lo, it is ended.

to the poet of New England agricultural life. From the appearance of this second book onward, Robert Frost developed those American traditional characteristics I have mentioned, in his own distinctive way. He had become the author of remarkable narrative poems – stories that would take a novelist three volumes to half-tell, done in dialogue within a few pages. He had become the poet of minute observation.

> Here's a patch of old snow in a corner
>   That I should have guessed
> Was a blow-away paper the rain
>   Had brought to rest.
>
> It is speckled with grime as if
>   Small print overspread it…

Compared with the previous passage quoted above, this poem (by no means the poet's most powerful one of this period) may illustrate where Robert Frost departed from the Georgian mode. His vision has become focused, presenting a clear outline of his object, in contrast to the blurred generalisation of fields, woods and highways of the earlier poem.

It is just this precise noticing of nature that makes Frost's most unique contribution to the tradition; this has been a constant factor in his work since he got clear of Georgianism. But his poetry is not static; it has acquired flexibility of form, it has deepened in meaning. A curiosity of nature, merely observed and noted, as in the last-quoted poem, later finds a more potent subjective equivalent, as in the poem 'Tree at my Window':

> But, tree, I have seen you taken and tossed
> And if you have seen me while I slept,
> You have seen me when I was taken and swept
> And all but lost.

> That day she put our heads together,
> Fate had her imagination about her,
> Your head so much concerned with outer,
> Mine with inner, weather.

Robert Frost's preciseness of vision is not attempted, nor intended to be conveyed by precise meaning. The reader is indeed aware of a system of thought, but the system operates with entire unconcern for rational premises. Such a statement as, for example,

> I have wished a bird would fly away,
> And not sing by my house all day;
>
> …
>
> The fault must partly be in me,
> The bird was not to blame for his key.
>
> And of course there must be something wrong
> In wanting to silence any song.

conveys the experience lucidly enough. But the last couplet is inaccurate – Ulysses stopped his ears against the sirens' song and was proved right.

To this, Frost might reply in one of his recent epigrams:

> I love to toy with the platonic notion
> That wisdom need not be of Athens Attic;
> But well may be Laconic, even Boeotian,
> At least I will not have it systematic.

[1951]

John Masefield

[…]

Towards the end of 1950 I was still a fairly unknown writer, a poet and critic. My poetry was moving more and more towards the narrative form. I was not yet ready to write novels. I thought in many ways that novels were a lazy way of writing poetry, and above all I didn't want to become a 'lady-novelist' with all the slop and sentimentalism that went with that classification. (In that aim, at least, I have the satisfaction of having been successful.)

Although I now write novels, and only occasional poems, I still think of myself as a narrative poet. My novels are not verse, they are not poetic in the flowery sense. But I claim a poetic perception, a poet's way of looking at the world, a synoptic vision.

Looking back at this work I wrote on Masefield, I feel a large amount of my writing on him can be applied generally; it is in many ways a statement of my position as a literary critic and I hope some readers will recognise it as such. Certainly I have changed over the intervening years, but my basic tenets remain surprisingly (even to me) constant.

***

I wrote to Masefield on 28th November, 1950, suggesting the book. He was the Poet Laureate, still in the public mind the 'sailor poet', but at that time not very widely read. I felt he was overlooked for the wrong reasons. Masefield replied immediately in his characteristically courteous manner:

> I am much honoured, that you should wish to write about my work, and much touched that you should have read so much of it and continue its friend.
>
> Would it be too much to ask, that you should first meet and talk with me?

I arranged to visit John Masefield at his house, Burcote Brook, Abingdon in Berkshire on 6 December 1950. He sent a car to meet me at Oxford Station. It was a freezing day. The snow was deep. Here is the account of my meeting with Masefield that I wrote in my Memorandum Book:

> Dec. 8 1950
>
> In bed with cold which was caught at Abingdon, and I can't help thinking that if Masefield were not so intemperately 'Temperant' I would not be snuffling and choking thus – i.e. if he had offered me a drink on frozen Wednesday last. But I have not the heart to blame him for in all else he is a generous and delightful host.
>
> He has a large house, much larger than I expected, with a lodge and drive. Somehow, I didn't expect to find the atmosphere of comfort and success. A lovely-looking old man. Rosy cheeks, white skin, pure-white hair and moustache and blue, blue eyes. A charming voice which carefully enunciates all vowels and speaks boldly. First I was shown

into his study which looks out on a long stretch of grass (frosted over on Wednesday) leading to a river running between clumps of trees. There was a large fire, comfortable chairs into one of which I was put, but M. chose a hard armless chair which he seemed to prefer (like the Admiral in 'Dead Ned'). He asked me kindly about my journey; then spoke about Mary Shelley (on whom I had told him by letter I had written), and whom he described as an excellent widow, whatever kind of wife she made. He spoke of Shelley and his admiration for his work, though he (M) 'did not think all priests and kings were evil'. Then of Godwin whom he disliked, he said, although he had read and enjoyed his novels when young. I asked if Caleb Williams had influenced 'Dead Ned' and he replied, yes possibly, though he was not aware of it & in fact could not remember the story. The idea of 'Dead Ned'; he told me, was given him by a story he was told when dining at Barber Surgeons' Hall. He was informed that the very table on which he was dining was that used formerly by the dissectors of hanged men, who had been condemned to be drawn and quartered, and exposed to public view. The surgeons who performed this office were under the secret oath of their society, to try to restore life whenever one of the hanged bodies showed signs of life (as frequently happened). M. was shown an oriental screen which had been sent by one of the criminals who had there been revived, to his surgeon-benefactors. It was the custom that when this reviving of the hanged took place, they were shipped abroad, just like Dead Ned. M. said that his brother had found some papers relating to some criminal who survived hanging and escaped rehanging through a pardon. These stories went to the making of the novel. He asked me a little about myself, but did not seem too curious. I told him a few brief details. He said how touched he was by my wishing to write the book, and I told him part of my plan. He said, in reference to *Dauber* that the story was told him exactly as it is recounted in the poem, even to the dying words of the *Dauber* 'It will go on.' He said he did not think much of *Dauber* either way, it was written so long ago. *The Everlasting Mercy*, he said, was of course a turning point in his career. (He did not seem keen to talk about his work, and so much that I wanted to ask him will now have to be put to him by letter.)

He spoke then of Rossetti and asked, I think, what is thought of him now. I said there is a tendency to think of him as a languishing aesthete. He said 'Oh but when I was a young poet we looked upon Rossetti as the life force of poetry. Without Rossetti, Swinburne could not have been, William Morris could not have been, Burne-Jones could not have been.' He went out to fetch Mrs Masefield whom I shall describe presently, then continued, 'Without Rossetti they would all have been clergymen – Swinburne would have been a curate.' Mrs M. laughed – a high cackle as is the laugh of the deaf, sometimes – and said, 'Imagine Swinburne a curate.' Masefield then spoke of Rossetti's discovery of Fitzgerald and the enormous success of *Rubaiyat*. Every copy was sold and they were selling at a pound a-piece (originally the book was a farthing) until the day the copyright was released when about six publishers brought out Omar and once again they went into edition after edition. Mrs Masefield left the study to go and finish her letter and about ten minutes before lunch we joined her in a smaller room which had a smaller fire, burning logs and peat. She, too, preferred a low hard chair as she said she always wanted to fall asleep in a soft chair. She was a small, kindly person, very weird-looking, with an ear-apparatus and glasses that looked as if they covered one glass eye – at least one eye had a special lens that magnified the eye to look like a marble. She was dressed in an antique black hat trimmed with velvet, a red jersey and shortish old-fashioned grey skirt. Her voice was rather appalling, being due no doubt to some deafness. I liked her; and Masefield behaved with natural courtesy towards her. I should think she has been a true companion to him. They talked of their travels, from time to time, speaking of the lion farm at Hollywood, which Masefield said was kept specially for film use. He had seen one shot of a film introducing lions and Christians in the Roman arena. The lions were trained not to eat people, only to look fierce, but, he said, the Christians in this particular film would have put any healthy lion off.

We went into lunch – had some fricassee, very well cooked, accompanied by vegetables and 'delights' as Masefield called them. These 'delights' were pecan nuts and raisins. During lunch Masefield told me how he had hung round Swinburne's door at Putney as a young man to see the poet – a queer figure with an aureole of red hair, tripping up Putney Hill. He asked, what did I think of Swinburne! I said I appreciated his technique but could not really extend my enjoyment beyond the words. He said, to the young poets at the end of the last century, Swinburne seemed to have released the language – he could do anything with language.

Meanwhile, I was feeling rather cold. We were all three provided with a black shiny round oil stove, reaching about 2 ft. But the other side was cold. Anyway, we returned to the smaller drawing-room after eating Christmas pudding which M. said he hoped was my first time this year. There in the smaller room, we had coffee which M. poured and served; and he was very assiduous in pressing me to further 'delights' – fruit, sweets, etc.

Other things he had told me during this time were: that he couldn't get beyond a few pages of *Wuthering Heights*, although he admired what Rossetti had said of it – 'The characters speak English but the scene is apparently laid in Hell.' *Jane Eyre*, he said, was considered a wicked book in his youth and his sister was forbidden to read it. He believed, he said, that he read a lot of books in his youth which would have been forbidden him 'had they known'; he told me, too, that he thought the present poor sales of poetry were due to the high prices of the books. He considered that the theory was wrong which attributed the unpopularity of poetry to inferior work by present-day poets, for, he said, the public for poetry has actually increased; Yeats, he said, estimated the British poetry-reading public at 4,000. To-day, there are one million BBC listeners to poetry programmes.

I left him at 2 p.m. – his car was waiting to take me into Oxford. I left him with a feeling of unexpected warmth. He had given me two of his photographs and his 'Book of Both Sorts' inscribed to me; and had said that he would give me every help with my book. A new autobiographical book by him is appearing in April – first in the *Atlantic Monthly* as a serial – but apart from my use of the material in this book, in 'The Conway' and 'In the Mill', he promised to 'think up' new material for me.

Throughout, he was most unaffectedly gracious, kind and sweet – an absolute poppet. I had rather expected to find a denunciatory reactionary somewhat out of sorts with the world & soured by neglect. Not a bit of it. His interest in all varieties of life's manifestations is still avid – much more so than mine or most of my generation's will ever be. The inner life of the man has not swallowed up the outer life. He is a poet of outwardness – of the essence of reality, not the essence of illusion. A born story-teller (as Herbert Palmer writes) – and this is true of his conversation as well as his art.

The car dropped me at Broad Street. It was just before 2.30. I dived into a basement tavern next door to Blackwell's and knocked back a double rum. Even so, I have a cold from my day's excursion.

One of the things I found very charming about Masefield was his interest in my tartan dress, which led him to look up the colours in a book, *Clans & Tartans of Scotland*: it is that of the MacKenzies. The war-cry was given as 'Tulach Ard', which fascinated Masefield. He repeated it over and over.

Dec. 9

Masefield also remarked on the true greatness of *Jude the Obscure*. I have remembered, too, that Masefield said that the theme of *Dauber* was that the artist is compelled to obey the law of his own being, no matter if death or disaster ensues.

Dec. 9 (evening)

I have just remembered more things about my visit to Masefield.

1) He began by asking me if I had a good journey, and had I much trouble getting from my home to Paddington.

2) He admires Peacock's poems, especially mentioning 'The Three Wise Men' and 'War Song'.

3) Re. 'Dead Ned' – he said he had a special interest in the Coast of Dead Ned, about which it is said,

Beware, beware, the Bight of Benin,
Few come out, though many go in

4) He said that recently he had been reading some of Tom Moore's poems, and found some of them surprisingly good, though, he said 'We used to mock them.'

5) He spoke about the suitability of the apron-stage to Elizabethan drama. He wondered why the Roman theatre at Verulamium had not been used for theatre purposes – for some open-air drama. Why not a circus – 'Bertram Mills at the Roman Theatre,' he said half-humorously.

6) When I told him I sometimes take a part-time job he said, 'All experience is good for an artist.' I felt flattered – about the 'artist' bit.

***

I wrote to thank the Masefields for their kindness. Masefield replied [...] reiterating the effect of Rossetti and Swinburne on a young poet like himself. He ended the letter hoping that the cry of 'Tulach Ard!' would continue to echo up the Old Brompton Road.

Masefield was born in 1878. He was 72 when I met him, at that time recovering from a serious illness. But he always found time to reply to my queries and to make helpful suggestions. When my book was finally completed I know he was pleased with it:

Please let me thank you for the patient care with which you have worked at my things, & for the generous things you have written.

Please forgive me, will you, if I add, after these thanks, (so well deserved by you), that I find a book about myself most difficult to read. 'What a pity,' I keep saying, 'that this Lady had not a better subject.'

I did not meet John Masefield again till the mid-sixties. He was now well over eighty and rather frail. He had attended a poetry reading and was sitting with some friends. I approached to greet him, begging him not to get up. But he stood up straight in his usual manner. He was brimming with pleasure about my successes, for by that time my early novels had been published. 'Your name is all over the place!' he said. We spoke for a while about those days, fifteen years before, when I wrote [his biography]: *John Masefield.*

[1950 & 1991]

Decorative Art

'Professor' George Burchett started his career as a tattooist in the 1880s, working his way from deck-hand in the Navy to a place of pre-eminence above all other professors of his trade. On his death in 1953 he left his life story in the form of miscellaneous papers which are edited and compiled by Peter Leighton under the title *Memoirs of a Tattooist*. Besides running his own prosperous 'surgery' in [London's] Waterloo Road, Burchett was, from Edwardian days, a Society tattooist, when he tinted the cheeks and lips of Mayfair women. Most of his trade, however, was done during the two wars. There was always a boom, too, just after the wars when home-going servicemen desired the removal of 'I love Mary', etc.

Royal weddings and coronations have always prompted loyal subjects to have their skins adorned with photographic emblems. We learn that tattooing was, for a while, fashionable amongst royalty and high-ranking Army officers. Edward VII was tattooed. So were Alfonso of Spain and Frederick of Sweden. George V bore a dragon on his forearm. Lord Montgomery's right arm was adorned with a 'rather frivolous little butterfly'. But these were small fry to Burchett, who liked to give full scope to his art. 'Over the years I tattooed my wife elaborately … I think that some of my finest efforts were dedicated to my wife. I have covered nearly every inch of her body …' The photographs are fearful in their revulsion-fascination.

[1958]

Poetry and Politics

From the very earliest times political affairs have influenced the poet in his work and, paradoxically, poetry of a political nature has flourished in times when it has been most dangerous for the author to be guilty of utterance for or against political factions. It is easier to write ambiguously in poetry than in prose and possibly this explains why surreptitious and sly comments on various forms of government have been made in verse throughout the centuries; this applies to the oldest of the nursery rhymes (most of which had a political significance) as well as to the poetry of the French resistance in World War II.

In the fourteenth century the political lyric was the favourite means by which gleemen and minstrels courted the people. These ballads are full of reference to the government of the day – usually in complaint against injustice. A political poem with a satirical flavour of the early fourteenth century denounces the violation of Magna Carta:

> For might is right, the land is lawless,
> for night is light, the land is loreless,
> for fight is flight, the land is nameless...

Poetic drama was the principal vehicle for political poetry in the reign of Elizabeth. Tongue in cheek, dramatists expressed, through the lips of court fool, gravedigger or courtier, what they would not have been able conveniently to write in straightforward prose. Shakespeare, of course, was an agile practitioner of this form of subtlety.

Political verse was popular, and reached its peak in the seventeenth century when it was a common thing for poets of genius such as Marvell (Member for Hull) and Milton (Foreign Secretary) to be active parliamentarians. Commonwealth supporters amongst the poets were responsible for eulogistic odes to Cromwell and his followers whilst the Royalists lay low, to emerge at the Restoration with elaborate panegyrics dedicated to the restored Monarch. Dryden, always adaptable, celebrated both Protector and King in their separate times with equally adulatory stanzas in the heroic measure. Pope, Dryden and Marvell were also keen satirists, the political satire being by far the best medium for the propagandist and pamphleteer; and a successful satire, published at an opportune moment, was often instrumental in influencing public opinion.

With the Romantic revival towards the end of the eighteenth century and the relaxation of the laws of treason, politics became less a subject for poetry than for the essay or tract, although there have been many outstanding examples of poems on the subject of government and parliamentary figures from Goldsmith to the present day.[*]

[1948]

---

[*]Originally, a selection of political poetry compiled by Muriel Spark followed this essay.

Emily Brontë

A panegyric by Swinburne on Charlotte Brontë* devotes no minor attention to Emily, and a negotiation of some tortuous sentences will reward the reader with a statement so elementary that to draw attention to it might seem unnecessary, were it not that sometimes Emily Brontë's creative *genre* seems in danger of being misdefined. Extensive references to Emily Brontë as mystic, as poet of Christianity, as heretic, as heathen, as intellectual thinker, as psychical hermaphrodite, as emotional writer, have all been made in this century, with some justification. It has also been suggested, without justification, that she was a lesbian, and that she was an intellectual writer. (This latter definition is here rejected since a distinction must be made between her intellect and her mode of writing.) But emphasis on any one of these aspects of her mind or nature, however diverting, may prove misleading, for none presents her as a creative writer in her integrity.

Charlotte Brontë's rhetorical and praiseworthy posthumous note on her sister notwithstanding, it was Swinburne possibly, who most exactly located the essence of Emily Brontë, and strangely enough, it was he who expressed it in the most concise terms: 'There was a dark unconscious instinct as of primitive nature-worship in the passionate great genius of Emily Brontë.'

Swinburne here noted three of the most important factors in her work: her *instinctiveness*, of a 'dark unconscious' order; her pantheism and its particular type – that of *primitive* nature-worship; and her *passion*.

Emily Brontë's approach to life, to people, places and things, was manifest in her work in quite original, because in so instinctive a way. That is also true of her approach to the literature of her past, for though it must be apparent that she was indebted to her reading of many poets earlier than, and including, Cowper, Burns, Wordsworth, Byron and Scott, she did not derive their various influences in any but an instinctive way. It would be surprising to find that she annotated, even mentally, the books she read; rather did she submit to the experience of her reading, allowing it to infiltrate, to become part of, her senses. Her instinct may be said to have acted as a filter, through which the varied modes and feelings of the past achieved that purification necessary to her own poetic genius.

---

*'A Note on Charlotte Brontë' (1877).

With the instinctive quality of her thought and expression, her pantheistic conception of life is closely associated. Her vision of nature was, as Swinburne wrote, a primitive one; her longing to become part of and one with the earth was not such that her intellect, more advanced, as is usually the case, than her instincts, could easily accede to.

> O thy bright eyes must answer now,
> When Reason, with a scornful brow,
> Is mocking at my overthrow;
> O thy sweet tongue must plead for me
> And tell why I have chosen thee!
>
> Stern Reason is to judgment come
> Arrayed in all her forms of gloom:
> Wilt thou my advocate be dumb?
> No, radiant angel, speak and say
> Why I did cast the world away;
>
> Speak, God of Visions, plead for me,
> And tell why I have chosen thee!

Thus she invoked her 'God of Visions', the nature-image that welded her being into unity; to this interrogation by her intellect, the only answer lies in her own definition of the possessing spirit,

> Thee, ever-present, phantom thing –
> My slave, my comrade and my king.

She did not find in nature, as did the Wordsworthians, a source merely of spiritual consolation or a philosophical springboard. Nor did she seek a moral lesson from nature, since her God of Visions represented a force which neither preached at nor indulged her, but simultaneously obeyed, befriended, challenged and enthralled. It was a conception of nature subject to no moral laws of the external world; it was a paradoxical, yet not chaotic concept, for the spirit of nature and its retinue, as conceived by her, observed their own peculiar *mores* operating on a transcendental plane. Her poetry was as much a product of the conflict between this and the outer world – of her sense of exile from her natural home, as was her obvious misanthropy.

'Emily Brontë's outlook is not immoral, but it is pre-moral', writes Lord David Cecil.[*] 'It concerns itself not with moral standards, but

---

[*] Essay on 'Emily Brontë and *Wuthering Heights*', in *Early Victorian Novelists* (1934). Though

with those conditioning forces of life on which the naïve erections of the human mind that we call moral standards are built up.' So that, while she, alike with nature, was moved by and was faithful to a strange and unique system of being, this was not entirely unrelated to external modes of behaviour. It was, in fact, their primitive basis: her originality of ideas and expression derived truly from origins.

Emily Brontë's occupation of a world existing in a transcendental dimension may lead to the conclusion that she was a mystic. But if she is so defined, it must be added that she was a mystic of passion, for passion informs the tempo and feeling of all her creative writing. Yet, once more, this was not the passion of the outward world, but was the vital and prevailing attribute of Emily Brontë's exceptional view of life. In her can be seen, as Arthur Symons described it, 'the paradox of passion without sensuousness'. To interpret this passion that drives and directs her work, as a reflection of her own or some other human being's objective experience, would be to misjudge the whole disposition of her thought. Arthur Symons might have reconciled his paradox had he considered how pre-human is her passion and her sensuousness; for the feelings and susceptibilities of Emily Brontë's creation are representative and archetypal rather than individual and specific as are human responses. It might be true to say that, had the events of her outward life evoked any great degree of emotional acknowledgment from her, the passion of her writings must have been of a much more chastened, less idealised, less emphasised order.

Emily Brontë died in 1848 in the thirty-first year of her life. The most gifted of a talented family, daughter of a clergyman, she received a good education according to current standards, tried school-teaching without success, and attended a finishing school in Brussels for some months; she wrote a novel and a considerable number of poems, and caught a chill at her brother's funeral which led to her death of consumption at Haworth Parsonage, where she had spent most of her days. That is the factual record of her existence of which little more is known.

But what of the thoughts, the spirit and temperament, the fierce and radiant genius that she embodied? Charlotte Brontë tells us, 'In Emily's nature the extremes of vigour and simplicity seemed to meet. Under an unsophisticated culture, inartificial tastes, and an unpretending outside, lay a secret power and fire that might have informed the

---

written with special reference to *Wuthering Heights*, this work presents an insight into Emily Brontë's mind, invaluable to readers of her poetry.

brain and kindled the imagination of a hero; but she had no worldly wisdom; her powers were unadapted to the practical business of life...'

Charlotte was often deceived by her own eloquence, yet, despite the fact that her letters often speak of Emily as being contentedly engaged in the 'practical business of life' – in housework, for example, Charlotte's words describe most convincingly such a mind as created *Wuthering Heights*.

Most readers of Brontë biography will know of the extraordinary imaginative activity of the Brontë family in childhood. Charlotte, Branwell, Emily and Anne, deprived at an early age of their mother, governed by a competent, if somewhat chilly aunt, and by a father elsewhere preoccupied, were largely free to find amusement in their own populous imaginations. Thus they came first to invent a series of adventure tales in which all four participated, and then to commit these games to writing with such prolific industry, that to-day those of Charlotte and Branwell fill two large volumes of the *Shakespeare Head Brontë*. The two eldest children, Charlotte and Branwell, seem later to have formed a literary alliance, while Emily collaborated likewise with Anne. Though the legends, romances and poems of Angria – the fabulous territory conceived by Charlotte and Branwell – are fortunately extant, those of Gondal, the country of the two younger Brontës' devising, remain to us only in the adult poems of Emily and Anne. For, long after the childhood partnership of Charlotte and Branwell had ceased, Emily and Anne continued to people their dream world with heroic, exotic figures, with whose loves, wars and destinies they became so closely involved that, in fact, they played the Gondal game all their lives; and this close association between Emily and Anne is one which many biographers have, in the present writer's opinion, underestimated. As we know from the messages they wrote to each other every four years in the ritualistic form of 'birthday papers', a strong sympathy existed between the two sisters: Anne, to whose lesser (though not inconsiderable) talent Emily provided a rich and vital stimulus, appears as Emily's confidante; Emily, as her younger sister's spiritual partisan.

Both Emily and Anne wrote poems that can be placed into the categories of 'Gondal' and 'personal'; the former do not, of course, describe their actual experiences. The isolated parsonage, exposed to the Yorkshire moorland, provided no such exhilaration, no such energetic scene of action as their Gondal poems portray; rather did their home's bare setting supply a negative contribution to their work, in failing to distract. Emily's Gondal poems are among her finest.

Derived, not from outward but from inner experience, they are as personal to her as are her 'personal' poems. The Gondal characters, *Julius Brenzaida, Alexander of Elbë, Augusta Geraldine Almeda, Rosina* and others, are caused to speak and act their parts, but Emily's own convictions, her judgments and all her tragic intimations, are implicit in their words and actions.

Throughout her poetry, the image of imprisonment and the vision of release by death prevail. Imprisonment she would equate with life; death represented her rehabilitation with nature. Death, for her, was not annihilation but a very positive force; not good, not evil, but at once the autonomous power whose victim she was, the submissive spirit whose victor.

There is a poem by Emily Brontë, as perfect a lyric as the nineteenth century produced, which seems strangely to have been ignored by anthologists. 'There let thy bleeding branch atone' has received little attention apart from being wrongly ascribed to Anne Brontë by an editor who later amended his sad fault. The import of this poem is not immediately recognisable since it belongs to the Gondal cycle whose framework can only be guessed. Nevertheless its atmospheric immediacy is undeniable; the diction is felicitous and pure; and its poetic idea – the association of a limb torn from a tree with the rough severance of an image from the memory – conveys the unusual degree of passion, embodied in traditional lyric formality, which makes this poem an outstanding one. The reason why such an important poem should have attracted scant notice is not, possibly, a matter of taste or opinion, but of the way in which Emily Brontë's critics have come to regard her; it is a question of what we are looking for, one that dictates what we shall find, and that affects the appreciation of all her work.

For in general, she is looked upon as a meteoric phenomenon, as a great romantic hermit, or as a profoundly individual heretic. Indeed, she was all these things. But for our own time, Emily Brontë is perhaps best seen as a part of the tradition of English poetry; and we shall not derive great advantage and pleasure from her work unless we notice and appreciate its traditional aspects.

Like Burns or Clare, Emily Brontë was an example of genius flourishing in isolation. It was this very physical and spiritual isolation that had a salutary effect on her writings: it was an isolation from the influences of contemporaneous social modes and from literary circles. But she was not isolated from literature; her solitary leisure was not spent entirely in day-dreaming and the composing of high fantasy, for Emily Brontë was a reader. While engaged in baking, we are told, she would have a book propped before her; she would enter a room full of people to snatch a book and retreat. The predominant characteristics of her poetry show how well she had assimilated her reading, and because the influence of Victorian literary criticism was never superimposed upon her, because her literary education was not drawn from current fashions, her assimilation of literature was instinctive, her natural discrimination and taste unadulterated. Like Burns or Clare, she is a poet in whom the tradition is manifest in an inevitable, because in so effortless, a way.

Now of *Wuthering Heights*, Lord David Cecil has justly written:

> So far from being the incoherent outpourings of an undisciplined imagination, it is the one perfect work of art amid all the vast and varied canvases of Victorian fiction.
>
> It seems odd that it should be so, considering the circumstances of its creation, considering that Emily Brontë's craftsmanship was self-taught, and that she evolved its principles unassisted by any common tradition.

There is no common tradition in which *Wuthering Heights* can be fixed, so far as the English novel is concerned. But does not the unique situation occur, in that Emily Brontë's novel is fed from traditional sources through the channels of her poetry? For, as many critics have observed, it is towards *Wuthering Heights* that her poems converge; they achieve fruition in that most poetic of structures.

It would be difficult to believe that the author of the lines

> Is he upon some distant shore
> Or is he on the sea
> Or is the heart thou dost adore
> A faithless heart to thee?

or of 'Douglas's Ride', was not acquainted with the border ballads. Scott, whom we know to have been a favourite source of reading in the Brontë household, had done much, with his *Minstrelsy of the Scottish Border*, to revive during the first part of the nineteenth century the interest aroused earlier by *Percy's Reliques*.

Not only do Emily Brontë's prototypal warriors and defiant female figures comply with the ballad tradition, but her tempo and metres, her phraseology, her occasional brutal irony, testify to her knowledge of ballad formulae. 'Douglas's Ride', for all it owes to 'John Gilpin' and possibly 'Tam O'Shanter', is so technically and suggestively indebted to the earlier forms, even in its conventional fireside opening, that it is, in fact, an excellent piece of ballad pastiche. Many of her Gondal pieces acquire their ballad flavour less directly. 'And now the house-dog stretched once more' has something of Cowper's handling of the classical couplet, eminently suited to the narrative; while the Marmionesque sense of chivalry, the recognition of family loyalties which take precedence over private friendships in 'Come, the wind may never again', is reminiscent of Scott's tenor of thought.

But Emily Brontë's poems are not entirely of the bardic type. In sentiment, in form and in diction, they more often resemble Elizabethan and Jacobean lyrics:

> Fall, leaves, fall; die, flowers, away
> lengthen night and shorten day.

The cadence echoes the seventeenth century, and only her acute auditory sensibility could have captured it. No later poet but Tennyson might have been capable of this lyric, though not of its final paradox, a fusion of the ballad influence and the lyric convention, and a strong metaphysical content:

> I shall smile when wreaths of snow
> Blossom where the rose should grow.

The metaphysical lyric, in fact, achieved by Emily Brontë its most important development since Shelley.

There is also evidence in Emily Brontë's verse of the romantic naturalism of her own time:

> The violet's eye might shyly flash

suggests the precision of Wordsworth. And though there is scarcely a poem by her that does not bear an implicit tribute to other poets, these various influences are not transparent. They are blended with instinctive craftsmanship, within the structure of her individual style; for Emily Brontë's own nobility of utterance, her manipulation of sounds, her percipient use of feminine endings, and her variable rhythms, direct and modulate all other elements.

It is her technical assimilation of influences that distinguishes her poetry, that endows it with the intensity, the emotional and somewhat ominous aura, which we associate with her as with no other poet:

> House to which the voice of life shall never more return
> Chambers roofless, desolate, where weeds and ivy grow.

Even in this earlier poem she achieved her characteristic tension with certainty and without conscious effort.

Many factors combine to condition the particular tendencies of a poet's style. In Emily Brontë we may well find some explanation of her strange, ebb-and-flow rhythms and her solemn, attenuated lines, in her own personality. For in these her pantheism is latent: her rhythms resemble the sweeping moorland and her language resounds with the storm and cataract.

[1952]

Part II

Autobiography and Travel

I was into my fifties, and getting old. How nerve-wracking
it is to be getting old, how much better to be old!
Memento Mori

I do not care to go about with nothing on my face
so that everyone can see what is written on it.
Robinson

My Most Memorable New Year's Eve

My most memorable New Year's Eve was when I was very small. I remember my mother and father waking me up. They took me to the window to see the fireworks. Church bells were ringing. In those days in Scotland New Year's Eve was more important than Christmas. My mother said, 'It's 1923!' She had a glass of port in her hand which I willingly sipped. I always loved a party.

[1982]

When I Was Ten

I was ten in 1928. My favourite reading was the Border Ballads, which in Edinburgh are best read in the long dark winters. In my childhood all my winter reading was done by gaslight.

I subscribed to *The Children's Newspaper* edited by Arthur Mee, famed in his time for educational publications. It was a real newspaper, packed with non-political information. Thanks to Arthur Mee, at ten I knew more about daily life in Baghdad than most British adults do to-day.[*]

My after-school life was divided between lending libraries and the corner of the kitchen where I curled up with my loot. When I was ten the cloth-bound *Joy Street* volumes (Nos. 1–14) appeared. Presented for children, the contents were an introduction to the poetry and prose of the day, featuring such modern young stars as Compton Mackenzie, Walter de la Mare, Laurence Housman, Algernon Blackwood, Edith Sitwell, A.A. Milne, G.K. Chesterton, Hilaire Belloc and a clever Katharine Tynan.[†]

My bookseller found me the whole *Joy Street* series, to refresh my memory, some years ago. As English writing they have worn quite well.

[2003]

---

[*]This was written at the outset of the disastrous war in Iraq.
[†]Muriel Spark asked whether she was related to Kenneth Tynan.

Pensée: Scottish Education

The Scottish education is famous for its rational and logical qualities. Logic was one of my subjects at school at a very early age. I always studied Latin and Greek. The Scots put a great moral accent on the virtue of honesty and I have always, myself, followed honesty of thought. I was impressed as a child by the Border Ballads. These are a large collection of anonymous songs and poems from ancient times, circulating by word of mouth mostly in the borderland between Scotland and England. They were collected in the nineteenth century by Sir Walter Scott. These ballads were very exciting and thrilling to me as a child. They were cruel and lyrical at the same time and I think it had a great effect on my later literary work.

I was reminded of the Border Ballads some years ago in Florence when one evening I heard about the *Guerrieri*, the heroic statues that had been found in the sea off Calabria. The *Guerrieri* were described to me as being very beautiful and terrible. I was so fascinated that my friend and I were to spend the night in Florence in order to see them the next morning in the Archaeological Museum where they were temporarily placed. I remember going along with my friend in my evening clothes to see these absolute marvels. They took my breath away and certainly do remind me of the great heroes in those old ballads, pitiless and beautiful.

[2003]

My Book of Life

When I was fifteen I was given as school prizes *The Oxford Book of Ballads* and Scott's *Minstrelsy of the Scottish Border*. I read them many times with increasing wonder; they entered my cognition as well as my emotional system, to stay there.

The characters who peopled these ballads seemed to me, persuaded as I was by the lovely lyricism of the ballad-forms and the language, microcosmic examples of real people whom I would expect to meet later in life, and essentially, did. They were a mysterious and irrational blend of people who could and would use their power to the utmost drop of blood, and those who, out of pure nobility, would refrain from using their power at all except for good. Lyricism, savagery, love and revenge: these were the undercurrents of life as those *Ballads* taught me. I have learned, am still learning, much more from life, but the basics of the *Ballads* go through all my works and ways of apprehending.

[2001]

Note on My Story 'The Gentile Jewesses'*

I find it impossible to separate the Jewess within myself from the Gentile, even for the sake of argument. The attempt is absurd in any case if the two strains exist uncomplainingly amongst one's own bones. Only, I like to analyse, to distinguish and compare. Otherwise, what is the point of all my labour and reading? I like to analyse, and then, as a reward, define myself. To embark on anything, even a train of thought, without hope of a satisfactory conclusion, is not in my nature.

I do not continually think of myself as a Gentile Jewess, or of the world as a specifically Gentile-Jewish complex. But what I felt as a child I now hold as a belief: the true dimensions of our lives are greater than they appear to be. This is a philosophical statement, a concept. By temperament I am unable to hold a concept without letting my imagination play upon it. And suddenly I return to the cycle of my grandmother's destiny, to the crossing of the Red Sea, and the history of all her activities throughout the Scriptures, Old Testament and New, from Genesis to Revelation. All the more since I discovered myself to be a Catholic animal am I a Gentile Jewess.

When it came to essential things the Jews and Jewesses of my youth considered me an alien. I was uninstructed in the Jewish religion and orthodox customs. Perhaps I was touchy. I always felt they considered me slightly unclean by my Gentile blood. I did not then realise how far Calvinism had penetrated into the Jewish life of Edinburgh and how deeply they had become involved with themselves as an Elect. It was not till later that I came across Jewesses of my grandmother's spiritual size.

Gentiles were mostly my friends, but I was alone because they could not understand my Jewishness which was nowhere on the surface. They thought it an accident of birth. Even then I knew it was

---

*The story 'The Gentile Jewesses' is published in *All the Stories of Muriel Spark* (New York: New Directions) and in Muriel Spark, *The Complete Short Stories* (Edinburgh: Canongate Books, 2001).

no accident, but something essential done on purpose. I knew a girl who was half Jewish. She, too, seemed lonely and set apart. We had no interest in each other. She died young.

At school, religion was taught from the Bible. Everyone read the Bible. I did so with a sense that it was specially mine. I had a strange conception of God, I thought him a charming and witty character with a ready answer, and with a lot of conflicting sides to his nature. I liked God, especially in his sophisticated moments, as when he spoke to Moses out of the burning bush, and Moses enquired his name, and God replied, 'I am who I am.'

That was a good answer, it inspired personal awe as well as purely technical admiration.

Am I a Gentile? Am I a Jewess? Both and neither. What am I? I am what I am.

It is said in the Catholic catechism that we are made in the likeness of God chiefly in the soul. In the final definition we are unique and indestructible. Who are you? You are who you are.

Already I am slipping into the scriptural style of questions and answers. My mind is full of my grandmother's environment stretching from her garden path in Watford to the Holy Land where my story begins.

Is it a spiritual autobiography or is it a novel? It is both and neither, the two are inseparable. I am not a literary commentator for the time being, I am a Gentile Jewess.

Is the story fact? Is it fiction? It is what it is.

[1963]

The Celestial Garden Party

There are some things that people should buy because they are so attractive, so irresistible in the shop; these should be bought but never worn or used.

I am a tie-watcher on the television. Especially do I watch the male announcers' ties. Vivid statements, they should certainly be acquired to content the restless soul of the purchaser, but they should be left to hang on the tie-rack until the moment arrives for the big periodic throw-out.

My mother had an analogous mania for hats. We lived in sober Edinburgh where, in the later 'twenties which I remember well, hats were pot-shaped, muted in colour, sometimes with tiny brims venturing an occasional feather or else made of straw for the summer, or [perhaps] light panama. Women's hats were a crown and a brim; sometimes adorned with a cotton flower or ruched with a black satin ribbon.

But my mother's hats were quite different. It is true that with her dark colouring and good features she looked well in those large, wavy-brimmed, shady and bedecked hats. But they were utterly impractical outside of Ascot races, and possibly the summer opening of London's Royal Academy: four hundred miles and many many more hundreds of cultural distances from our puritanical Scottish capital. But my mother could not resist them. 'Why,' I asked, 'do you buy these hats?' She could never pass a hat-shop, particularly if the milliner gave her cash-credit. I recall my mother trying on her latest acquisition, holding a hand-mirror in front of the dressing-table glass so that she could see all sides. 'It would do lovely for a garden party,' she would invariably reply.

It was always a garden party she had in mind when she acquired and tried on those hats. I never thought of her as really wanting anything else but a garden party hat, although she did, for every day, wear a sensible head-hugging cloche. The fashionable Scottish tam-o-shanters she eschewed entirely. She wore these sensible hats out of pure obligation. In the 'twenties and early 'thirties in Edinburgh, where everything was passionless and only the weather was full of consternation, nobody left home hatless. Even the poor women of the then High Street slums wore black shawls which covered their heads. I was about ten at the time of my most vivid hat memories, but a few years later, the same hats were still occupying shelves and hat-boxes in our house. (We were never asked to a garden party, that I recall.) But I was now doing classics at school and the elements of Plato's philosophy were seeping in. I formed the opinion that my mother's hats were designed for an ideal Garden Party which took place somewhere in the sky. I thought of my mother's celestial garden party many years later when I explained to dear Iris Murdoch, that most professional of Platonists, how a desire to design an automobile could start, in the Platonic sense, with a little motor-car in the sky. She was very intrigued, repeating my phrase, trying it out on herself: 'A little motor-car in the sky...'

Like most people outside of France I had not read Proust in the hey-day of my mother's hats. If I had, I would have seen in my mind's eye Odette promenading in the Bois with her author, Marcel. In fact, so wonderful were the hats of duchesses and lesser girls in Proust's experience it is recorded that, as he aged, and was writing *A La Recherche*, he sent round to one of his titled ladies to ask, would she kindly send her maid to him with that delightful hat she had worn on some distinguished occasion years and years before. 'My dear fellow,' she replied, 'it is gone and disposed of long ago.' Proust, it is said, could hardly believe that the poetic hat of his memory no longer existed.

We had a family friend, Sheila Fagan,* who, being widowed, sometimes came to give my mother a hand in the house. Sheila was tall, slim and naturally fair-haired. My father always had a soft spot for Sheila, a very genial, kind woman. One day my mother and I returned home to find my father and Sheila having reasonably innocent fun with my mother's fantastic hat collection. Sheila was trying them on, one by one. I don't remember the outcome. I suppose I went off to play, but I felt something in the air.

Sheila eventually married again, to a prosperous man. But I think she had a soft spot for my father. In the 'seventies I was the go-between on the phone for Sheila and my father. 'Yes, Sheila, he was asking for you, Sheila.' (He wasn't.) After his death Sheila and my mother got together and were the best of friends from then on.

In the late 'thirties I went to the then Southern Rhodesia, now Zimbabwe. My mother wrote exultantly that she had been asked to a garden party. Letters were then sent by sea; they took two weeks to arrive. I wondered what hat my mother would wear and waited anxiously for the next mail. I had misgivings. The garden party was in aid of a Jewish benefit. The Jewish community of Edinburgh had, like minorities everywhere, taken on some of the habits, forms and social colourings of their neighbours.

I had written in time, as I thought, to remind her that in wartime the fashions were somewhat subdued, but I have no doubt she went to the party crowned with one of her floral tributes and a dress to match. 'It was very dreary,' she wrote. 'They were all wearing tweeds.'

Have I inherited any of this garden party tendency? – Perhaps. The other day, going through my clothes, I noticed a preponderance of drifting chiffon. I tend to grab off the peg things that look good. Years ago I underwent a phase of haute couture but the numerous fittings that the Diva-like dressmakers demanded piteously ate up my precious working mornings. 'Madame, I could not possibly let you leave my atelier without a half-centimetre off each shoulder…' I had work to do. So I got to snatching my clothes without even trying them on. Hence, when I rummage for a pair of jeans, all these floating-island

---

*Not her real name.

chiffons come to light. There is little one can do with them. Where I live, in Tuscany, women pass on their clothes to a house of nuns who pass them on to the needy, or even wear them under their habits. (They looked up their Rules, which limited themselves to prescribing 'warm stuff' for underclothes.) But clouds of transparent nylon and beaded velvets? They are called for from time to time, it is true. But mainly they beautifully hang there for some useless celestial occasion, as should the ties of the TV announcers.

As for the hats, I was so fascinated by a multi-hat shop in Venice that I started writing a poem about it. My handbag was snatched later, in Florence, with my poem in it. 'How did the poem go?' asked the policeman, his pencil poised.

'I wish I knew,' I replied.

[2002]

What Images Return

In the spring of this year I was obliged to spend some weeks in the North British Hotel* in Edinburgh, isolated and saddened by many things, while my father's last illness ran its course in the Royal Infirmary. It was necessary for me to be within call. I do not like the public rooms and plushy lounges of hotels anywhere in the world, I do not sit in them; and least of all in one's native city is it spiritually becoming to sit in the lounges of big hotels.

I spent most of my time in my room waiting for the hours of visiting my father to come round. I think at such times in one's life one tends to look out of the window oftener and longer than usual. I left my work and my books and spent my time at the window. It was a high, wide window, with an inside ledge, broad and long enough for me to sit in comfortably with my legs stretched out. The days before Easter were suddenly warm and sunny. From where I sat propped in the open window frame, I could look straight on to Arthur's Seat and the Salisbury Crags, its girdle. When I sat the other way round I could see part of the Old City, the east corner of Princes Street Gardens, and the black Castle Rock. In those days I experienced an inpouring of love for the place of my birth, which I am aware was psychologically

---

*Now called the Balmoral.

connected with my love for my father and with the exiled sensation of occupying a hotel room [instead of my family home] which was really meant for strangers.

Edinburgh is the place that I, a constitutional exile,* am essentially exiled from. I spent the first 18 years of my life, during the 'twenties and 'thirties, there. It was Edinburgh that bred within me the conditions of exiledom; and what have I been doing since then but moving from exile into exile? It has ceased to be a fate, it has become a calling.

My frequent visits to Edinburgh for a few weeks at a time throughout the years have been the visits of an exile in heart and mind – cautious, affectionate, critical. It is a place where I could not hope to be understood. The only sons and daughters of Edinburgh with whom I can find a common understanding are exiles like myself. By exiles I do not mean Edinburgh-born members of Caledonian Societies. I do not consort in fellowship with the Edinburgh native abroad merely on the Edinburgh basis. It is precisely the Caledonian Society aspect of Edinburgh which cannot accommodate me as an adult person.

Nevertheless, it is the place where I was first understood. James Gillespie's Girls' School, set in solid state among the green Meadows, showed an energetic faith in my literary life. I was the school's Poet and Dreamer, with appropriate perquisites and concessions. I took this for granted, and have never since quite accustomed myself to the world's indifference to art and the process of art, and to the special needs of the artist.

I have started the preceding paragraph with the word 'nevertheless' and am reminded how my whole education, in and out of school, seemed even then to pivot around this word. My teachers used it a great deal. All grades of society constructed sentences bridged by 'nevertheless'. It is my own instinct to associate the word, as the core of a thought-pattern, with Edinburgh particularly. I can see the lips of tough elderly women in musquash coats taking tea at McVittie's enunciating this word of final justification, I can see the exact gesture of head and chin and gleam of the eye that accompanied it. The sound was roughly 'niverthelace' and the emphasis was a heartfelt one. I

---

*Muriel Spark did not actually think of herself as 'exiled'. The *OED* gives the definition of 'exile' as: '(1) Penal banishment, long absence from one's country, also figuratively, and (2) a banished person (literally and figuratively)'. Muriel Spark was not, of course, banished literally, and although she may occasionally have felt figuratively in exile, she returned to Scotland to visit throughout her long life, although she did not live there again. It was a place she knew but was no longer part of. She declared herself, however, to be Scottish by formation.

believe myself to be fairly indoctrinated by the habit of thought which calls for this word. In fact I approve of the ceremonious accumulation of weather forecasts and barometer readings that pronounce for a fine day, before letting rip on the statement 'nevertheless, it's raining'. I find that much of my literary composition is based on the nevertheless idea. I act upon it. It was on the nevertheless principle that I turned Catholic.

It is impossible to know how much one gets from one's early environment by way of a distinctive character, or whether for better or worse. I think the puritanical strain of the Edinburgh ethos is inescapable, but this is not necessarily a bad thing. In the south of England the puritanical virtues tend to be regarded as quaint eccentricities: industriousness, for instance, or a horror of debt. A polite reticence about sex is often mistaken for repression. On the other hand, spiritual joy does not come in an easy consistent flow to the puritanically-nurtured soul. Myself, I have had to put up a psychological fight for my spiritual joy.

Most Edinburgh-born people, of my generation at least, must have been brought up with a sense of civic superiority. We were definitely given to understand that we were citizens of no mean city. In time, and with experience of other cities, one would have discovered the beautiful uniqueness of Edinburgh for oneself as the visitors do. But the physical features of the place surely had an effect as special as themselves on the outlook of the people. The Castle Rock is something, rising up as it does, from pre-history between the formal grace of the New Town and the noble network of the Old. To have a great primitive black crag rising up in the middle of populated streets of commerce, stately squares and winding closes, is like the statement of an unmitigated fact preceded by 'nevertheless'. In my time the society existing around it generally regarded the government and bureaucracy of Whitehall as just a bit ridiculous. The influence of a place varies according to the individual. I imbibed, through no particular mentor, but just by breathing the informed air of the place, its haughty and remote anarchism. I can never now suffer from a shattered faith in politics and politicians, because I never had any.

When the shrill telephone in my hotel room woke me at four in the morning, and a nurse told me that my father was dead, I noticed, with that particular disconnected concentration of the fuddled mind, that the rock and its castle loomed as usual in the early light. I noticed this, as if one might have expected otherwise.

[1962]

Comment on 'The Poet's House'

In July 1960 I was asked to talk on the wireless about how I became a writer. 'The Poet's House' describes an actual experience in 1944, when, during the bombing, I took refuge for a night in a house that turned out to belong to a well-known poet who was absent at the time with his wife and family. It was a small enough incident, but the experience was important to me. I used it first in 1952, as a starting-point for a short story, 'The House of the Famous Poet', which I put aside until this year, when it was published.

When I wrote the present piece for broadcasting I did not let my imagination elaborate on the actual event. I left some things out, partly to save myself embarrassment. I left out the name of the poet whose house I had made so free with. It was Louis MacNeice. I am sure he would not have been embarrassed by the story, for his part, but rather amused...

[1960]

The Poet's House

I think most writers have started their literary careers at a very early age. They've discovered at school that they can write good essays or poems, even if they're no good at anything else. But many and many people who've shown an aptitude for writing even in their teens stop writing when they grow up and find themselves occupied with something else.

But I've always been interested in what makes the adult writer start to write. Is it something compulsive within the person? Or is it, perhaps, some outward combination of circumstances? Because it's one thing to feel quite certain within oneself that one has the ability to write and to be full of ideas and visions, but it's quite another thing actually to get down to it. I think the getting down to it is the most difficult part. Even now, after years of practice I always have the greatest difficulty in lifting up a pen and sitting down to write. I can always think of other things to do which look more attractive at the time. But I always do get down to it in the end. It's a sort of obsession. And once I've started to write, everything becomes easy, everything else is forgotten, and the hours I spend writing my novels or stories are perhaps the happiest hours of my life.

Now I've been asked what it was that made me get down to writing in the first place, and actually put pen to paper and see what I could do. It was a curious adventure that I had in the summer of 1944. Before that I'd been in Central Africa for some years, and couldn't get home because of the outbreak of war. Africa was full of astonishing and marvellous things, but I had felt very strongly the lack of communication with the world to which I belonged. There was no advanced cultural life in Africa by which to measure all I experienced there – because I had even then a satirical cast of mind. So I'd longed throughout the early years of the war to get back to a place of books and ideas even though the bombs were falling. Above all I was passionately fond of poetry; I'd managed to read the modern poets in *Penguin New Writing* and felt they were tremendously exciting.

It was early in 1944 that I managed to get a passage home, and like everyone else I was immediately sent to a war job. This was with the Foreign Office in the country, but whenever I got leave to come up to London I made straight for the bookshops. Very soon I'd read all the poets of the 'thirties and early 'forties. You must understand that these writers seemed like giants to me at that time; remote, almost unreal people bearing glamorous names – Auden, Spender, Day Lewis, MacNeice. These are poets whom I now read with a more or less critical enjoyment. But at this time I thought them superbly beyond criticism because of the new doors they seemed to be opening everywhere.

***

One day in the summer of 1944 I was returning from a visit to Edinburgh by train. Those war-time trains were terribly crowded. I sat next to a girl who told me she was working in London as a mother's help at a house in St John's Wood. She was very good company, and we whiled away the long hours talking about our lives before the war, which was always good common talking-ground in those days. If you travelled long distances by train during the war you'll probably remember how the trains used to stop at some big station like Crewe or York, or at some large junction, and seem to forget to go on. Sometimes a train would simply wait at a place for four or five hours at a time. One supposed this was due to troop movements or air raids. This was the time of the V-1 bombs – robots that buzzed across the London skies, then shut off their engines, hovered for a moment and fell like a thunderbolt. Our train had stopped at one station for about three hours and we watched the comings and goings of soldiers, and families laden with shabby bags and children on the platform; there was a sort of dingy poetry about the scene, and I wanted to be a writer and make it permanent. I remember especially a young private soldier standing on the platform drinking a large cup of railway tea, drinking it all up, then staring for a long time into the empty cup with no expression at all on his face.

We were about five hours late arriving in London. The sirens were wailing. It was a horrible sound, whoever thought it up. I was always more afraid of the sirens than of the bombs. I'd missed my last train back to the country and I was undecided where to spend the night, because I was quite poor. The girl I'd met on the train asked me to come and spend the night with her at St John's Wood. 'It's all right,' she said, 'because *they're* away just now.' She meant the master and mistress of the house. We got a taxi to St John's Wood and on the way she told me their name, which didn't mean anything special to me just then.

***

The house had a small front garden, which I remember in the waning summer light as a mass of tangled greenery, rather neglected. My friend opened the front door and we entered a darkish room almost wholly taken up with a long plain wood work-table. On this was a half-empty marmalade jar, a pile of papers and a dried-up ink bottle. I remember there was a steel Morrison shelter in one corner and some photographs on the mantelpiece, one of a school-boy wearing glasses. We opened our bags to get out our little packets of food rations and I asked her about the owner of the house. She said he was something in a university.

The room in which I was to sleep was a large light room on the first floor, partly a study, with several windows. I noticed it was far more orderly than the rest of the house. The bed was merely a fairly thick mattress neatly made up on the floor. I thought the owner of the study was probably an elderly cranky professor. Then of course I looked at the books. I can't remember many of the titles but I saw that it was an enterprising sort of library, not at all consistent with the idea of an old scholar. But in fact I think I was rather irritated by the unconventional quality of the whole house, and now of these books, because I couldn't see any meaning for it. Eccentricity for its own sake always seems to me a very boring thing, but it ceases to be merely eccentricity when it's the expression of a new and living system of thought.

I took down one or two books. An inscription in one of them was signed by its author; a well-known novelist. I found another inscribed copy, and this was dedicated on the fly-leaf to a famous poet, one of those whose work I'd been reading again and again. I recalled the name of the owner of the house which my friend, the nurse-maid, had told me in the taxi. She was having a bath at that moment. I shouted to her through the bathroom door, 'Is this the house of the famous poet?' Through her splashes, in a bored sort of way she said, 'Yes, he writes poetry.'

***

I don't want to exaggerate the importance in itself of this incident; to most people I think it would have been interesting and perhaps amusing to find themselves lodged in the house of a well-known writer. But on me at that particular point in my life it had an intense imaginative effect. I had no wish to meet or see the poet; on the contrary I began to be afraid that the family would return suddenly from wherever they were, and I asked my friend very urgently to assure me there was no chance of them coming back. Now it was the house itself which fascinated me.

I went round it touching everything. I sat at the poet's desk. I lifted the pencils and smelt them. I wanted to draw the virtue out of everything, and make it my own. In the attic I found a pile of shabby books. These were mostly novels and volumes of nineteenth-century poets, the sort of books that might once have been prescribed school reading. But I didn't bother much about the titles, I was intent on touching the books. I think I must have felt that by some sympathetic magic I could draw from the poet's possessions some essence which would enable me to get down to my writing. Perhaps I ought to say here that I haven't been particularly influenced in my work by this poet. It was merely the will to write that I wanted to acquire.

During the night the sirens went frequently and one heard the thud of the V-1s near or far. I didn't take shelter, I didn't see any need to on that occasion. I felt it was impossible that the poet's house could be hit by a bomb.

Next morning early I went outside and stood exactly where I'd been when I first saw the garden from the door of the taxi. I wanted to get my first impressions for the second time. And this time I saw an absolute purpose in everything both outside and inside the house. I was intensely curious, and greatly impressed now by the unconventional quality of the house.

At this particular moment my life could have taken several courses. Everyone was thinking of what they were going to do after the war. A number of lively prospects involving whole new ways of life were opening before me at that moment. But suddenly in the poet's house they all seemed unattractive beside the possibility of becoming a writer.

One never knows if any particular decision is a right or a wrong one. But whatever its value, I came to this determination, and I was filled with a feeling of freedom and complete dedication which has never left me. And so this poet's house in which I found myself by chance became for me a symbol of what I was to attempt to make of my life. Perhaps if I'd foreseen the difficulties I wouldn't have had the courage to choose this particular vocation. But at that time I felt so confident that I would become a writer that before I left for the country I lifted the poet's telephone and rang up a literary agent. I enquired if they would like my new book. So far I hadn't written any book, but still I said: would they like to have it? I added that I was speaking from the house of the poet, whose name I didn't hesitate to mention. Possibly on the strength of this the literary agent said, yes, yes they would like to see the book. I promised to send it the following week.

Of course it was some years before I wrote anything like a book and before I even discovered what kind of writing I could do best. But that evening when I was back in the country I started writing a poem. It was a terrible poem. But I made two copies of it and sent it to two magazines at once. Amazingly – because it really was a frightful poem – both magazines accepted it, which put me into a most encouraging dilemma. And I felt I was really set up in my literary career.

Since that time I've been in the houses of many poets and writers, though not as a trespasser. There's always something special and something simple about a writer's house. I've never met a really good writer who lives in high style. I think a stylish life is unsuitable to the writer, and very often in the house where there's a mild disorder one finds the writer with the best powers of organising his work. Order where order is due.

[1960]

Footnote to 'The Poet's House'

The houses of famous writers have, to me, an ambiguous quality. First, they are houses like anyone else's. If they had not been lived in by famous people there would be no plaque on the wall, no visitors to roam round the rooms. In some cases ordinary people are living there, hardly aware of the past illustrious occupants; one can easily see such a house in the light of everyday life, and the practical requirements of real estate.

But also, these houses invite an imaginative surrender. Lamb House at Rye, Sussex, for instance: a desirable small residence, especially in these days when large houses are a burden. But when we place Henry James in those rooms, in his study, assiduously composing his voluminous, his lovely novels, stories and long letters, entertaining Edith Wharton in the dining room, pacing round the garden, the very ordinariness of the scene gives place to a sense of wonder.

And the Brontës' house at Haworth – if it had not been preserved as a museum it would surely by now be completely restructured inside. No-one could wander round these rooms without being struck by the smallness of their living space. The three Brontë sisters shared a bedroom hardly larger than a linen-cupboard; their workroom was the common living room.

The Casa Magni near Lerici where the poet Shelley lived, and from the terrace of which Mary Shelley looked out over the bay in her vigil for the boat which never returned, is now, from one point of view, merely a desirable property on the Ligurian coast. The windows of Byron's apartments in Venice look out on the Grand Canal with modern eyes peering from behind the curtains.

But the fascination of a writer's house arises from a combination of the spiritual and the concrete. We know that out of that bleak rectory in Yorkshire came *Wuthering Heights*, *Jane Eyre*, *The Tenant of Wildfell Hall*, and all the richly imaginative works of the Brontë sisters. We know that there in the Casa Magni, on the terrace, in the garden, Shelley wrote his last poems and filled the house with his febrile energy.

To me, a famous writer's house is irresistible; I find sheer magic in the rooms, in the staircases, in the gardens. The more ordinary the scene, in fact, the more I succumb to sensation, wonder and awe.

***

Once I found myself in the house of a famous living poet without at first realising it. The memory of that experience still returns to me, although it was over forty years ago.

Memory is not a straight line. It is like a tree, spreading its branches in all directions. The more I remember this episode the more it ramifies in my mind.

The experience took place in 1944.

[...]

'It was a small enough incident, but the experience was important to me,' I wrote at that time. Indeed, it was in that house that I finally determined to become a writer by profession.

The famous poet was Louis MacNeice whose work I loved and admired tremendously. I had just been reading his poem 'The Trolls', written after an air-raid.

> Death has a look of finality;
> We think we lose something but if it were not for
> Death we should have nothing to lose, existence
> Because unlimited would merely be existence
> Without incarnate value…

We thought a lot about death in those days. We didn't speak much of our fear because we were all in it together. But certainly we were aware of the imminence of death, and felt the penetrating chill that accompanied the howl of the sirens.

[…]

I have always known that this occasion vitally strengthened my resolve to become a writer. In the short story I wrote eight years later, and my broadcast of sixteen years later, I reproduced some of the actual scenes of that event. The story tells of an imaginative meeting with a soldier, and a brush with death. It has taken me over forty years to realise that the quality of the experience was intensified by fear of those flying bombs and the knowledge that destruction might fall at any moment, even on the house of the famous poet.

Louis MacNeice is dead now. He would have recognised how the resolve to be a writer, to create, can be fortified by the coincidence of a certain time, a certain place. To me, this is conveyed in his poem 'Off the Peg':

> The same tunes hang on pegs in the cloakrooms of the mind
> That fitted us ten or twenty or thirty years ago
> On occasions of love or grief; tin pan alley or folk
> Or Lieder or nursery rhyme, when we open the door we find
> The same tunes hanging in wait…

Many years later Louis MacNeice asked me to read a poem of mine, which he admired, at a poetry reading. I didn't tell him, and I don't think he ever knew, that I had been his uninvited guest, or how much the 'house of the famous poet' had inspired the course of my life.

[1985]

My Madeleine

Proust's madeleine fetish is well known. He dipped a small cake in a cup of tea; he put it to his lips; and the past came flooding back. He experienced the same effect when he tripped over a cobblestone in a courtyard.

Memory touchstones are most often connected with smells. Who is not moved to recall some previous experience by, for instance, a waft of honeysuckle, or the smoky whiff of a coal fire?

My Madeleine is an empty notebook. A friend who accompanied me one time into a stationer's shop remarked, 'You examine a notebook like a housewife in the market examining a fish.' As soon as I see one (and I acquire many and many), I desire to fill it in. Whenever I am stuck for a new subject or something to write I go to my stock of notebooks and select a new one.

Long ago, in 1951, I saw advertised a prize for a short story on the subject of Christmas. The prize was two hundred and fifty pounds, a handsome sum in those days. It was a Saturday. I went out and bought a new notebook and then sat looking at the empty pages. My lovely school notebook, all ready to be written in, filled my mind.

I started writing a story on my favourite subjects, which at that time were angelology (the fascinating study of the order of angels) and the French poet Baudelaire. To make the story unusual, I placed it in Africa, on the River Zambesi, where I had lived for some years. The result was a story entitled 'The Seraph, the Zambesi, and the Fanfarlo' (since reduced to 'The Seraph and the Zambesi'). I finished writing it at about three o'clock on the Saturday afternoon, then set about to type it. But I found I had too little typing paper. Saturday afternoon, all the stationer shops were shut. I walked round the streets of London's South Kensington, where I was living at that time, and found nothing open which could possibly furnish me with typing paper. My friends, better off than I, were away for the weekend.

I felt an inner compulsion, an obsession, about finishing the story and mailing it off that day. Then I saw that there was a small art dealer's shop with the owner inside. I had been in the shop before, merely to look at his modern paintings and discuss them, for I was much too poor to buy paintings.

No, he told me, he didn't sell typing paper.

'But you must have some of your own. Do give me, lend me, some,' I said. 'I need it, for a story.'

So he gave me a little sheaf of paper, and I finished and mailed the story. I promised I would buy a picture if I won the prize. It was stipulated that the author's real name should be put in an envelope to accompany the entry, with a pseudonym on the outside. I chose the name Aquarius, my sign of the zodiac. I was lucky, and won the competition.

I bought from my art-dealer friend, for thirteen pounds, a charcoal drawing of a boy listening to a radio, by Stanley Spencer. I bought a dress for six pounds, the first new dress I had had in four years. I gave my mother fifty pounds to pay for my son's bar mitzvah (we were a mixed-origin family, and my son wanted to be a Jew), and another fifty pounds went to another needy author, who, strangely enough, began to detest me from that day.[*]

[2000]

How I Became a Novelist

Although I have written five novels[†] I still have difficulty in thinking of myself as a novelist. Before I became a novelist I was a writer, and I have been attracted to writing ever since I could hold a pencil in my hand. In a sense I think it's more accurate to call myself a writer than a novelist, because what I actually enjoy most of all about novel-writing is the act of putting pen to paper: writing away, and forgetting everything except my subject-matter.

The reason why I have turned to novels in the last few years goes back a long way. As a child I used to enjoy telling myself stories in which I, of course, always took the principal part. There were many exciting adventures and always a happy ending. And as I grew older I read every scrap of fiction I could lay my hands on. I was allowed to read anything I liked from the Sunday newspapers to *The Pilgrim's Progress*. We had at home some bound volumes of Victorian ladies' magazines, and I read all the romantic love stories most avidly. I was especially fond of Robert Louis Stevenson's novels of adventure. There was no censorship, and there was a public library not far away. Sometimes, when I read a particularly impressive book, I used to extend the story

---
[*]Derek Stanford, who thought Muriel Spark was wasting her time writing fiction.
[†]By the end of her life Muriel Spark had written 22 novels.

in my imagination and make the characters live on in my own world of invention.

Also ever since I can remember I have had the habit of going over conversations which I have overheard, or in which I have taken part, and re-casting them in a neater form. You know the occasions when someone has said something provocative, or silly, or perhaps something pleasant – you do not think of the really good, appropriate, answer until afterwards, when it's too late. I sometimes think, 'I shouldn't have said this or that. What I should have said was…' and so on. This may be a silly habit, but it has had one practical purpose for me as a novelist: it has helped me with my dialogue. What I like doing is to make the characters in my novels say as nearly as possible what they ought to say, one remark thus provoking another. I enjoy making a foolish character say a very silly thing, and a clever character say something really intelligent. And sometimes a character can have a double-edged tongue and say something with two meanings. I enjoy contrasting such characters and seeing what happens, always in the hope that everything will be said and done more clearly and appropriately than in real life.

Up to 1955 I had been writing and editing books about nineteenth-century writers, particularly the Brontës whom I admired greatly, and Mary Shelley, the author of that thrilling novel, *Frankenstein*. I read and wrote a great deal of poetry and was especially enthusiastic about the narrative poems of John Masefield, particularly *Reynard the Fox* and *Dauber*. Later, when I was writing a book about Masefield and went to visit him I found his zest for life and dedication to the art of story-telling very stimulating and, in a way, infectious. I felt that I, too, wanted to write stories, but I was not sure how to begin.

One day I wrote a short story – it was my first – for a competition announced in the *Observer*. It was a very peculiar kind of story and it puzzled a lot of people, but it won the prize. The story was about an angel that appeared on the Zambesi river. I do not know what gave me the idea for the story, but certainly I believe in angels and I had been up the Zambesi on a boat.

Some time after this a publisher wrote to me and suggested that I should write a novel. I had been ill and was to be convalescent for some time. I had written nothing for over a year and in the meantime had entered the Roman Catholic Church – an important step for me, because from that time I began to see life as a whole rather than as a series of disconnected happenings. I think it was this combination of circumstances which made it possible for me to attempt my first novel. On the practical side, my publishers gave me some money to start this non-existent novel, and I was also assisted by one or two generous patrons, including Graham Greene. I took a lonely cottage in the country and started writing *The Comforters*. I wrote the first sentence on the day I moved in, while the rooms were still a jumble of packing-paper and saucepans and books.

I soon found that novel-writing was the easiest thing I had ever done – far easier than writing a short story or a poem or a piece of criticism. I found that the novel enabled me to express the comic side of my mind and at the same time work out some serious theme. But because it came so easily I was in some doubt about its value. I still have the decided feeling that anything worth while is done with difficulty. And since I write my novels so quickly and easily I sometimes feel I am cheating. Of course, after finishing a novel I am always exhausted, and life seems unbearable for a week or two. But the actual writing is more like play than work.

The Comforters was published in 1957 and the reviews were very encouraging. It was made into a play for the wireless, and I think the play was an improvement on the book, because it showed the plot more clearly. When I started my next novel I was in an adventurous mood and I wrote a desert-island story called *Robinson*.

Then I decided to write a book about old people. It happened that a number of old people whom I had known as a child in Edinburgh were dying from one cause or another, and on my visits to Edinburgh I sometimes accompanied my mother to see them in hospital. When I saw them I was impressed by the power and persistence of the human spirit. They were paralysed or crippled in body, yet were still exerting characteristic influences on those around them and in the world outside. I saw a tragic side to this situation and a comic side as well. I called this novel *Memento Mori*.

Next I wanted to give my mind a holiday and to write something light and lyrical – as near a poem as a novel could get, and in as few words as possible. So I wrote *The Ballad of Peckham Rye*, the story of a curious young man who causes trouble and high jinks wherever he goes. I set the story among the young people of Peckham, which is near my home.

My fifth novel – *The Bachelors* – was published in October. There are so many confirmed bachelors living in London, with their funny little ways and eccentric ideas – doing their own shopping and washing out their socks in hand-basins, and I thought the subject might make an amusing book.

But having finished it I had to revise it thoroughly. One of the scenes in the book is a criminal trial, and court procedure must be accurately described. I do not enjoy going over a novel once I have written it, nor revising pieces here and there. On the whole I do very little re-writing. I dislike going back over my work – I always feel I might turn into a pillar of salt, like Lot's wife. Once a thing is written I like to finish with it, because so many other ideas come to me.

[1960]

The Writing Life

'The Editor thanks you for your kind contribution but regrets he is unable to publish it.' My mail was full of such messages in those early days in the 1950s, when 'I commenced author', as the phrase went.

What came with the rejection slips were poems and essays. I hadn't yet got around to stories.

At the time I was sharing part of my meagre life with a man my own age, a literary critic; he possessed lots of literary information, which I found fascinating, even useful. (But I suspected he had no idea what to do with his knowledge, and so it proved.)

We sent out our productions always accompanied by a stamped and addressed envelope; otherwise we wouldn't see our pieces of work again. (I must interpose a memory of the then poet laureate John Masefield, already old and famous and honoured, whose exquisite manners were expressed even to the point of sending that stamped, addressed envelope every time he sent a poem to, say, the *Times Literary Supplement*, although of course he knew full well that the grateful editor would receive his poem with joy.)

I must say that my rejection slips, if they fell out of the envelopes at the rate of more than two in one day, depressed me greatly. However, I had a list of possible weeklies and little magazines to hand, and immediately I put the poem or article into a new envelope with a new letter to the editor and a new SAE. If the work I was offering looked shop-worn, I would type it out again. The money for these stamps for my outgoing mail was a pressing part of my budget in those days.

Thinking back, it is surprising how many – almost all, in fact – of my once-rejected pieces were subsequently published, as I began to make my name. Among the rejects, of course, I found some which, on reflection, I was not quite happy with. Those I put aside. But the majority of those one-time rejects have become a part of my oeuvre, studied in universities.

I started writing stories after my first story, 'The Seraph and the Zambesi', won first place in a competition run by the London *Observer*. My companion blew up when he heard that I had 'wasted my time' writing the story for the competition, and was quite put out when I won the prize, although he didn't mind sharing it.

At that time I found it really good to have a literary companion. Sharing the same profession, though in conditions of considerable poverty, gave me the courage to resist any other course of action. Occasionally I took office jobs to help out, but I was always drawn back to freelance writing, especially when eventually I obtained some advance money for books from various publishers. I was given fifty pounds to write my book on Mary Shelley. Somehow I managed to do it well and thoroughly. I revised it a few years ago, and it is in print to-day; I can honestly say I am proud of this work.

Sharing my working life with the man in question in the early '50s was, however, a great problem. Severe rationing of food was still in force, and as he was mainly living at home with his parents, they kept his ration book. Roughly three days a week he stayed and worked with me, and he shared my food rations. I was really hungry and undernourished in those days and had to pay the price in a few years' time in the mid-1950s, when my health broke down.

Some good emerged from that, however. I broke with the man I had shared with, and felt the wonderful breath of freedom. Soon I recovered from my illness, wrote stories and started a novel. It was commissioned by Macmillan, London – an act that brought a great deal of criticism down on their heads: in those days publishers did not commission first novels. They gave me one hundred pounds. Graham Greene, who admired my stories, heard of my difficulties through my ex-companion; he voluntarily sent me a monthly cheque with some bottles of wine for two years to enable me to write without economic stress. My first novel, *The Comforters*, was a success. I was suddenly 'the new young thing'. Graham was delighted, and of course from that time on I was able to fend for myself. I shall never forget Graham's sweet thoughtfulness.

The success of my creative work was a great relief to me. I was reminded of the marvellous Italian author Leonardo Sciascia's advice to writers: 'Want as much money as you like, but be careful not to need it.'

I was now, also, Evelyn Waugh's favourite author, since *The Comforters* touched on a subject, hallucinations, which he himself was working on in his novel, *The Ordeal of Gilbert Pinfold*; he was generous enough to write a review of my novel in the *Spectator*, in which he said that I had handled the subject better than he had done. Imagine the effect this had on a penniless first-novel author.

I find it difficult to re-read the novels and abundant stories I have written in the many years since then. Each one represents the convictions and humours of the writing personality I was at the time.

Thought is the main ingredient of a creative work, and thought goes with intention of some sort. I remember visiting Auden at his house in Austria some years before he died. He was re-writing some of his poems. He said to me, 'I'm not changing my first intentions, but getting closer to what I really meant.'

What a writer really means can come to light in a great many mysterious ways. On that same visit Auden told me that a typist had rendered the words 'foreign ports' in a poem in his handwriting as 'foreign poets'. 'I realised that "poets" was the word I really meant,' Auden said.

I found that once I've started on a work, the subject acts as a magnet, almost as if I were consciously surfing the Internet for information. I suppose this has to do with a functioning of our powers of observation. So many facts and phenomena that would normally go unnoticed in the course of a day simply present themselves, as if they positively wanted to be in the book. On occasion this selective process can even influence a book. As an example I can even cite one of my novels, *The Only Problem*.

It deals with the problem of good and evil as it is expressed in the biblical Book of Job. The main character in the book is studying the biblical text and the mysterious problems involved in God's relation to humankind depicted by the patriarch Job. I had come to a part of the book where nothing seemed to square. I had, for some reason quite unknown to myself, placed the scene of action near Epinal in France. Then I went there en route to England with my artist friend Penelope Jardine.

Soon after our arrival at Epinal, my friend was looking at one of the numerous tourist brochures littered about the hotel room. Suddenly she said, 'There is a museum here at Epinal containing a famous painting of Job and his wife by Georges de La Tour.' It was the turning point of my book. We went to look at the painting, and I could see that it would give me all the impetus and logic I needed for continuing with my story. But why had I already chosen Epinal? I know I had never before heard of this painting. And why did Penelope happen to look at that brochure?

Creativity is mysterious. I have been writing since the age of nine, when, on a corner of the kitchen table I wrote an 'improved' version of Robert Browning's 'The Pied Piper'. (I called him 'the Piper pied' to rhyme with 'he cried'.) I gave my poem a happy ending, not being at all satisfied with the children of Hamelin disappearing into a mountainside forever, as Browning made them do.

Since then I have learned that happiness or unhappiness in endings is irrelevant. The main thing about a story is that it should end well, and perhaps it is not too much to say that a story's ending casts its voice, colour, tone and shade over the whole work.

[2001]

Living in Rome

I settled in Rome long ago in 1967 because I found myself returning there, staying longer and longer. I think what attracted me most was the immediate touch of antiquity on everyday life. If you live in central Rome you only have to walk down the street and you come to a fountain by Bernini in which children are playing or a Michelangelo embassy or some fine fifteenth-century building with to-day's washing hanging out. The names Bramante, Raphael and Borromini become like familiar friends. One comes into the territory of the Republican ages, the Caesars, the emperors and the medieval popes at any turn in the road, and any bus stop; and there is the Rome of Garibaldi's troops, of Keats and Shelley, of Arthur Hugh Clough (whose narrative poem *Amours de Voyage* contains one of the funniest descriptions of the English in Rome during the troubles of 1848). Byron's Rome, Henry James's Rome is here; and Mussolini's big fat dream Rome with grandiose popular centres and concepts.

The first apartment I occupied was in the Piazza di Tor Sanguigna not far from the Tiber on the corner of Via Coronari, an ancient street of antique furniture shops. I was at that time dazzled by the adjacent Piazza Navona, and indeed I still am; I greatly desired to find a more permanent home in the Piazza. I did find a flat there, with a picturesque view of the marvellous Bernini fountain, but devoid of everything else including water. The bathroom and the kitchen, explained the landlord, and the plumbing, electricity and other trivialities were to be laid on by the lucky tenant who succeeded in obtaining from him a contract limited to one year's residence. The rent alone was high. I knew right away that the project was impossible, but I still enjoy the memory, as I did the experience, of standing in that dark vaulted cave-like apartment while the landlord explained in a mixture of Italian, French and English those terms which I discerned by careful deciphering were exorbitant. I fairly egged him on as far as my powers in Italian permitted, so keen was I to see with my novelist's curiosity how far he would go. The tenant had to be an American, he said. I replied that I was a Scot, but that I doubted if he would find an American to pour capital into his property with a tenure of one year. He replied that the apartment was in a famous fifteenth-century building in which many famous lords had lived, which was true enough. So he went on, while I looked out of the window watching the baroque fountain playing in the fine October light of Rome. The theatrical figure representing the Nile, with his great hand held up as if to ward off some falling masonry, seemed apt to my situation. 'Speak to me,' Michelangelo is said to have challenged his Roman statue of Moses; and indeed, the sculptures of Rome do speak.

[...]

I moved to an apartment full of history in the Palazzo Taverna and I radiated out from there. The palazzo was at the top of the Via Coronari overlooking Castel Sant'Angelo. The main room was enormous, a renaissance Cardinal Orsini's library. The upper walls and the ceilings were painted with classical scenes and Orsini emblems. I didn't try to furnish it, but made a sitting room in a remote corner while the rest of the room with its polished Roman tiles was for going for walks. It would have made a good skating rink. In one of the corridors a Roman pillar had been let into the wall. By this time I was used to permanent residence in historic Rome. Part of the excitement of visiting one's friends was to see what portion of history their living-space occupied. It is practically impossible to live in Rome without finding oneself encamped in history and often overwhelmed by beauty; a statue, a fresco, the perspective of a scene through an archway, with always the busy *portière* at the door-lodge, making no nonsense about it.

The wives of ambassadors to Rome are hard put to it to seat their guests according to protocol; there are several different hierarchies. In the first place, Italy is a republic. Then, there is an Old Aristocracy whose ancestors were Popes; they were, up to the early 1970s, very much on ceremony if they deigned to go outside their palace walls at all. The New Aristocracy comprise the hurly-burly of princes and counts who have sprung up since the time of Napoleon. Bourbon descendants fall somewhere among this category but I know neither where nor who does know. Ex-monarchs usually find their way to Rome which is another headache for the embassies; and the Vatican with its cardinals and ambassadors top the cake. Fortunately these were not my problems, for whenever I throw a party, high or low as it may include, I make it a buffet.

[...]

The Palazzo Taverna with its fountain in the great courtyard, its arches and small courtyards was fun to live in and my echoing Cardinal's room was to many of my friends one of the wonders of the world. My cats used to love to sit on a rug while we whizzed them round the vast floor. After dinner everyone in the Palazzo would go down to the courtyard to take the air with the neighbours. One of the fascinations of Old Rome is that there are no exclusive neighbourhoods. Rich and poor live on top of each other.

I go to the Rome opera in the winter. Each year on the night the opera opens there is always a great embracing and greeting of fellow ticket-holders, and '*Bentornato*' ('Welcome back') all round. One never sees these people anywhere else; they are one's opera friends.

Whether it was a good or a bad performance on the Opera's second night the film director Luchino Visconti was always there with his friends or rather, as is the way with Italian film directors, his court. 'Good or bad, I like opera,' he said. On one special evening, when Montserrat Caballé was singing in a Bellini opera, the rain started coming in the roof. Now, a well-known Roman of that time was the late Mario Praz, a critic and scholar of English literature. (He wrote *The Romantic Agony*.) He was said to have the Evil Eye and was known as the Malocchio. This nickname wasn't attributed with any repugnance, but rather as an affectionately recorded and realistic fact (for such people are regarded as carriers rather than operators of the Evil Eye). He was extremely generous-minded towards young writers. Naturally, everyone noticed when Mario Praz was present at a party, and if so, waited for the disaster. There was usually a stolen car at the end of the evening, or someone was called away because his uncle had died. Well, when I saw the rain coming in the roof of the Opera, and heard the commotion behind me, I looked round instinctively for Mario Praz. Sure enough, there was our dear Malocchio and party sitting under the afflicted spot. When he died he was mourned on a national scale. (The Italians put their artists and people of letters on a higher level than anywhere else I have known.) Before his house could be unsealed for his heirs, the robbers got in and looted his lifetime's collection of museum pieces and memorabilia.

In the summer I always try to see the open-air performance of *Aida* at the Caracalla Baths. These mighty ruins are extremely well adapted to a mammoth spectacle. The ancient Romans, for whom the Baths were built as a social and cultural centre, would have loved *Aida* in this setting with its superabundance of camels and cavalry, its luxurious scenery and massed troops.

[...]

I think it is a great blessing to us that the Baths have fallen into ruin, nature's magnificent sculptures that they are. The original must have been of decidedly totalitarian dimensions. Against a late afternoon October light all Rome looks sublime and especially the ruins of Caracalla. They are flood-lit at night; the environs used to be a favourite night-walk but nobody takes lonely walks in Rome any more. The footpads are rife. Even the girls of the night, with their picturesque road-side bonfires, have deserted the vicinity of the Baths, and the nightingales sing to the ghosts.

Wherever I live I am in the writer's condition: work is pleasure and pleasure is work. I find Rome a good place to work. The ordinary Roman is nearly always a 'character', which is to say there are no ordinary Romans and therefore life among them, although it may be exasperating at times, is never boring. The extraordinary Byzantine bureaucracy of Italian living, and the usual bothers of life are always present, but if I can get a glimpse of the Pantheon even passing in a taxi on my way to fulfil some banal commission I find the journey worthwhile. At night, if I go to dine in one of the excellent *trattorie* near the Pantheon, I love to walk round in the great solid portico for a while. It is sheer harmony: the bulk is practically airborne.

My stay at the Palazzo Taverna came to an end after three years when the landlady wanted the flat 'for her daughter'. My next flat looked out on the Tiber at the front, and, at the back, on the roof-tops and winding alleys of ancient Trastevere. Here again I had one big room surrounded by a few small rooms. The best thing about it was the view of the river at night with a moving bracelet of traffic on either side of the Tiber and over the bridges; and if I was working very late at night I loved to go for a walk in my big room and look out at the three flood-lit monuments of my window view: the clock-tower of Santa Maria in Trastevere; up on the Janiculum hill the Fountain of Acqua Paola; and behind it the church of St Peter in Montorio. Eventually my landlady wanted this apartment, too, 'for her daughter'. Tired of landladies' daughters I acquired for my own the apartment I live in now, a small but very exciting place just emerging from slumdom. It is in a street between Piazza Farnese, where Michelangelo added a floor to what is now the French Embassy, and the great Campo dei Fiori, the colourful flower and fruit market. This is deep in the Rome of the Renaissance. My apartment dates from the fourteenth century at the back and fifteenth at the front. It belonged to an inn called La Vacca owned by La Vanozza, mistress of the Borgia Pope, Alexander VI and mother of Cesare Borgia. Her coat of arms, those of her husband and those of the Pope, all three joined, are set in the outside wall near my windows. When the workmen were getting this apartment ready for me they tore down some paper which covered the ceilings to reveal beautiful woodwork. A window was found in a wall leading to the main part of La Vanozza's property. Embedded in the old tiles of the floor they found the remains of a speaking tube that communicated with the street door. Whether or not this was used by La Vanozza's fifteenth-century call-girls I will never know.

[1983]

Venice

Most people who write about Venice do not tell you what they think of it but how they feel. Venice is a city not to inspire thought but sensations. I think it is something to do with the compound of air, water, architecture and the acoustics. Like the effect of these elements on the ear, there are acoustics of the heart. One can think in Venice, but not about Venice. One absorbs the marvellous place, often while thinking about something else.

I have never been to Venice in summer time, nor in Festival time, nor at the time of any of the cinema and great art shows. My Venice belongs to late autumn and winter, the Venice of meagre tourism, the Venetians' everyday city.

I have never known Venice to be crowded or hurried. Perhaps for this reason, when I published a novel set in autumnal Venice, someone was puzzled by the facility with which some of my characters encountered each other in the street. It transpired he had only been in Venice during the crowded and stifling tourist seasons, when you couldn't very likely meet the same face two days running. In the winter it's quite different. After a week of walking around Venice – and one does have to walk a lot – or of waiting at the landing-stage for the diesel-run *vaporetto*, the same laughing students are there, the same solemn goodwives with their shopping bags and well-preserved fur collars, the same retired gentlemen with righteous blue eyes and brown hats. This is everyday Venice where the passers-by are sparse, where eventually they say good-morning.

My first visit to Venice was on a cold, bright morning in February, with a friend who had been there before. However much one has read and heard about the visual impact of Venice, it never fails to take one by surprise. After five visits I still gasp. It isn't merely the architecture, the palaces, the bridges and the general splendour, it is the combination of architecture with water, space, light and colour that causes amazement; especially I think the element of water. The first impression of the waterways of Venice is acoustic, so that normal sensations subliminally cease and new ones take their place. Voices, footsteps, bird-cries, a cough from the window on the other side of the canal – all are different from the sounds of the land one has left. The traffic is entirely watery. A greengrocer's shop piled high with colourful vegetables is a ship floating past your window. After a few days of this estrangement from normal life I begin to feel at home with it. Some people tell me they can never settle down to a feeling of familiarity with Venice. Sometimes those are people who frequent the super hotels where everything is done to comfort and console the visitors who come with their usual bag of worries. I don't say that this isn't a very good thing for a holiday. But the very nature of Venice is such that the things that usually preoccupy us, from which we are attempting to get away, undergo a shift of perspective after about three days.

I have known Venice in a mist and drizzle, where everything is depressed and soaking, every bridge is a bridge of sighs. But it is not the usual personal depression one is experiencing, it is something else, something belonging to Venice, it is collective. I think this is something the reverse of Ruskin's 'Pathetic Fallacy' in which he holds that artists and poets tend to attribute to nature our human responses; Venice would be 'brooding' or 'smiling' according as we feel. On the contrary, I think we are sad when majestic Venice is in gloom; and if we are depressed already the fine thing about those gloomy days of Venice is that you forget what you are personally depressed about. Venice is a very good place to be sad. On days of mist, it is like a trip to the Shades. But winter often sparkles and these are the days one can sit warmly in Florian's café while outside the hardy musicians perform their nostalgic palm court pieces.

Venice has been declining for some hundreds of years. Decline is now of its essence, and I don't think it would be anything like as attractive to ourselves if it were on the way up in the modern sense and flourishing. The Venetians themselves talk little about Venice, never unless you ask. They are proud of their native city and attached to it, but it doesn't go to their heads as it does with the rest of us.

There was a time when wealthy foreigners like Milly in Henry James's *The Wings of the Dove* could take on a romantic palace, and play at princesses. Poor Milly got what she demanded, and this was, of course, how James made fun of his contemporaries in Venice:

> At Venice, please, if possible, no dreadful, no vulgar hotel; but if it can be at all managed – you know what I mean – some fine old rooms, wholly independent, for a series of months. Plenty of them, too, and the more interesting the better: part of a palace, historic and picturesque, but strictly inodorous, where we shall be to ourselves, with a cook, don't you know? – with servants, frescoes, tapestries, antiquities, the thorough make-believe of a settlement.

Byron thought seriously of settling permanently in Venice to spend the winters there. Permanently is not a good idea; it's bad for our bones, and also, the sort of infatuation a foreigner feels about Venice cannot last. Henry James's American girlfriend, if one can stretch a phrase, settled in Venice only to throw herself out of a window one dark night, to her death. Byron's Venetian girl, who threw herself into the canal, was careful to be rescued.

However, it is difficult not to be romantic about Venice. Myself, I arrived on one of my visits – it was early in November – nearly midnight. All the river traffic, including the taxis, were on strike in solidarity with the gondoliers who had notices up demanding that gondoliers' claims should be dealt with 'globally'. There was a squall blowing in from the lagoon. It was quite a plight for me, there on the landing-stage, for my luggage was heavy with some reference books (I was correcting the proofs of my Venetian novel *Territorial*

Rights). But it was really exciting to strike a bargain with some men on a coal barge which rocked and plunged in the wind and surge, with me and my books among the sooty cargo, up the Grand Canal where doges and dowagers were once wont to ride in state. The night porter at my lodgings showed no surprise; he merely came down to the landing-stage to collect me and my goods, dripping rags that we were, and to make sure that the men had not overcharged me. I will always remember that midnight journey through the black water, and the calling of the bargemen, wild sea-bird noises, as every now and again they passed another laden vessel. The palaces were mostly in darkness with the water splashing their sides, the painted mooring poles gleaming suddenly in the light of our passing; the few lights from the windows were dim and greenish, always from tiny windows at the top. Nobody walked on the banks, and yet a strange effect that I can only describe as water-voices came from those sidewalks and landing-stages. Perhaps they were ghosts, wet and cold.

I usually stay at a charming, fairly old *pensione* near the Accademia, which sits on an angle of the Grand Canal and a side canal. In time, after I had taken in day by day all the sights and spectacles of Venice – the incredible St Mark's church, the happy square with its shops full of expensive junk, the Tintorettos, museums and galleries and all those already hyper-described stones of Venice, I began to form a Venice of my own. It is rather as one does with acquaintances when one goes to live for a length of time in a new country – eventually one whittles them down to an affectionate few. These I visit again and again in my winter walks and excursions, well wrapped up and wearing boots like everyone else. Most men and women wear warm hats, too.

Since one of the advantages of an off-season visit is that there are no crowds, it is possible to sit without interruption almost alone in the church of the Frari looking at Titian's *Assumption*. I love to walk round the Ducal Palace, to see those four charming Tetrarchs, timid and proper and quietly influential, modestly embracing each other in a formal half-huddle. Giorgione's mysterious *Tempest* in the Accademia is another of my best-loved familiars. And I remember a sunny winter trip, and also a cold bleak one, with a friend in the ferry-boat to Torcello, one of the islands in the Venetian lagoon where very little goes on now except the magnificent Cathedral, part Gothic, part Byzantine. There is a vast biblical narrative done in seventh-century mosaics at one end, and a golden-backed mosaic of the Madonna behind the altar, hypnotically radiant. But going behind the altar to snoop we waded into a deep pool of water which had seeped into that glorious building. We were glad of our boots. In winter there are no restaurants on the smaller islands, no bar on the ferry-boats. But sweet visitors don't care, and the sour ones don't matter.

The art-treasures apart, what I return to again and again are the more homely friends of my walks through the windy *calles* and the placid, sometimes leafy squares of Venice. These include a men's hat shop standing all alone in a small square house on the canal near Santa Maria Formosa; in the windows, and piled up inside, is a vast variety of men's hats; straw boaters, Breton sailors' berets, felt hats, black velour hats, fedoras, Stetsons, hats for hunting and hats for going to funerals.

Funerals in Venice, of course, are a stately procession. The city lays on a great show, with gilt-edged barges and coffins carved within an inch of their lives. In vain have the last two Popes set the example of being buried in plain pinewood boxes, there in St Peter's for all the world to see. Venice sails on regardless. In Venice the ambulance service too is interesting: it provides a sedan chair to run a less than stretcher-case down to the boat.

Often, in Venice, getting lost, as everyone does, I have come across a type of that high blank wall of *The Aspern Papers*:

> ... a high blank wall which appeared to confirm an expanse of ground on one side of the house. Blank I call it, but it was figured over with the patches that please a painter, repaired breaches, crumblings of plaster, extrusions of brick that had turned pink with time; and a few thin trees, with the poles of certain rickety trellises, were visible over the top. The place was a garden and apparently it belonged to the house.

I like the term 'apparently'. Because, in Venice, anything can or might lie behind those high blank walls. It is well to say 'apparently'. One never knows.

It is true that, for myself, I never cease to feel a certain amazement that all that sheer visual goodness and aural sublimity was in fact based on commerce. Culture follows gold, somebody said. Indeed, in Venice, it apparently has done so. To-day in Venice you could never live and follow a culture in the sort of style that gave birth to it. In a Venetian palace you could never live a modern life, you would have to be serving the walls, serving the servants, giving orders for your private motor-boat to be repaired, the mooring-posts to be painted, the crystal chandeliers to be cleaned piece by piece. To own a Venetian palace must be simply awful. Some people still do it.

It was comparatively late in a much-travelled life that I made my first trip to Venice. That was in 1975. I was vaguely saving it up for a romantic occasion. Special and romantic occasions were not wanting in my life but they never coincided with the possibility of a trip to Venice. So in the winter of 1975 I suddenly went. Venice itself was the romantic occasion: the medium is the message.

[1981]

Istanbul

Istanbul is what I imagine the cellars, crypts and warehouses of the great art museums – the Tate, the National Gallery – to be like; full of discarded rubbish amongst which can be found, without a doubt, occasional treasures beyond price, sometimes badly framed or in need of restoration, but lying there in wait for their moment to arrive, for a discerning mind to make them flower. It is not that much of Istanbul is not already on display or that much remains to be exploited. It is rather that what is on show is not yet, in a sense, truly itself.

The first impact on Western eyes is surely the element of shape and of spatial harmony. Suleiman the Magnificent's mighty mosque, the great architectural triumph of the sixteenth-century Ottoman regime, sprawls like a round and bulging sultan and his court, with its minarets rising like maces and spears.

The Blue Mosque, or the Mosque of Sultan Achmet I of the early seventeenth century, is quite wonderful. It is doubtfully reputed to have been built by a music-master turned architect, and the legend is understandable: the sheer harmony of the exterior, its domes upon domes, its six minarets, have a symphonic rhythm and flow. The glowing decorative ceramic tiles of the interior are particularly lovely. The principal dome rests on four massive pillars rightly called 'elephant legs'. And yet these give a curiously airborne effect to the building, rather reminiscent of the bulky Pantheon in Rome. The Blue Mosque struck me as a place of great holiness.

Different as were the religions of the Christians of Constantinople and the Turks who conquered in 1453, the outward sign of change is very slight; evidence of the abrupt takeover is mainly to be seen in the interiors of the former churches.

Kemal Atatürk had the genius to secularise the Hagia Sophia. 'It has been a church,' he said, 'it has been a mosque, and now it is a museum.' This made it possible for the plastered-over Christian mosaics of

Justinian and Theodora and their descendants to be uncovered. But to have done so in style the city would have needed the means of the sixth-century Emperor and his fabulous bride; and this Istanbul has not got.

Hagia Sophia still has an air of punitive religions hanging about the place. In those colossal halls I shivered with a sense of cruelty and fear as I do in the Colosseum in Rome. Standing in the women's gallery one can see in one's mind's eye, as did the women of former days in actuality, the barbaric hordes of crusaders and invaders below, wrecking the place and liquidating the worshippers.

The Byzantine element lingers in the vastness of the architectural conception, and the impassive quality of those glorious mosaics which have been uncovered. Justinian and Theodora embodied the Byzantine state of mind. In Hagia Sophia, and in the great site of the Hippodrome I kept thinking of that couple, who stand immortally preserved in mosaics in the Church of St Vitale in Ravenna, on opposite walls, flanked by their respective courts, observing each other placidly as if butter wouldn't melt in their mouth. And yet it was Theodora herself, the story goes, who won over the generals to loose the army and put to death her thirty thousand best friends who had foregathered in the Hippodrome to massacre her and her munificent husband.

Hagia Sophia and the Blue Mosque are both in the old city. Nearby are the third-century Hippodrome from whence the famous horses of St Mark's in Venice are looted, and in the same area the Palace of Topkapi, which houses the world's grandest collection of china, precious stones, jewelled daggers, diamond-embedded jars, gilded furnishings, burnished thrones, tapestries, and vestments, painted miniatures, manuscripts – all of which testify to the residence in these sumptuously decorated rooms of the learned, artistic and treasure-loving sultans of the Ottoman Empire from the fifteenth to the nineteenth centuries.

This plethora of wealth and dazzle at Topkapi must always in a sense have constituted a mighty museum: a house of the sensual arts, a showplace of the all-powerful, all-sufficient and all-possessing life of a single potentate, his family and his court.

While anxious to see as much as I could of Istanbul, I was specially on the look-out for mosaics, an art-form dear to my heart. They are like the suddenly halted images of modern film – stills of a special moment frozen in time. It was from Constantinople that the mosaic material went by sea-route to Venice and Ravenna. We owe St Mark's in Venice and the jewel-box of mosaics that make up the churches and baptisteries of Ravenna, to the Byzantine genius.

Nothing at all in Istanbul can now compare with the Italian wonders that reached their peak in the sixth century. What has been uncovered in the Hagia Sophia can give only a small indication of what the dazzling whole must have been up to the conquest of Constantinople and the immediate plastering over of all Christian art.

The interior of St Saviour in Chora is a decorated whole, following a definite iconographic design and a planned narrative. It is thanks to the Byzantine Institute of America that the extensive fourteenth-century mosaic picture-sequence has been uncovered. These late pictures are more expressive and humanised, and at the same time more sentimental, than the still and stylised early Byzantine examples, but their portraiture, movement and colours are truly superb. A genealogy of Christ is depicted, and a legendary life of Mary from her infancy to her death ('the Dormition'). This latter mosaic picture, beautifully constructed, is of great mystical-theological interest. The Virgin is shown lying in the sleep of death, watched by Christ who also holds Mary as an infant in his arms so that the images of Mary as mother and daughter of Christ appear simultaneously. In another mosaic, the Virgin and child are placed in a central position within a fluted dome, with ancestral figures of the House of David portrayed on each rib.

Another church with beautifully restored mosaics is St Mary Pammakaristos (The All-Beatific Virgin). This church is in the Fener district, difficult to find through teeming slumland, but well worth the search. It was said to been used by the Christians for some years even after the Turkish conquest, but by the late sixteenth century it had been converted into a mosque like other Byzantine churches. The restored mosaics are in a side-chapel which has been set apart as a museum. The main building is still used as a mosque.

Portions of the sixth-century mosaic pavement of the Great Palace, home of the Byzantine Emperors, belong to the great and lovely period of Byzantine art. The Mosaic Museum, as it is called, is an excavated section of the Great Palace, entered through a door in a back street near the Blue Mosque. These mosaics represent secular hunting scenes. What pictures remain are full of fun and movement. A bear, a stag, a donkey, a wolf, a tiger, a horse, a camel with two children taking a ride, a man falling from a horse loaded with fruit, and, best of all, a wonderful green-bearded man of the woods with a ruddy face and bright eyes, his hair and beard blending into the foliage.

From the historical point of view, nearly every single item of interest in Istanbul would be worth going specially to see: the city walls date from Theodosius II in the fifth century. They have been well restored in recent times, and dramatically stretch over six kilometres from the Golden Horn to the Sea of Marmara. Most of the sites and monuments deserve far more attention than the average visitor can give. The Archaeological Museum is worth many visits for many reasons, not the least being the presence there of the famous sarcophagus of Alexander. The reality of this much-photographed tomb with its dramatic battle and hunting scenes carved in great movement and detail is one of those treasures which alone it would be worth going to Istanbul especially to see.

The ancient aqueducts are one of the city's most impressive landmarks. I found the old tombs and extensive graveyards with their tall, thin, ghostly stones particularly haunting. For a trip back in time to Byzantium a descent to the underground network of cisterns is convincing, and is now enhanced by a *son et lumière* show; wooden bridges lead in all directions over floors of water which were once the much-beleaguered city's water supply. Ancient pillars hold up the roof. Light plays on the majestic scene to the strains of Beethoven.

It is amazing that so much has survived when the city and its monuments, its churches, mosques, palaces, towers and walls have been so repeatedly attacked and destroyed by invaders, crusaders, plunderers, earthquakes, fire and sheer neglect. Timelessness often seems to possess the streets and shops: pavement vendors, old men with spices on a stick over their shoulders, boys pushing handcarts everywhere and the bazaars themselves, give the impression of long, long, ago. The much-celebrated Covered Bazaar of Istanbul stretches for miles of interleading streets; there, the shops are altogether repetitive, and to my mind it is a great bore and a fire hazard.

History and politics, religion and philosophy are the focal and commanding centre based on which mosque architecture, the main feature of the city, has flourished, while music, the visual arts, literature and theatre, and that greatest of all the arts and sciences, daily life, have not.

The secularisation of Turkey, Atatürk's dream, started to work, but stopped. One looks in vain for that Pera Palace atmosphere of pre-war culture and sophisticated fun, but it is nowhere to be found, least of all at the Pera Palace, now merely a one-time grand hotel. Alexandria, Carthage, are the cities that come to mind when one thinks of Istanbul in its decline. But Istanbul's new opportunities lie in its annual multitudes of tourists. If it can learn to take care of them, which it can't at present, the city might have a promising future.

But in the streets and bazaars something smoulders; perhaps it is a dying fire, perhaps an incipient one. I would never be surprised if there was not a spontaneous Turkish rising, a revolution. The official handout is that there are no extremists at large, right or left. They are all in prison, 'all 23 of them'. Meanwhile, Prime Minister Turgut Özal is said to be working towards a one-party system. His mother had a dream before she died. The venerated Sultan, Suleiman the Magnificent, appeared to her and invited her to be buried within the royal and sacred precincts of his great mosque and splendid mausoleum. The dream was put to parliament who ratified the request for the Prime Minister's mother to be buried there. And there she is in the royal cemetery, occupying the only modern grave.

Typical of the city, the dying hillside at Eyüp, where Pierre Loti, the French writer, liked to spend time at a coffee house, is still covered with ancient tombstones, but there are shanty towns and crude factory buildings of more recent growth to amaze the view.

These reflections, negative and sad, are however the best frame for sightseeing in Istanbul. There is no point in going round with western illusions and aesthetic standards, merely gaping and gasping. The rubble piled up everywhere in the streets, the aimlessness of the millions who march in the streets all day, going nowhere, young men waiting for the time to go home, do have a bearing on the Blue Mosque, the Palace of Topkapi, the brilliant newly restored narrative mosaic of the Chora. The fact that within a few feet of the Blue Mosque and its elegant surroundings, people are living in holes in the rubble, with only a row of pathetic washing for a curtain, is part of the total experience. If this were not so, a visit to the Byzantine department of any of our great western museums would do just as well.

Up the Bosphorus on the European bank, bask sumptuous private houses and elegant highly priced apartments, but on the opposite banks, on the Asian side, bulldozers have been busy everywhere.

The best part of a trip up the Bosphorus from Istanbul towards the Black Sea are the distant views, and the hovering warships both Turkish and Soviet. How close geography is to history!

Generally in Istanbul and its environs, both on the European and Asian flanks, whole mountain-sides, entire street corners have been bulldozed away. Whether this is part of some huge reconstruction plan or an endeavour to forestall earthquake damage, there is nothing to show; only huge piles of rubble are in evidence, and occasionally a solitary workman with a wheelbarrow and spade shovelling at it; sometimes, an idle bulldozer seemed to await orders. The scene reminded me of wartime London but without its defiant energy. I was reminded, too, of Bombay's seething millions. There is no alley-charm, no back-street vivacity as one might see even in the direst quarters of Naples. The smell of bad drains is a constant factor. A few characteristic wooden houses have been attractively restored but most are falling to pieces. If one asked about these demolition sites the answers were vague and without conviction: 'a mosque is going up', or 'that space is for a new hotel'. No-one seemed to know much; no-one appeared to have the right to know. Modern Turkey raises a vast number of questions; the answers savour of schoolroom propaganda. The present life of Istanbul is entirely in the past.

[1988]

Tuscany By Chance

It was by chance, not choice, that I came to Tuscany to spend several months of the year at the house of a friend in the olive groves between Arezzo and Siena. So that I have never been properly 'on tour' in Tuscany. It is a place where I work and live, visit friends or go for day-trips for a special reason – to hear a concert, look at a picture or a building, or a square, or to eat at a newly discovered *trattoria*, coming upon a small hill-town or an old parish church on the way. Although Florence is not far away it is another world from rural Tuscany. Florence is Florentine. The same with Siena and all its glories; it is Sienese.

It isn't necessarily the great and famous beauty spots that we fall in love with. As with people, so with places: love is unforeseen, and we can all find ourselves affectionately attached to the minor and the less obvious.

I don't have an art-historian's response to places. I can discern and admire a late renaissance gate, a medieval street, a Romanesque church or an Etruscan wall, but my first thoughts are for the warmth of the stone, the bright yellow broom covering the hill-sides in early summer, the clouds when they look like a fifteenth-century painting with a chariot or a saint zooming up into them; I notice the light and shade on buildings grouped on a hilltop, the rich skin-colours and the shapes of the people around me. I love to watch people, to sit in a *trattoria* listening-in to their talk, imagining the rest, and to take country roads lined with woods of pine, ilex, forest-oak, chestnut.

Nearly every evening I go somewhere in the countryside. Early summer is good, August generally hot in Tuscany, but the autumn up to Christmas is comfortable. For people too busy to cook, as I am, it is easy to eat out all through the year.

One of my shortest drives is to the castle-hamlet of Gargonza, passing the medieval market town of Monte San Savino. Dante Alighieri stopped at the Castle of Gargonza on the first few days of his exile. It is an intimate fortification, well restored, with an ancient tower and an airy forest view. Once at sunset I saw a wild boar (*cinghiale*) sauntering down one of the tarmac roads outside the restaurant. It was a beautiful rippling beast. It looked around as it walked like a tourist taking the air.

I return again and again to lovely Pienza, originally a medieval town which was re-planned by Pius II in the fifteenth century. Its central square is small, enclosed by a church and three palaces, all of appropriate and elegant proportions – an attractive example of urban planning. Walking round the square of Pienza I often have the illusion of being in a roofless temple, as in the Parthenon.

Near Pienza are several *terme* or sulphur-bath resorts. Chianciano is one of the best-known in this vicinity. For me, these towns have too much an air of people caring greatly for their own health, and really quite healthy people at that. At Bagno Vignoni a fountain in the piazza takes the form of an ancient bath filled with the hot curative waters.

When people come to visit me I usually take them to see the majestic *Madonna del Parto* of Piero della Francesca. This fresco was to be found entirely on its own in a small cemetery chapel at Monterchi.[*] The surrounding countryside, with its broad sweep of cultivated, undulating fields, seems to be out of a painting of the fifteenth century. Peasant-like and noble, the picture is planned to represent a stage, the Virgin herself both dramatic protagonist and actual theatre, as she opens her dress to prepare for the historic curtain-rise of the Incarnation. In parallel action two angels on either side hold back the curtains of the canopy where she stands.[†] Throughout this part of the Tuscan countryside one can still see indigenous faces resembling that of Piero della Francesca's famous model; there is something, too, in the setting of the head on the sturdy neck which is still typical of the Tuscan to-day.

From Monterchi it is only five kilometres to Sansepolcro, home of Piero della Francesca. His stupendous *Resurrection* is in the museum.

---

[*]The fresco has been moved to a modern school-house in the village of Monterchi.
[†]The additional painting of a *baldacchino* (canopy or tent), not the work of Piero della Francesca, has now been removed.

The streets of the old city are characteristically medieval to renaissance. There are good hotel restaurants in Sansepolcro; and, between Monterchi and Anghiari at Castello di Sorci, there is an old, capacious farmhouse where a good fixed menu is served at a reasonable price including local wine. Here again, as in so many hidden places of Tuscany, there is a feeling of timelessness. In the ground-floor kitchens the cooks can be seen skilfully making the pasta, by hand, in different designs.

The city of Cortona is too well-known, too crowded, for the comfort of a long-term resident in the area. For some reason, when in Tuscany, I find an abundance of English and American voices around me an irritant; not so in Rome which is cosmopolitan from its foundation. But to be in the midst of an English-speaking fraternity in this wild and natural Italy depresses me greatly. I wonder: What am I doing here? I could just as well have stayed there at home. Did I come all this way to hear phrases like, 'Why do they close the museums at the lunch hour?', an innocent question that opens a huge cultural gulf; the long mid-day meal and repose is sacred to the Italians; only catering establishments are absolved from the near-religious duty of going home to eat at *il tocco* (one o'clock). And I remember an English visitor asking me, 'Are you stationed out here?' Recalling this, I look out of the window and see Gino the horse-coper riding by proudly with his beasts; nobody has told him he lives 'out here', and as for me, there's nothing in my life that corresponds to being stationed. Cortona, then, is one of the places I avoid, despite its art treasures and antiquities. Even in winter. Because, when the flocks of visitors have gone home, the wintery streets are all the more deserted, all the more gloomy. Like Edinburgh after the Festival. Better the places that never have this swarming influx. I take Cortona as my convenient example of this phenomenon; there are many many more.

But to me there is a fascination about Cortona: the road to it that leads south from Arezzo. This indeed is one of the classic Tuscan drives, through the rolling basin of the Valdichiana. From where I live, one comes first to Castiglion Fiorentino, a charming small town mainly composed of one street rising up to the very fine municipal arcade of Vasari, an old market-place, from which there is an impressive view framed by the arches. In the picture gallery, modestly displayed, is a strange, hypnotic painting, *Stigmate di S. Francesco*, beloved of Kenneth Clark. It is by a little-known mid-fifteenth-century artist, Bartolomeo della Gatta. St Francis and his companion are unusually represented in green habits among an almost cubistic formation of rocks.

Also on the way to Cortona it is worth stopping to see Montecchio, the recently restored stronghold of Sir John Hawkwood, a fourteenth-century English *condottiere*.*

Up the valley of the Casentino a grand mountain view is to be seen on the way to Camaldoli, where there is a hermitage and monastery, with a few souvenir shops and two unexceptional restaurants. The church has been much restored since its foundation in the thirteenth century; it is now predominantly eighteenth-century baroque and contains some minor Tuscan paintings and frescoes. The main attraction for me is the old monastic pharmacy. Here you can purchase such potions as Amaro Tonico, which is described as a neurotonic and digestive and is recommended for 'nervous exhaustion, for disturbances of the liver and for physical and intellectual stress'. It is prepared from 'a basis of roots and aromatic herbs'. Try it if you like; I haven't. The air and stillness of this great forest are enough balm for physical and mental stress; like so many of the vast valley and mountain scenes of Tuscany, the prospect from the heights of Camaldoli makes for a generous heart; it is one where mean thoughts are out of place, where the human spirit responds easily to the expansive benevolence of nature and its silence.

The long, shady, forest road to Vallombrosa is another place I sally forth to, glorious in the leafy autumn. This is on the Pratomagno, a mountain ridge, and leads up to the seventeenth-century Benedictine Abbey of Vallombrosa, quite modern for these parts; the original foundation was eleventh-century. Here, too, is a scene of wooded hills, canyons, crags and rivers which belongs to no century at all. A short way above Vallombrosa, on the site of a thirteenth-century hermitage, is a modern edifice, now a forestry school; this is Paradisino; the building bears a plaque to commemorate the sojourn of 'the supreme English poet Giovanni Milton in 1630'. The inscription goes on to say that he was 'enamoured of this forest and these skies'; and one can well believe it. The view from Paradisino has a feeling of *Paradise Lost*.

Arezzo is the nearest big town to the spot where I spend part of my life. The remains of the original walls are Etruscan, it has a number of notable medieval and renaissance churches and *palazzi*, and much of the town is modern. The overwhelming attractions of the city are the abundant frescoes of Piero della Francesca. In the Cathedral is the famous *Magdalen*. In the church of San Francesco are the frescoes

---

*Giovanni Acuto in Italian. His portrait by Paolo Uccello may be seen in the Duomo, Florence.

depicting those biblical subjects which made church-going such a wonderful picture-show for the faithful. I often think, as I look at them, how fortunate it is for us that so few people could read in those days, and were obligingly informed by these wonderful stories in pictures. The same Tuscan face of the *Madonna del Parto* is here in other roles.

Even closer to my second home are the two hill-towns I visit most for practical purposes of shopping or eating out, Monte San Savino and Lucignano. I have grown fond of them.

At Monte San Savino for several years I used to be invited with a friend to lunch every Thursday at the home of an elderly Signora of that place. She was in her eighties and had wonderful and terrible stories to tell as we made our leisurely way through Tuscan rarities, cunningly prepared with the herbs and flavourings she knew were the right ones. Thrilling and terrible were her stories. The Germans had taken her villa during the war; it still stands high on a hill-side, but her house at the time I knew her was in the piazza. The Germans had shot her 19-year-old son; a street bears his name. She herself with her daughter had been put on a truck bound for a train-connection to dreaded Germany; but one of the officers on guard, noted for his rigid toughness, nevertheless put them off in the countryside before they got to Florence, on the basis of a mutual love and knowledge of music. Love stories, escape stories, stories of wars and occupations, of her youth, provincial balls, visits to the opera: those Thursday lunches were unforgettable. After lunch our friend Carolina would play the piano and sing romantic songs from the turn of the century. My favourite was called 'Tormento' which she rendered with her whole heart. When she returned the visit, she would bring with her those things befitting a day in the country; these were her embroidery, her sketch book, and a book of poems by Leopardi. Carolina died on her nineteenth birthday. She seemed to sum up my Tuscan experience. A whole people, the product of civilised time past, the product of the dramatic landscape, the Tuscans are also the progenitors of what one finds there. It is this spirit of endurance and rejoicing in the goodness of life which inspired the architecture, the paintings, the churches and those ancient cultures of olive groves and vineyards, which are the essence of Tuscany.

[1984]

The Sitter's Tale

The Director of the Scottish National Portrait Gallery wrote to me and asked if I'd sit for Sandy Moffat. I asked if I could think about it, but in the meantime they booked it up. At the time there was a very nice curator, Duncan Thomson, whom I liked very much, so I didn't mind.

Sandy Moffat's portrait of me is a striking picture but bears no likeness to myself. Nobody recognises me. I spent one week in Edinburgh about 15 years ago with five sittings. Objectively I think it looks like a good poster. The artist didn't try to get to know me; in fact, he seemed only to want to fill in sessions with extra sketches.

He has given me yellow hair with a navy blue parting. It looks like dyed hair, but I've never coloured my hair, I've never needed to do so. Although I'm 81 I still have my natural light reddish hair and freckles, which is part of my 'look'. The portrait has somehow altered all that.

Sandy Moffat didn't know what I should wear. I had a black suit and a sweater with a thin black-and-grey stripe which he made into broad footballer's stripes. I put on a red scarf through my own intuition; it cheered the artist up, he was quite gloomy. He said to me, the picture is called *The Red Scarf*, and that, in fact, is what it is. I was just a model for *The Red Scarf* by Sandy Moffat. It isn't me at all; the author of my books is just not there.

Sandy gave me the name of a good restaurant in Leith, and recommended some brands of whisky to take home, for which I'm grateful. I don't regret it, I never regret anything like that. But I hope to do another portrait some time. I would like to be in the National Portrait Gallery in England as well.

[1999]

Italian Days

In those days, the late 1960s, I had a play on the West End of London and also on Broadway, and, although this was very acceptable for my working life, it drew a great deal of attention upon myself and I was looking for a place to live where I was comparatively unknown so that I could pursue my art in peace. I had been to Italy twice, once in the early 1960s to receive the Italia Prize for the radio dramatisation of my novel *The Ballad of Peckham Rye* at Verona and the second time I spent some days in Rome on my return from the Holy Land where I had gone to gather information for my novel *The Mandelbaum Gate*.

As I was a Catholic, I was attracted by the evidence of the early Christian church in Rome, mixed with the history of the Roman Empire up to the Renaissance. I could walk in the streets feeling that I was living in the fifth century or the fifteenth century as the case might be. I also felt that I could manage the Italian language having studied Latin. I can now read Italian very well, but my spoken Italian is not good.

I met a great many people when I came to Rome; mostly, at first, they were visiting writers and I soon found myself in an artistic environment. However I got to know many Italians, not only writers like Alberto Moravia, Alberto Arbasino and Luigi Barzini, but also the people in the shops with whom I became very friendly: hairdressers, dressmakers and electricians. I was particularly attracted by Italian fashions at that time, so much more creative than the English and American styles and more informal than the French. I had a season ticket to the opera and I used to go every year on the second night, where I would meet the director Visconti, always surrounded by his little court. Visconti, by the way, was very keen to make a film of my book *The Driver's Seat* and had arranged for it to be especially translated for him by Masolino Cecchi d'Amico, who did it beautifully. Visconti was on the point of discussing this film, I believe in the Raffaello Hotel, when he took ill and died. It was a great loss to the whole world of the cinema.

The Driver's Seat, under the translated title *Identikit*, was ultimately made by Giuseppe Patroni-Griffi with Elizabeth Taylor. I think Patroni-Griffi had difficulty in coaxing Elizabeth Taylor down to the street from her hotel room when he was ready to film but he managed the proceedings very professionally.

In Rome I met many people with whom I have formed a lifetime's friendship. And others, acquaintances like the Doria family or that Alessandro Torlonia who was married to an Infanta of Spain, I was many times in their houses, but more fun was the other Torlonia, the Duchessa Gioia of whose house in the Via Coronari I have so many happy memories. I often used to go to Nemi near Rome to visit the remains of Diana's temple, which was the basis of a book I was writing called *The Takeover*.

My Roman days ended at about the time of the Moro tragedy. I had met Aldo Moro and found him very charming. He had just come from my home town, Edinburgh, and had picked up an amusing Scottish tune from the Duke of Hamilton, with whom he had stayed. I think the death of Moro had a terrible effect upon everybody. It was a dreadful summer.

My friend Penelope had a house in Tuscany and invited me to stay with her to finish my book *The Takeover*. I moved in for a few weeks and have remained ever since. At first I was accepted with a certain reserve, but as my friend worked hard on her land it was quite obvious that we were two working women, so I think that we gained some respect from our neighbours. Certainly we soon made some very good friends. The Tuscans are very reliable, less demonstrative than the Romans, but, of course, I am talking of a rustic society as opposed to an urban people. I have always been able to work quietly in this part of the world. It is known that I am a writer and I was very touched last Easter when the priest asked me to address a few words to the congregation. It gave me great pleasure to thank them for the kindness they had shown me over these nearly thirty years.

A great many foreigners come to settle in Italy. I think the reason is that the Italians are very relaxing people to be with. They talk continually about 'stress', but in fact there is very little stress compared with other countries. And besides, there is a built-in court of appeal in every Italian that helps to bridge gaps of formality and class. There is also the factor that Italy is a very beautiful country to live in. I do know that there are pockets of foreign nationals who form self-contained colonies, but I don't belong to any of those. It would be contrary to my nature as a writer to restrict myself only, for instance, to English-speaking people – and what a bore it would be. I do love a good ethnic and national mixture. I like my country better when I visit it than when I stay in it. I quite enjoy going to London for visits and to Edinburgh, my native city, but I would not wish to live there again. Without its empire, Britain is insular and that is a plain geographical fact.

I think that the Italians have changed at exactly the same pace and in exactly the same style as in any other civilised country. I don't see that the Italians have fundamentally changed. It is only that they have washing-machines now and they didn't have before and I think this is the same everywhere. There is a greater moral permissiveness, not only in Italy but elsewhere in western civilisation.

It was my reading of a great writer, Cardinal John Henry Newman, that first attracted me to the Catholic Church and on reflection it seemed the most rational and practical of all religions. I was never able to believe nothing. I am a believer by nature. I would rather believe everything than nothing. I am a Catholic writer in the same sense that I can be called an English writer so far as I write in English and I think in terms of the Catholic Faith. I am not in agreement with all of the church doctrine. In fact I feel myself free to differ on subjects such as birth control and divorce.

I believe, as Cardinal Newman claimed, that it is impossible to write a novel that does not contain evil if one is writing about human beings and their destiny. Evil is absolutely necessary for dramatic presentation. A novel without evil would be like the white of an egg without the yolk – insipid.

[2003]

The David Cohen British Literature Prize, 1997

Your warm endorsement of this most important prize has made me very happy. The stated purpose of the award – 'For a lifetime's achievement' – is one that appeals greatly to me, for I have indeed dedicated a lifetime to the art of letters and to perfecting it to the utmost of my talents and capacities.

In fact, it is exactly seventy years ago that, at the age of nine, I set forth upon my literary life. My first work, a poem, was an intended improvement on Robert Browning's 'The Pied Piper of Hamelin'. My elders and teachers were somewhat intrigued by this ruthless re-writing of the 'Piper Pied' as I called him (so as to rhyme with 'he cried'). And so, where angels feared to tread I continued to rush in with my improvements on many such examples of English literature, available in plenty as they were in the Edinburgh Public Libraries.

Eventually I settled down to producing original work of my own – poems and stories – and have been at it ever since, with the result that I stand here this evening to thank you from the bottom of my heart for this great honour, the British Literature: David Cohen Award.

A few years ago I was called to Aberdeen University to receive an honorary degree. It was conferred on me by the then Chancellor, Sir Kenneth Alexander. After the ceremony he asked me, 'Do you remember Miss Kissock?' With a little thought I did indeed remember kindly Miss Kissock, our first infant teacher at Gillespie's school, Edinburgh. Sir Kenneth, about my age, had shared those warm experiences with me when we were little more than toddlers – the play-boxes and the coloured plasticine. And here he was in his glittering robes and there was I in my scarlet gown. What does one do with the best part of a lifetime? I thought of the lines of Robert Louis Stevenson:

> Honoured and old and all gaily apparelled,
> Here we shall meet and remember the past.
>
> (from 'Keepsake Mill')

I feel fortunate in having been born in a rich century for literature. It is the century that produced the gate-crashing *Waste Land* of T.S. Eliot, the spellbinding *A la Recherche du Temps Perdu* of Marcel Proust. It is a century that stretches from Chekhov, Pirandello and Sciascia to García Márquez; from E.M. Forster, Joseph Conrad, Virginia Woolf and Graham Greene to Milan Kundera, Iris Murdoch, Saul Bellow and John Updike. We have had critics of art and literature, indispensable to civilisation – scholars of brilliance and wit, such as Lytton Strachey, Herbert Read, Allen Tate, Lionel Trilling, and onward to Frank Kermode and Gabriel Josipovici, the more to enrich our powers of appreciation and discernment. The list is a long and dazzling one.

As for the novel itself, often as it is pronounced dead I am convinced that it is very much alive. So long as experiments in prose continue, so does novelty of thought, so do invention and imagination.

The twentieth century, in fact, has been buoyed up with an abundance of literary talent and originality – pressed down and flowing over. To be a writer in such an atmosphere of achievement has been, to me, a fulfilling and fully rewarding activity. To have been able to contribute to such a great tradition is in itself a high privilege.

What turn will literature take in the century to come? – Drama? Poetry? – a lot depends on the pathways opened by communicative technology. Let's hope it will be as inspiring in the field of creative writing as was, for example, the development of printing methods in the West in the fifteenth century.

One thing I am persuaded of: the world of communications has to be fed by travel. Nothing can be done without it. Marcel Proust wrote: 'the real voyage of discovery consists not in seeking new lands, but in seeking with new eyes'. This is an ultimate truth, never to be overlooked. But it has surely to be qualified by the likelihood that 'new eyes' are very greatly stimulated by new faces, new sights and sounds. To me, travel is the life-blood of literature. We have to find at first hand how other people live and die, what they say, how they smell, how they are made. I recommend travel to young authors.

And also to authors not so young. So far, you have been too polite to ask me how I intend to use the handsome prize-money that goes with the British Literature Award. I can say right away that I intend it for my travels, starting with a lovely, new, suitable motor car, which I hope will bear me in and out of our famous tunnel with ever more ease and pleasure.

Thank you again, and again.

[1997]

Part III

Literature

Who are you to say what's good for my mind?
Robinson

It is my first aim always to give pleasure. That is not to say that a book cannot make the reader think in a melancholy way or in a thoughtful way. Even tears can bring pleasure.
Il Messaggero, Rome

How to Write a Letter

In the middle of a house-move I came across many books I didn't know I had, among them pamphlets that I had picked up for their curiosity value as long as twenty years ago, and tucked out of sight among the overpowering hardbacks. Busy as I was, now, in the turmoil, I couldn't resist sitting down among the packing-cases to read *How to Write a Good Letter: A Complete Guide to the Correct Manner of Letter Writing* by John Barter, F.S.Sc., Revised and Enlarged by Gilbert Foyle (London, W. & G. Foyle, 135 Charing Cross Road, W.C., 1912).

At the time I picked up this treasure, I was reminded of Max Beerbohm's essay of 1910, 'How Shall I Word It?', he having come across a complete letter-writing manual at a railway bookstall; I feel it was rather more old-fashioned than mine. In Max's booklet a young man writes to 'Father of Girl he wishes to Marry'. In mine, the young man may alternatively write to the girl herself, but not, be it noted, addressing her by her first name.

The ever-incomparable Max, in his essay, was led on to compose some 'model' letters of his own, such as Letter from Poor Man to Obtain Money from Rich One and Letter to Thank Author for Inscribed Copy of Book, each with its Beerbohmesque sardonic twist.

In my case, my novelist's imagination takes over. For example, 'Leslie Dale of 328 Brondesbury Road, Kilburn N.W.' writes the following Proposal of Marriage.

5th April 1907

Dear Miss Hall

As I take my pen in my hand, I am wondering if you will think this letter rather premature, but the gist of the matter is that you and you alone are the one ideal woman in all the world for me. My mind is in a chaos as to whether your sentiments are the same concerning myself, and I cannot rest until you send me your answer to this question. Are you willing to share my lot?

...I will try my utmost to do all that is in my power to make your life happy and free from care, that there may never occur one moment of regret in taking the step I wish. You are to me my guiding star. Now please tell me whether you are going to make me the happiest or most miserable man on earth. Do as your heart dictates.

Awaiting with impatience your reply.

Yours hopefully,

Leslie Dale.

It does not take a great deal of novelist's imagination to conceive that Miss Hall is mightily thrilled by this fairly passionless missive, and loses no time to take it along to show her bosom friend, Miss Bellamy. She finds the latter lady, however, in a state of acute palpitation, having herself just received a Proposal of Marriage from her admirer, Herbert Clark. With trembling hands the girls exchange letters, only to find, on perusal, exactly the same wording, their suitors having both had recourse to the model letter in Messrs. Foyles' popular publication. Naturally, they decline their respective proposals. An example of the most dignified wording for that occasion is ready to hand in the manual:

> I am truly sorry if my letter causes you pain, but through circumstances over which I have no control, I am obliged to decline the great honour you offer me...

We do have a Reply of a Gentleman in Explanation of his Conduct, but it does not apply to Miss Hall's young man:

26 Albert Square,
London, N.W.
13th August, 1907.

My own Darling,

For so I must still address you, has cruelty entered into your tender nature, or has some designing wretch imposed on your credulity? My Dear, I am neither false nor perjured. My sole reason for walking with Miss Brown was that I had been on a visit to her brother, who you know is my Solicitor. And was it any harm to take a walk in the fields along with him and his sister? Surely no; in you are centred all my hopes of happiness; my affections never so much as wander from the dear object of my love. Do not entertain for a moment these groundless jealousies against one who loves you in a manner superior to the whole of your sex; let me beg of you an answer by return, as I will be most miserable until I hear from you.

Yours, for ever,

Herbert.

In an aside, our Gentleman is warned never to write 'My Dearest Katie', lest the loved one be moved to reply 'Am I to understand that you have other Katies?'

Although the Love and Matrimony section is crowned by a charming letter from Napoleon to Josephine, 1796, other headings are well represented. There are business letters such as that concerning 'the machinery that you made for our grinding department twelve months ago' which makes one go into a dream of wonder over grinding departments. There are specimen letters 'Requesting Payment of an Account', and a 'Reply to an Advertisement for a Governess', which are the soul of tact and good breeding.

We are a long way from the twelfth-century father of epistolary rhetoric Boncompagno da Signa, and further still from that immortal letter-writer, Paul of Tarsus. We are in the more modest daily lives of our great-grandfathers, grandfathers or even our fathers as the case may be. Our handbook has something for everybody, the stationer, the railway company; and if you should chance to be the Queen of England at a loss how to frame a letter to the President of the United States, this is what you write:

> Buckingham Palace,
> 22nd June 1860.
>
> My good Friend,
>
> I have been much gratified at the feelings which prompted you to write to me, inviting the Prince of Wales to come to Washington. He intends to return from Canada through the United States, and it will give him great pleasure to have an opportunity of testifying to you in person that these feelings are fully reciprocated by him. He will thus be able, at the same time, to remark the respect which he entertains for the Chief Magistrate of a great and friendly State and kindred nation.
>
> The Prince of Wales will drop all Royal State on leaving my dominions, and travel under the name of Lord Renfrew, as he has done when travelling on the Continent of Europe.
>
> The Prince Consort wishes to be kindly remembered to you.
>
> I remain ever, your good friend
>
> Victoria R.

[1990]

Our Dearest Emma

Emma Hamilton's rapid progress from scullery maid to wife of the British Ambassador at the Court of Naples, and thence to everlasting notoriety as Nelson's mistress, is transformed by Miss Prole into a tale which might have been more pertinently named 'Forever Emma'.

Her one true love, we are told, was Charles Greville, a worthless pervert who later sold her to his uncle, Sir William Hamilton; and Miss Prole is hard put to it to prove Emma's fidelity to his image, throughout her voluptuous career. Greville, in fact, seems to have been no less deceived than the reader will be.

This technicolour rendering of Emma's life and background shows her as a woman 'made for love', tiresomely unaccountable to herself for the frequent betrayals she suffered at the hands of her lovers; a fashionable trollop who was none the less a simple girl at heart. Whether Emma is shown exhibiting herself, nude, in the Health-and-Beauty pornographic racket where she was employed; whether she is trailing her provocative petticoats around the Royal Palace of Naples; partaking in violent flagellation scenes; or romping with Romney in the studio; Emma is always the seduced, never the seducer.

According to Lozania Prole, the Regency male must surely be the most single-minded in the whole history of society, since one and all who cross Emma's path are moved by her beauty to a common intent to possess her, by means no matter how foul.

And it was Emma, of course, not Nelson, who saved England from the French.

[1949]

Passionate Humbugs

The time for debunking the Victorians, we now hear from high quarters, is over. Let us take them seriously then. It may be, of course, that these authorities mean only the Eminent in Victorian life; but I propose to take them at their literal word because Thackeray, Tennyson and, say, Gladstone and Florence Nightingale do not add up to something that means 'the Victorians'.

The Victorians were a large number of people called 'the poor'; a small but immensely materially powerful number, the middle class;

and an even smaller number, influential but impotent, the aristocracy. I make this obvious statement because it should be clear that, when we are asked not to debunk the Victorians, it is not Matthew Arnold who is in question. It is the powerful middle class with whom we have to deal so far as 'the Victorians' and their tastes are concerned. It was they who bought up *In Memoriam*, very wisely, in edition after edition; it was they above whose heads Thackeray would have liked to write but dared not; and it was they who created something unknown in England in previous centuries, called a 'demand'.

The demand was supplied. But what was its nature? The very fact that it was a 'demand' and not merely a 'wide interest' (as there had been not long since in Scott, Mrs Radcliffe and even Jane Austen) suggests it was something pretty vigorous. In fact, it was full-blooded and passionate; and I suggest that the Victorian age can only be rivalled for passion by the Elizabethan. The difference is that while Elizabethan passions were still regulated by a cultural and religious unity, Victorian passions were all over the place, like their religion. The Victorian passion was for everything they did – eating, dressing, talking, money-making, writing, worshipping and sex. They indulged these passions unrestrainedly and promiscuously, with the exception of sexual passion which was counteracted by what we know as Victorian morals. These morals derived from many things besides Puritanism, but mostly I think, from the material desire of the middle class to secure its strength and protect its unity by disciplining itself to a rigid code of outward behaviour. What went on in their emotions – in their inward behaviour – was nobody's business so long as it did not come out and menace the structure of things. And it was this undisciplined emotion that created the demand for a type of popular literature.

Alan Walbank has collected an anthology of excerpts from the work of women novelists between 1850 and 1900. They do not bear considering as art, but they do confirm the type of demand these literary ladies supplied. What was wanted, particularly by women readers, was a violent emotional catharsis. That is nothing new in art. But this catharsis was required to be vitiated – and the art was consequently debased – by the introduction of material sentiments. Virtue has explicitly to be its own reward here on earth. You could vicariously murder your husband, set fire to a house, 'take' a lover, but you would receive your reckoning in Vol. III. So that, what I assert to be the intensely erotic instincts of the Victorian reader were left unassuaged by what I find to be the peep-show obscenity of Victorian popular reading. Hence the craving for more and yet more emotion-through-fiction. It is not satisfied yet. What is more, literature is becoming increasingly a matter of a meeting of demands mainly emotional, rather than a stimulus of interest, emotional and otherwise. For which we have to thank the Victorians. Alan Walbank's selection is useful mainly for easy reference to this aspect of popular Victorian taste. The authors represented include Charlotte Yonge, Mrs Henry Wood, Mrs Oliphant, Marie Corelli, Mrs Humphrey Ward (surely out of place in this company) and Ouida. They differ widely, but all meet on the materialist-moral level.

What I am quite seriously getting at is that I don't see that we can do other than debunk 'the Victorians', even admitting it would be nice to prove our grandfathers misjudged our great-grandfathers. I think, in fact, they did misjudge them, for they denounced the Victorians for the wrong reasons. They failed to realise that the Victorians had the advantage of being far more passionate in every way, and I repeat, more promiscuous in non-sexual matters, than their descendants who made such a fuss about emancipation. But the Victorians were humbugs, and they bequeathed us a more vicious sort of humbug – emotional chaos.

If we are looking for a typical example of this emotional excess in the powerful element of Victorian society, we can do no better than read Walbank's extracts from Ouida and Eileen Bigland's biography of that author. As Eileen Bigland says, Ouida gave the middle class a sensational though inaccurate account of high society. But an accurate account would never have satisfied this insatiate public. Ouida only offered what they craved. That frightful female's activities, as Eileen Bigland capably displays them, and her literary output, are all of a parcel with her times.

[1951]

Pensée: Biography

The sort of biographical writing that adheres relentlessly to fact, faithfully recounting all that undoubtedly happened and nothing that perhaps happened, can give a terribly distorted picture of the subject and times in question, because facts strung together present the truth only where simple people and events are involved; and the only people and events worth reading about are complex. There is another biographical approach in which the author's imagination rampages across history, mercilessly getting up our ancestors in all sorts of fancy dress and imbuing them with our latest notions of love, psychology and hygiene.

[…]

[1950]

Fuzzy Young Person

Bettina Brentano is one of the most fascinating ecstatics and line-shooters that one could hope to meet in the annals of the Romantic Movement. She was born at Frankfurt in 1785; her father was a prosperous Italian merchant and her mother, Maxe de la Roche, with whom Goethe had an amorous affair, a cultivated German.

Everything about Bettina, all that happened to her, is piled on, like an historical film. She was for ever finding herself in Gothic situations: she rescues and conceals a fugitive soldier, licks his wounds clean, no less; she finds herself abandoned by the coachman in a dark forest in the middle of the night; as a schoolgirl, she roams the convent grounds when all are asleep, is caught in a thunderstorm, clings to a tree, is wonderfully terrified. Or so she claimed in her delightful letters. These letters are intelligently arranged and linked by the authors' explanatory text.

Bettina lost no time in seeking out her mother's lover, Goethe, whom, one gathers, she began by enchanting and ended by boring. She was observed, dry-eyed, by the visiting Crabb Robinson; she cultivated Beethoven, Schelling (of whom she said, 'There is something about him I do not like, and that is his wife'), Schiller (who said of her that when she had left he felt as if he had recovered from a severe illness), and in fact everyone in politics and art. Her husband, Achim von Arnim, thought twice and thrice before marrying her, and hesitated to introduce her to his family lest she should lie down upon the table. 'Who is this fuzzy young person?' said Napoleon. She published, without embellishments, her correspondence with Goethe. He was undoubtedly the presiding genius of her imagination, and the authors are wisely uncertain whether she consciously modelled herself on Mignon, the child character in 'Wilhelm Meister', or whether

Bettina was simply born to fit the part. She kept up the frisky young attitude till quite late in life. An unfriendly friend of Bettina's enquires, 'What is the use of an elf in a commercial age? Who wants her trick dances, her tree-top games…? … dances are unsuited to the greying locks.'

This is a splendid biography, one of whose many incidental qualities is the light it casts on the Germany of the period.

[1957]

The Brontës as Teachers

The general feeling about the incursion into teaching of Charlotte, Branwell, Emily and Anne Brontë is that it was little short of martyrdom. The letters of Charlotte, the diaries of Anne, the novels of both, abound with evidence that the experience of being teachers was an agony to all four. Nothing, we are given to understand, could be worse than to be a private governess, a tutor or a school teacher to such pupils as came the Brontës' way; nothing worse than to be employed by such people as engaged the Brontës.

I am in sympathy with the view that their enforced choice of careers was a pity (except that it provided marvellous material for fiction) and rejoice with everyone else that at least three of them discovered their true vocation in time to write their unique, unconformable books. But were the Brontës mere lambs among wolves when they set forth to teach? I suggest that if anything could equal the misfortune of their lot as teachers it was the lot of the respective pupils and employers of Charlotte, Branwell, Emily and Anne.

Charlotte was the first to teach. Having practised for a while on her sisters she left Haworth Parsonage in 1835 to become a resident mistress at Roe Head school where previously she had been a pupil. Her formal education had covered little more than two years' schooling supplemented by home tuition from her maiden aunt. When, just turned nineteen, she became a mistress at Roe Head, her main qualification as an instructor of the young was a protected upbringing; this was, after all, judged to be the highest qualification a girl could produce. The headmistress (that Miss Wooler who remained a life-long friend to Charlotte) began by treating her as a friend. Charlotte stayed with Miss Wooler for over two years, but according to her letters and diaries she was miserable most of the time, as she well might be. Here is one of her diary entries:

> All this day I have been in a dream, half miserable, half ecstatic... I had been toiling for nearly an hour with Miss Lister, Miss Marriot, and Ellen Cook, striving to teach them the distinction between an article and a substantive. The parsing lesson was completed; a dead silence had succeeded it in the schoolroom, and I sat sinking from irritation and weariness into a kind of lethargy. The thought came to me: Am I to spend all the best part of my life in this wretched bondage, forcibly suppressing my rage at the idleness, the apathy, and the hyperbolical and most asinine stupidity of these fat-headed oafs, and of compulsion assuming an air of kindness, patience and assiduity? Must I from day to day sit chained to this chair, prisoned within these four bare walls, while these glorious summer suns are burning in heaven and the year is revolving in its richest glow? Stung to the heart with this reflection I started up and mechanically walked to the window. A sweet August morning was smiling without... I felt as if I could have written gloriously... If I had had time to indulge it I felt that the vague suggestion of that moment would have settled down into some narrative better at least than anything I ever produced before. But just then a dolt came up with a lesson.

Now, all this did violence to Charlotte, who wanted to write, not teach. But what we are concerned with here is the effect of her frustration on the Misses Lister, Marriot and Cook, not to mention the unfortunate 'dolt' who interrupted Charlotte's reverie. Were they all so unlike normal children, were they all such 'fat-headed oafs' that they failed to sense Miss Brontë's contempt and fury? One cannot help feeling that they gained less from Charlotte's instruction than she expended upon it by way of 'suppressing my rage'.

But poor Charlotte was to fare worse. She presented herself in 1839 as governess to the children of a Mrs Sidgwick who, poor soul, did not dream she was about to harbour an eminent Victorian. Charlotte immediately transferred her dislike of the job to Mrs Sidgwick and her children, though she was not averse to Mr Sidgwick. Charlotte's complaints were many and bitter: Mrs Sidgwick never left her a free moment to enjoy the spacious grounds and neighbouring countryside; Mrs Sidgwick would not allow the children, 'riotous, perverse, unmanageable cubs', to be corrected (a charge which Charlotte was to bring against her next employer and Anne against hers, somewhat contrary to notions of middle-class rearing of children in the nineteenth century); Mrs Sidgwick took Charlotte to task for sulking, whereupon Charlotte wept; Mrs Sidgwick expected Charlotte to love the children; and, final indignity, Mrs Sidgwick 'overwhelms me with oceans of needlework, yards of cambric to hem, muslin nightcaps to make, and, above all things, dolls to dress'.

It sounds quite drastic. Certainly the patent misery of the new governess must have seemed so to Mrs Sidgwick who, from other accounts, is said to have been an amiable woman. No doubt she loaded on the needlework with a view to keeping Charlotte from brooding, to give her something to occupy her mind, for it is remarkable how often in those days melancholy was equated with vacancy of purpose and cheerfulness with a full life. Still, we cannot blame Mrs Sidgwick for being an average mediocre nonentity; she never claimed to be other. If anything was to blame it was the system which included needlework among other semi-domestic tasks in the normal duties of a governess. Unless we look upon Charlotte as a famous author, which we are not doing at the moment, the sewing was no real outrage. And whether it was any more degrading, any greater a bore, than is the supervision of conducted tours and school lunches to the present-day teaching profession, is a question.

This record of Charlotte's brief sojourn with the Sidgwicks would be incomplete without the testimony of one of the Sidgwick pupils in later years, after Charlotte's distaste for his family had been made public by Mrs Gaskell. He declared that 'if Miss Brontë was desired to accompany them to Church – "Oh, Miss Brontë, do run up and put on your things, we want to start" – she was plunged in dudgeon because she was being treated like a hireling. If, in consequence, she was not invited to accompany them, she was infinitely depressed because she was treated as an outcast and a friendless dependant'. Since most of the Brontë victims were inarticulate, locked forever in the pillories of the Brontë letters and novels, I find this brief protest rather touching, coming from the otherwise mute and admittedly inglorious Sidgwick child.

As this was a temporary post Charlotte only had to endure it for less than three months. Before she left, one of the little Sidgwicks threw a Bible at her. He later became a clergyman.

Next comes Mrs White. Charlotte soon discovered that 'she does not scruple to give way to anger in a very coarse, unladylike manner'. Charlotte preferred Mr White, in spite of her conviction that 'his extraction is very low'. Meanwhile, she said, she was trying hard to like Mrs White. This effort was fruitful, notwithstanding Mrs White's bad grammar of which Charlotte is critical, and the fact that Charlotte feared her to be an exciseman's daughter. In the end, Mrs White won over the parson's daughter, who came to admit that she was intrigued by the 'fat baby', and called her pupils 'well-disposed' though of course, 'indulged'.

Behold now Charlotte in her last teaching post. The Pensionnat Héger in Brussels is the scene, and Charlotte, having gone there to study French and German, has now become an English mistress in this school for young ladies. Her employer, Mme Héger, has grown rather suspicious of the English teacher and spies upon her; Charlotte apparently cannot think why. She prefers M. Héger. The schoolgirls are 'selfish, animal and inferior'. And we are further delightfully informed that 'their principles are rotten to the core'. Charlotte's colleagues hate each other, and she them. So her letters go on. One of her fellow mistresses, worse than the rest, acts as a spy for Mme Héger, is false, is contemptible, is Catholic. In fact they are all Catholic, and in fact, as Charlotte writes to Branwell, 'the people here are no go whatsoever'.

As the months proceed, Charlotte is giving English lessons to M. Héger, who seems well satisfied with her work and gives her presents of books occasionally. Charlotte declares that his goodness towards her compensates for the 'deprivations and humiliations' which are her lot, but on which she is not explicit.

But presently M. Héger takes to avoiding Charlotte, having first lectured her on the subject of 'universal *Bienveillance*'. She, however, is no universalist; her *bienveillance* is focused on the object of her master whom she observes is 'wonderfully influenced' by his wife. With curious logic Charlotte now finds she can 'no longer trust' Mme Héger, and driven back to Haworth by that lady's suspicions, proceeds to confirm them by writing a series of impassioned letters to M. Héger until he implores her to stop.

Let us now look at the teaching career of Branwell Brontë. At the age of twenty he joined the staff of a local school from which he retreated within six months. The small boys made fun of his red hair. After fortifying his dignity with a long interval of writing, painting, hard drinking and opium eating, he became tutor, in 1840, to the children of a Mr and Mrs Postlethwaite. Branwell's view of his job can best be savoured from his own account of it written to one of his former drinking cronies:

> If you saw me now you would not know me, and you would laugh to hear the character the people give me... Well, what am I? That is, what do they think I am? – a most sober, abstemious, patient, mild-

hearted, virtuous, gentlemanly philosopher, the picture of good works, the treasure-house of righteous thought. Cards are shuffled under the tablecloth, glasses are thrust into the cupboard, if I enter the room. I take neither spirit, wine, nor malt liquors. I dress in black, and smile like a saint or martyr. Every lady says, 'What a good young gentleman is the Postlethwaites' tutor.' This is a fact, as I am a living soul, and right comfortably do I laugh at them; but in this humour do I mean them to continue.

Branwell ends by saying that as he writes one of the Postlethwaites' daughters is sitting close by… 'She little thinks the Devil is as near her…'

Branwell's attitude to these folk, whatever else it amounts to, does make a welcome contrast with that expressed by his sisters in similar circumstances. The sons of the family he describes as 'fine spirited lads' – these being, no doubt, merely Charlotte's 'riotous, perverse, unmanageable cubs' in a lighter aspect. And Branwell depicts Mr Postlethwaite as 'of a right hearty, generous disposition' and his wife as 'a quiet, silent, amiable woman'. But within a few months Branwell's restless ambitions tore him from the Postlethwaites to visit Hartley Coleridge, and thence back to Haworth.

His next and last post as tutor came three years later. Anne introduced him into the household where she was employed as a governess. He was to teach the son of the house. His employer, Mr Robinson, was an aging invalid; Mrs Robinson was much younger. Branwell preferred Mrs Robinson. 'This lady,' he wrote later, '(though her husband detested me) showed me a degree of kindness which, when I was deeply grieved one day at her husband's conduct, ripened into declarations of more than ordinary feeling.' It took Mr Robinson two-and-a-half years to confirm his suspicions, whereupon he wrote to Branwell, then on holiday, 'intimating' as Charlotte reported, 'that he had discovered his proceedings … and charging him on pain of exposure to break off instantly and forever all communication with every member of his family'. Branwell insisted that Mrs Robinson returned his passion. Years afterwards, when Brontë biography began its voluminous course, she took occasion to deny it.

Anne's post with the Robinsons was her second. The youngest Brontë proved the most patient of the four, and though by no means devoid of talent and the will to write, endured her teaching career for a longer period than the others. However, in proportion as she exercised restraint, so did her novels reveal exactly what she had restrained in the way of spleen. At the age of nineteen Anne took charge of the two eldest children of a Mrs Ingham. Before long, Charlotte was busy passing on Anne's news: her pupils were 'desperate little dunces', 'excessively indulged', 'violent' and 'modern'. Anne left this family after eighteen months' attempt to cope with them; she was somewhat the worse for the experience.

Anne was twenty-one when she went to the Robinsons. Charlotte, who exaggerated most things, gave out that Anne was 'a patient, persecuted stranger' amongst 'grossly insolent, proud and tyrannical' people. Direct evidence from Anne has not survived beyond two diary fragments, the first of which commits her no further than 'I dislike the situation and wish to change it for another.' (Her novels provide the usual terrible children.) She remained four years, during which time her pupils had become very fond of her. In fact, the Robinson girls continued to visit and write to Anne, long after she had left the family and her brother had been dismissed in disgrace from it. Anne's only other direct comment on the job refers to her earlier dislike of it. 'I was wishing to leave it then, and if I had known that I had four years longer to stay, how wretched I should have been; but during my stay I have had some very unpleasant and undreamt-of experience of human nature.' This last lament is taken to refer to Branwell's intrigue with Mrs Robinson and can be found precisely stated in *The Tenant of Wildfell Hall*.

Emily, like her sisters, was nineteen when she set off to be a teacher at Law Hill School and it seems fairly certain that Emily was still nineteen when she did the sensible thing and returned. All we know of her stay at Law Hill is that she wrote a letter which, according to Charlotte, 'gives an appalling account of her duties – hard labour from six in the morning until near eleven at night, with only one half-hour exercise between. This is slavery.' 'I fear,' Charlotte adds, 'she will never stand it.' Emily did not stand it. But the curious thing is, that during this period Emily's poetic output was higher than at any other time, which seems to indicate that she was not entirely starved of leisure.

Emily did not long endure her job as a music-teacher at the Héger establishment. When she was called back to Haworth with Charlotte on the death of her aunt, Emily showed no desire to return with her sister to Brussels. Much has been made of the fact that M. Héger expressed approval of Emily (after she was dead and famous) declaring, somewhat ambiguously I have always thought, that she should have been a navigator. He also gave the opinions that she might have been a great historian and she should have been a man. Nowhere does he say that she should have been a music-teacher. And at the time, M. Héger felt moved only to inform Emily's father, 'She was losing whatever remained of her ignorance, and also of what was worse – timidity.'

For the three sisters it was torture while it lasted. For Branwell, fun while it lasted. Their frail constitutions were damaged and much of their creative energy dissipated in the uncongenial schoolroom. They did their best to earn a living in the only way open to them. But from the point of view which it has been my purpose to adopt, it might also be thought that genius, if thwarted, resolves itself in an infinite capacity for inflicting trouble, or at least for finding fault. It is asking too much of genius to ask it to keep its personality out of anything; even the lesser talent can seldom do so.

Branwell's conduct was unprofessional, to say the least. Charlotte was not, to say the least, proof against those states of mind which the most protected upbringing will not protect. Anne's reaction was to hoard her resentment. Emily's way, by far the most successful, was to get out of the predicament with all speed (and note: she shows no obsession in her work with the governess theme). The Brontës, however, gained ample revenge for all injustices real or imagined.

So one might, therefore, without compunction enquire whether their employers – the Sidgwicks and Inghams and Whites – did in fact fail in their duty to their employees; or were they merely unfortunate in crossing the Brontës' path? I should say that if their sense of duty were wanting, it was to their children. And along with this thought comes the realisation, supported from other sources besides the Brontës, that the wealthy middle class of England during the last century were willing to hand over their children to any young woman who came out of a clergyman's home, neurotic or ailing as she might be.

The Brontës once planned to start a school of their own. The project, as mercifully for others as for themselves, came to nothing. Branwell's wasted life gave a warning signal to his sisters, and miraculously they asserted their creative powers.

I have not depended on their novels to support this essay, since I believe that fiction is a suspect witness; (and if it is not stranger than truth, it ought to be). But, of course, unmistakable versions of Brontë pupils and employers are to be found in the novels of Charlotte and Anne.

Perhaps the lesson to be drawn, for any writer with the necessary will of iron, who lacks only the opportunity to write, is that he should prove himself no good at anything else.

[1966]

My Favourite Villain: Heathcliff

Heathcliff of *Wuthering Heights* is quite the most fascinating villain I have encountered in fiction. He's an arch-villain – there's no doubt at all about his evil nature. And yet he is not repulsive; everything he does is on a scale larger than life; if he lies it is not a petty lie, it is the sort of lie that brings ruin on someone's head; if he steals, it is a whole family heritage that he steals – you couldn't imagine Heathcliff as a shoplifter. In a modern novel such a character would be depicted as at least partially mad. Emily Brontë succeeds in making him perfectly sane and utterly bad.

To me, most villains of nineteenth-century literature are slightly ridiculous, and I think that is because they are little, mean men. Heathcliff is a big bad man, he is never ridiculous, he is terrible, a real Prince of Darkness. He is not only the villain, he is the hero of the book in the grand Homeric sense.

The action, already noted, which according to Rossetti's famous comment is laid in Hell, is in fact laid very much in Yorkshire, in two remote mansions of the moors. It is a small rustic world in which the scene is set, a world of secluded landed gentry whose occupations are shooting and riding and farming. It is Heathcliff who dominates and colours the world of *Wuthering Heights* and who gives it all its fiendish magnitude. He carries hell about with him, so that one feels as the novel progresses, that the familiar moorlands have somehow become dislocated from their natural time and place; the inhabitants are outside of the ordinary law of the land: there are no magistrates to appeal to. An ordinary love affair becomes a blood pact lasting beyond the grave.

Heathcliff comes on the scene as a foundling child – in Emily Brontë's words, 'a little black-haired swarthy thing, as dark as if it came from the Devil', and from that moment he radiates an influence on all the other characters, at first attracting hatred and violence and then exerting them.

One thing I find curious is the fact that the mere physical action of the novel is not sufficient to explain Heathcliff's influence and power over the other characters. Sometimes he captures them physically, of course – Isabella Linton, the young Catherine, and even the solid Ellen Dean are at one point or another made prisoners behind locked doors at Wuthering Heights. But sooner or later they find some means of escape – and one has the impression that with their wits about them, they might have escaped sooner. Certainly, they walk very easily into the traps Heathcliff prepares for them.

But it is obvious that in Heathcliff's presence, they haven't really got their wits about them. His real power goes far beyond that of property and physical possession: he is a kind of moral hypnotist, and it is in some deep hidden way that he is able to manoeuvre his victims. Even those who find his appearance repulsive, and who, like Edgar Linton, have every reason to detest him, unfailingly permit themselves to fall in with his huge plan for vengeance, they seem almost to collaborate unwillingly with him. And these are not weak characters. Ellen Dean, the housekeeper, and the older Catherine are each in their own way as strong and spirited as Heathcliff. And yet they find him finally irresistible.

Of course, it was brilliant of Emily Brontë to conceive Heathcliff's physical appearance in the way she did. The flesh-and-blood Heathcliff is tremendously endowed with male attractiveness of the dark brooding order. Even Mr Lockwood, whose reactions are so invariably sane and normal, reveals a definite admiration for him: 'He is a dark skinned gipsy, in aspect,' he reports, 'in dress, and manners a gentleman, that is, as much a gentleman as many a country squire: rather slovenly, perhaps, yet not looking amiss with his negligence, because he has an erect and handsome figure, and rather morose...'

And we see the well-bred, dainty Isabella Linton simply throwing herself at him. 'Is Mr. Heathcliff a man?' she asks after their marriage, 'If so, is he mad? And if not, is he a devil?' That he is, for the most part, a devil seems to be recognised only by two people in the novel, the older Catherine and Ellen Dean. Catherine puts up a fight before she accepts the destiny of this demon-lover. Ellen Dean's response is a peculiar mixture of homeliness and deep fear. She has been Heathcliff's childhood nurse, and when she finds him on his deathbed she can hardly keep away from him, terrified as she is. 'I combed his black long hair from his forehead,' she says, 'I tried to close his eyes – to extinguish, if possible, that frightful life-like gaze of exultation, before anyone else beheld it. They would not shut – they seemed to sneer at my attempts, and his parted lips, and sharp, white teeth sneered too!'

From first to last Heathcliff reveals this power of drawing strange, uncharacteristic passions out of the people of his environment; whenever he appears there is not only trouble, but wild agitation, frantic behaviour and violence. Emily Brontë's sister, Charlotte, wrote of *Wuthering Heights*, 'Whether it is right or advisable to create beings like Heathcliff, I do not know; I scarcely think it is.'

This seems to me an irrelevant statement, because the invention of a being so elemental as Heathcliff doesn't seem to come within the scope of things that are right or advisable. He is what he is: a giant character of high fiction. It is true that one is not likely to meet a full-scale Heathcliff in ordinary life, but that is because most of the Heathcliffs of the civilised world are subject to the restraints of society. In fact, I think we do occasionally come across the type of person Heathcliff represents – the obsessed spirit which infects everyone around it, the moral blackmailer, people of terrifying psychological influence; and of course, in ordinary life, one is best out of their way.

But Emily Brontë was not dealing with ordinary life and society. It is not the plain truth of realism, but the paradoxical truth of imaginative fiction which draws us to the immortal *Wuthering Heights* and its nightmare hero.

[1960]

Mrs Gaskell

Despite the devoted tone of this long and laboured biography, Mrs Gaskell emerges as a provincial, materialistic, self-satisfied humbug.

As an author she has surely had her due; she never wrote 'a great, a profoundly moving scene' in her life, far less in the passage so designated by Miss Hopkins. Mrs Gaskell possessed an interesting minor talent. She wrote badly most of the time. In spite of her social zeal it is impossible to take her altogether seriously. These are facts to which Miss Hopkins, in her solemn and burning faith, is blind.

Mrs Gaskell was transported by signs of affluence in people: 'My word! authorship must bring them in a pretty penny' was her response to seeing someone's art collection. At a dinner party, while smiling until her face ached, Mrs Gaskell's inward eye would be weighing and pricing the beef: 'More than 40 lb. we had at the bottom of the table and 2 turkeys at the top.' She wrote endless letters about food. Not a green pea went uncounted by her.

And what a scandalmonger she was!

About George Eliot she wrote: 'I shut my eyes to the awkward blot in her life' and 'Mrs. Lewes… (what do people call her?)'.

About Mrs Robinson (Branwell Brontë's employer): 'mature and wicked woman', 'profligate woman', 'depraved woman'.

But not everyone adored Mrs Gaskell.

Mary Shelley said of her: '...the Beau ideal of a Country Blue grafted on a sort of Lady Bountiful... pretension animates her to perpetual talk'; and Jane Carlyle: '...there was an air of moral dullness about her'.

Ladies! Ladies!

[1953]

Mary Shelley

Author's Note
The following, which I wrote in 1950, is a scheme of work on Mary Shelley which I offered to publishers with a book in mind for the 100th anniversary of her death in 1851.

Whether my subsequent book *Child of Light* (1951) – later revised as *Mary Shelley* (1987)[*] – fulfils the ambitious aims that I set forth in this outline, or not, it does now seem to me to fully incorporate and summarise my past and present opinions on the subject.

Proposal for a Critical Biography of Mary Shelley (1797–1851)

The centenary of the death of Mary Shelley will be 1st February, 1951, and this might be a suitable occasion on which to publish a definitive biography which is, I feel, long overdue.

So far, there have been only three studies of this writer. The first appeared in 1890, by Lucy Madox Rossetti; the second (a very brief outline of her life numbering 80 pages) by Richard Church was published in 1928; and the third, by R. Glynn Grylls appeared in 1938. All of these biographies have dwelt upon the outward circumstances of Mary Shelley's life – she has been portrayed rather as the daughter of Mary Wollstonecraft and William Godwin, and as the wife of Shelley, than as an important nineteenth-century literary figure in her own right. The first of the works mentioned above has been superseded

---

[*]Reissued in 2013 by Carcanet Press, with a new introduction by Michael Schmidt and including Muriel Spark's original 'Proposal...', reproduced here.

by the discovery of fresh material; the second is perhaps too short to have allowed sufficient scope to the biographer; and the third, whilst providing footnotes and appendices useful to the student, does not seem to me to offer a fluent and convincing study of the inner and outward life of its subject, hampered as it is by frequent quotations and notes. Added to this, the two latter volumes do not incorporate material made available since their publication, which reveals new aspects of Mary Shelley's character during and after Shelley's lifetime.

The biography I now propose would take into account all the known facts of Mary Shelley's life, interpreting her character in the light of this new material, and also considering her work as an indispensable source of illumination. So far, her autobiographical novel *Lodore*, which reflects the characters of her circle and many events of her life, has not been incorporated into biographical studies of Mary Shelley. And, apart from her best-known novel, *Frankenstein*, her other powerful and imaginative novels and stories have been neglected. In the critical-biography I have in mind, I would propose to examine all her works in assessing the personality that motivated them; and would compare her life and works with those of other women writers of the nineteenth century. This is not to suggest that I would give her a place in English literature superior to that which she deserves; she had not the craftsmanship, for instance, of Jane Austen, nor the emotional force of the Brontës; but a comparative study such as I have in view would bring to light those qualities in her work which have been overlooked, and which other women writers do not possess. Her novels *Frankenstein* and *The Last Man*, for example, are almost entirely without their counterpart in feminine literature, being the prototypes of the scientific extravaganza popularised by H.G. Wells, and recently reflected in the novels of Aldous Huxley and George Orwell.

I would also trace, in her emotional and intellectual attitudes, the influence of her parents Mary Wollstonecraft and William Godwin; whilst the effect of Shelley on her life I would show to be manifest in the idealisation and ennoblement with which she invested her own tragic situation, and in the ruthless pursuit of her vocation after Shelley's death.

It has been said that Mary Shelley lapsed into the conventional salon habituée. This, I would argue, is questionable, since an attentive examination of her letters would indicate that her social activities were undertaken simply to further her literary ambitions, and that never was she misled in the matter of basic values. Her letters show, too, an intellectual breadth remarkable in a woman of her times, or indeed, of any time; despite her essential femininity – and she was often frivolous and flirtatious – she handled Shelley's romantic fluctuations with composure and not a little humour.

Her mother, Mary Wollstonecraft, had been an ardent feminist who, although she was at pains to set forth her theories on the rights of women, was herself temperamentally unsuited to the application of her doctrines. It was her daughter, Mary Shelley, who realised these ideals by a natural acceptance of her status as a creature the equal of, yet different from, the male of her times.

[written 1950]

Mary Shelley: Wife to a Genius

A hundred years ago, on the first of February, 1851, Mary Wollstonecraft Shelley died, aged fifty-four. She had started life with some unique advantages and some commonplace disadvantages. Her parents, William Godwin and Mary Wollstonecraft, were both famous literary figures of the day. People like Lamb, Hazlitt and Coleridge were among the old familiar faces of her childhood, and she heard a rendering of *The Ancient Mariner* from the poet's own lips. These were her initial advantages. Of the disadvantages the most unfortunate was the death of her mother in giving her birth, and then the advent of Godwin's second wife. It was probably partly because her home life was so distasteful that Godwin's daughter eloped with the most unique advantage offered by the Godwin ménage. This was the poet Shelley whom she later married.

Being Shelley's wife was a mixed blessing, he being a genius. On the whole, Mary Shelley counted it a blessing, with a conviction which increased throughout her long widowhood. At the same time, this talented, sensitive, reserved woman suffered keenly from a sense that she was unpopular; for the most part she was justified in this belief. It was the sensitivity and the reserve (as often is the case) which made her unpopular, but some of her acquaintance resented her talent – or at least the use to which she put it after Shelley's death. It was remembered that her father Godwin was the rationalist philosopher whose principal work, *Political Justice*, had made him the idol of the Progressives. It was remembered that her mother, Mary Wollstonecraft, was the perpetrator of *The Rights of Women* and of a passionate, one-sided love affair the documents of which had been placed on record for the more exclusive spirits of enlightenment to exult in. It was remembered still more of Mary Shelley that she was Shelley's widow, and he in turn was then remembered rather for his libertarian views than for his poetry. These were the things that Mary Shelley's friends considered when they considered her. They observed she was not visibly warm and passionate like her mother; that she was neither an advocate for the rights of women nor of men. They looked upon her, in fact, as a reactionary; and this is still often said of her in various ways.

My own admiration for Mary Shelley is based on her quite exceptional writings; as for her personality, those very qualities seem now to commend her, which made her unpopular in her time. I mean, of course, unpopular among the small group of lesser intellectuals who exalted Shelley for the wrong reasons. Other eminent or talented people whom she met after Shelley's death – the poet Beddoes was one of them – held her and her work in great respect, if they did not offer her close friendships. What I like about her, then, is that she had the strength of character to reject what she thought immoderate in the doctrines in which she had been scrupulously educated. Mary Shelley's life was unusually beset all along with frustration, disappointment and tragedy. In her widowhood she had to support herself and her son Percy by her writing. Yet she refused to mitigate her hardships by turning out propaganda for the family 'cause'. It would have secured her many friends and relieved her bitter loneliness had she done so. But she even refused to defend herself against criticisms on this score. She did, however, record her case privately and at length in her diary; the following few sentences of which are representative:

> … with regard to 'the good cause' – the cause of the advancement of freedom and knowledge, of the rights of women, etc. – I am not a person of opinions. That my parents and Shelley were of the former class, makes me respect it. I respect such when joined to real disinterestedness, toleration, and a clear understanding. My accusers, after such as these, appear to be mere drivellers. For myself, I earnestly desire the good and enlightenment of my fellow creatures, and see all in the present course, tending to the same, and rejoice, but I am not for violent extremes, which only bring on an injurious reaction.

This is plain sense. But though she did not respect her accusers, she felt bitter about their attitude to her:

> To hang back, as I do, brings a penalty. I was nursed and fed with a love of glory. To be something great and good was the precept given me

by my Father: Shelley reiterated it... If I had raved and ranted about what I did not understand; had I adopted a set of opinions, and propagated them with enthusiasm; had I been careless of attack, and eager for notoriety; then the party to which I belonged had gathered round me, and I had not been alone. But since I had lost Shelley I have no wish to ally myself to the Radicals – they are full of repulsion to me – violent without any sense of Justice – selfish in the extreme – talking without knowledge – rude, envious and insolent – I wish to have nothing to do with them.

It was difficult for her to turn her back on the Progressive set; it was more difficult still to enter another set. She was not very clear, in any case, about what she wanted of life – her statement only makes it clear what she did not want. If asked what she wanted, she would have answered, 'friends, society', but though she often lamented the lack of these, her notions of society were very vague, and she had no positive ideas about the type of people she wanted to make friends with. Shelley's friends, Hogg, Jane Williams, and even Hunt and Trelawney, all failed her in varying degrees. The upper-middle-class, recalling the scandal of her elopement with Shelley, Harriet Shelley's suicide, Shelley's atheism, etc., would have nothing to do with her. She would have despised them anyway; serious, studious and intelligent as she was.

Many have observed that her diaries and letters give the effect of a singularly dissatisfied temperament. They do give this effect, though her diaries and letters are not the whole story; they tell only of her somewhat disordered, though genuinely exacting, outward existence. She had opportunities for marriage after Shelley's death, but could not bring herself to consider anyone not of Shelley's stature. She had intimated that she would consider Washington Irving, whom she had met; but when he learned of this he did not seem interested. Prosper Mérimée, however, who sent her an amorous letter, received a polite snub. She turned down Trelawney with emphasis.

It is true that she had a melancholy nature, and she knew it. But she would have had to be extremely optimistic not to have been affected by the extraordinary disasters that beset her. Three out of her four children died in infancy. Then Shelley's death was followed by a long struggle to educate their son Percy, whom she sent to Harrow and Cambridge. The meanness of Shelley's father towards her is well known; a small allowance was granted her as a loan on account of Shelley's inheritance. This fell due when Sir Timothy died, he having lingered till it was too late for Mary Shelley to benefit from it. In the few remaining years of her life, when for the first time she was relieved from financial anxiety, she was subjected to a series of blackmails that finally wrecked her. Even Percy was a disappointment. He was a good, dull son whom she dragged all over Europe in an effort to launch him in society. But Shelley's son bought a trumpet to play on while his mother was visiting the art galleries; pined for England and a sight of 'the new flying machine', and on his return talked and thought of entering Parliament. He finally gave up the idea, married a nice girl who had some money, and settled down to do practically nothing.

Was Mary Shelley's life a failure, then? She would have denied this. The eight years she spent with Shelley were constantly in her mind – too constantly, and in too idealised a form for her own peace, perhaps, but this memory was her chief consolation. But there is another, very important factor in her life, which her letters and diaries do not reveal, and which commentators on Mary Shelley are apt to forget. That is, her constant creative activity. She was well aware that her life was not turning out as she had hoped; but she loved, and lived in, her work when her power was at its height, and before her life encroached altogether upon it. As early as 1834, when she was looking through the pages of her diary she wrote, 'It has struck me what a very imperfect picture...these querulous pages afford of *me*. This arises from their being a record of my feelings, and not of my imagination...'

The record of her imagination is to be found in its most successful forms in her novels *Frankenstein* and *The Last Man* (a work which deserves to be better known). *Frankenstein*, the first English novel in which a scientific theme had been combined with the Gothic horror convention, made Mary Shelley's name as a writer, and was highly and lengthily applauded by Sir Walter Scott in *Blackwood's*. The book is now an English classic, and even pre-war film-goers will remember the story of the scientist who, discovering the principle of life, created a monster who pursued him to ruin. It is a horrifying interpretation of science as man's destroyer, an anticipation of what we now know in our own time.

Mary Shelley was in her teens when she wrote *Frankenstein*, which was inspired by conversations between Shelley and Byron. But it was not until after both Shelley and Byron were dead that her very fine work *The Last Man* was written. This is an amazingly powerful story about a plague which gradually spreads across the earth, annihilating all but one man. None of her subsequent novels and stories approach these two books for imaginative strength. The themes alone outweigh their many artistic defects; they are remarkable works, greatly neglected by students of nineteenth-century fiction.

Apart from the valuable and extensive notes written by Mary Shelley when she edited Shelley's complete poems in 1839, her writing declined. She lost her creative will; she lost vigour; in her search for 'life' and a nebulous 'society', she lost her vision of life and society. (That she did have this vision, is clear from her admirable handling of vast social issues in *The Last Man*.) Outward circumstance partly contributed to this condition, but also there was the fact that she could never formulate, or even follow instinctively, any positive philosophy. The themes of her novels bear this out – they show her strong and lucid intellect moving slowly towards negative conclusions.

[1951]

Frankenstein and *The Last Man*

Mary Wollstonecraft Shelley was [for many years after her death] best known as the second wife of the poet Shelley; and she was remembered also as the child of that exceptional couple – William Godwin the rationalist philosopher, and Mary Wollstonecraft, the passionate, not-so-rational reasoner on behalf of the Rights of Women. It is [still] as well to remember these facts, for they help to explain the most memorable thing [now recognised] about Mary Shelley: she was the author of two remarkable novels, one being the well-known *Frankenstein* and the other, [for many years] hardly known at all, *The Last Man*. She wrote other books, of course, besides editing Shelley's poems with extensive notes, but in these two novels she did something in English fiction which had not been done before; and that was to combine rational and natural (as distinct from supernatural) themes with the imaginative elements of Gothic fiction. She initiated, in these books, that fictional species which H.G. Wells made popular in his early novels, and which he called 'fantasies of possibility' and we call science fiction.

Frankenstein, like those early books by Wells, is a novel of scientific speculation, in which the germ of prophecy necessarily resides; and while *The Last Man* isn't concerned with science, it perpetuates the central prophetic idea of *Frankenstein*. Wells later came to the conclusion that fiction is not a suitable vehicle for prophecy, but I think he had something more literal in mind than I have when I suggest that *Frankenstein* and *The Last Man* belong to prophetic fiction. What Wells meant was the sort of hit-or-miss gamble of conjecture that enabled him to prophesy television as early as 1898, but which also led him to announce that 'long before the year A.D. 2000, and very probably before 1950, a successful aeroplane will have soared and come home safe and sound'. Mary Shelley also tried her hand at this sort of thing. In *The Last Man*, published in 1826, she describes the Royal Family as adopting the name of Windsor; but her calculations were out when she said that by the end of the twenty-first century a sailing-balloon would be the swiftest means of travel, plying between London and Scotland in only forty-eight hours.

This isn't the type of prophecy I mean. Mary Shelley had a certain intuitive far-sightedness by which she anticipated the ultimate conclusions to which the ideas of her epoch were heading – an epoch in which fixed religious beliefs had been shaken by eighteenth-century rationalism, and were now being challenged by science and progress.

Her association by birth with Godwin and by marriage with his disciple Shelley were, of course, conditioning factors to her way of thought. She was educated to think according to the principles of her father's monumental work, *Political Justice*, and to approach all ideas with rigid logic. But she was also gifted with a fertile imagination, well-nurtured by Shelley, and she was embarrassed by a pessimistic temperament. Her thought was pragmatical where Shelley's was abstract. These factors combined, in her work, to produce something far removed from Godwinism. In fact, as I shall try to show, *Frankenstein* and *The Last Man* are unconscious satires of Godwin's brand of humanism.

Frankenstein carries the glorification of man by man to its rational extreme. That had been Godwin's aim in *Political Justice* where his theories evolved from his belief in the perfectibility of man. But his daughter showed that the rational extension of a theory isn't necessarily, in practice, the inevitable one; she showed how far the simplicity of a theory fell short of the complexity of man. Her conclusions were arrived at imaginatively, but because she used a rational method to demonstrate them, her critique of rationalism was cogent. There are many improbabilities in *Frankenstein* but nothing that could not be explained by natural processes; the horror of Gothicism is there, but none of its supernatural devices. In *The Last Man*, this blend of horror and realism is employed too; and there the humanist concept is made to lose all meaning. Both novels are prophetic in an implicit and allegorical sense; by which I mean also that the strictures of Godwinism implied in them are proved to have been sound. But to get at these implications I should like to look briefly at the stories themselves.

The story of *Frankenstein* occurred to Mary Shelley, when, still in her teens, she visited Switzerland with Shelley. They had Byron for a neighbour, and 'many and long' she tells us, 'were the conversations between Byron and Shelley, to which I was a devout but nearly silent listener'. They spoke of some ghost stories they had been reading and also discussed recent scientific theories. These two topics, Mary Shelley says, formed the direct inspiration of *Frankenstein*; and in fact, these talks contained all that was needed for the Gothic-rational synthesis she afterwards brought about.

The story tells how Frankenstein, while a young student, discovers the principle of life and dedicates himself to manufacture a human creature. There was plenty of scope in this situation for harrowing-up the reader. The narrative is invested with the murk and mist – it reaches the fever-pitch – of Gothic atmospherics, as Frankenstein records his task of assembling the component parts of the body. All of which, however, is directed towards other ends than just the raising of a shudder, as Gothic fiction had tended to do. The effect here is to show the incongruity between Frankenstein, an educated, civilised being, and the desperate lengths he is prepared to go to realise his ambition. To assemble the body, he tells us,

> I dabbled among the unhallowed damps of the grave ... tortured the living animal to lifeless clay ... I collected bones from charnel-houses; and disturbed, with profane fingers, the tremendous secrets of the human frame ... The dissecting room and the slaughter-house furnished many of my materials ...

Frankenstein, then, creates this being, a man who breathes and moves. Only then are the consequences apparent to him; the scientist feels an abrupt revulsion when he sees what a hideous monster he has brought to life.

The theme, from this point, is one of pursuit, in which Frankenstein and his Monster alternately occupy the roles of hunter and hunted; until finally pursuit becomes the obsession of both. The Monster, stalked by Frankenstein across the frozen Arctic, urges and even sustains his creator for the chase, by leaving messages to say where food can be found, or to warn Frankenstein to wrap himself in furs.

Now the notable thing about Frankenstein, is that after the creation of his Monster, his own character changes. No longer detached, no longer following a way of life he has ordered for himself, Frankenstein becomes a weak, vacillating figure. He is, in fact, no longer free, but is bound to the Monster, as the Monster is to him, by a relationship which renders Frankenstein at once master and slave. Master, in his role of creator, yet slave in that a portion of his faculties are lost to him, and embodied in his creature. Frankenstein says,

> through the whole period during which I was the slave of my creature, I allowed myself to be governed by the impulse of the moment.

The Monster is, significantly I think, given no name. He is referred to variously as fiend, daemon and monster; though from the time of the book's appearance it has been a common error to call the Monster 'Frankenstein'. This is not really a surprising error, since the relationship of identity and conflict between the Monster and Frankenstein tends to show that the creature is a projection of his creator. The two are complementary yet antithetical figures; for the rational faculty which Frankenstein has lost can be found in the Monster, who is a symbol of the intellect. The Monster is also shown as the perpetrator of evil motivated by revenge for Frankenstein's neglect of him. And I suggest his conflict with Frankenstein represents the forces which, by the beginning of the nineteenth century, had started to pit reason against imagination, instinct, faith. Mary Shelley equated those rational forces with evil.

The real subject of the novel can perhaps best be found in its sub-title. The book was called *Frankenstein, or The Modern Prometheus*. In the humanist image of Prometheus, she saw Frankenstein perpetrating the ultra-humanistic act of creation of life, and she used every device of horror that her imagination could conceive, to express the ghastliness of Frankenstein's action and its consequence. Its consequence is the real subject, and the real subject is the disintegration of the individual personality, as Frankenstein was disintegrated, following the practice of rational humanism in its last and dehumanising degree. Her story culminates in the romantic motif of man in search of himself and in conflict with himself.

I don't think Mary Shelley was intellectually aware of these conclusions I have drawn; but it's worth noting that Shelley, who wrote the Preface to the first edition of *Frankenstein*, seems to have felt uneasy about its underlying meaning. Here are Shelley's strangely equivocal words, made to appear, incidentally, as if coming from the author:

> The opinions which naturally spring from the character and situation of the hero are by no means to be conceived as existing always in my own convictions; nor is any inference justly to be drawn from the following pages as prejudicing any philosophical doctrine whatsoever.

They are strange words, and in a way, meaningless, since Shelley well understood that any consummate creative work has for its basis a system of thought, if only a temporary one.

But I don't think this was merely a temporary attitude which Mary Shelley adopted for the duration of her story, for the other novel of hers I have mentioned, presents us with conclusions entirely consistent with those of *Frankenstein*.

The Last Man, a long, panoramic work, is the story of a plague that sweeps across the earth, annihilating all but one man. The book unfortunately is almost unobtainable to-day.[*] It isn't neat enough for modern tastes, and as a work of art it hardly meets with the standards set by the best nineteenth-century English novels – the language has a solemnity that often defeats itself, and since the story is not really about people but about mankind, the characters are neither here nor there. The merits of *The Last Man* are in the development of its tremendous theme. Only there, does the novel give us something new in nineteenth-century fiction.

But it needed a more objective intellect yet a more sympathetic imagination than Mary Shelley's to make a great book of it. All the same, I regret being unable to do justice here to the detail and scruple with which, incident by incident, she shows the encroachment of disaster. And one of the compensating features of the book is the way in which she copes with vastness. Mary Shelley had a grip on social ideas, and though she could never comfortably bring off a domestic scene, she was able to manipulate people in a mass, she could depict a social trend.

The subject of *The Last Man* occupied many creative thinkers of the time; the poets Campbell, Beddoes and Hood wrote poems of that name, and the theme was treated by contemporary painters. It was a general pessimistic reaction to the progressive time-spirit. But Mary Shelley was not so much concerned, as were these poets, with the fate and feelings of the one survivor, as she was with the cause of

---

[*]Since the first edition of *The Last Man* was published in 1826, the novel had not been published again at the time of this essay (1951). This essay was originally broadcast by the BBC Third Programme and set up in type by the Falcon Press in 1951 as an Editor's Foreword introducing the novel, but it was never published as the publisher failed. Eventually a new edition of the novel was published by the University of Nebraska Press (1965) and in the UK by the Hogarth Press with an introduction by Brian Aldiss (1985). This, Muriel Spark's introduction, was published by *The Listener* as 'Mary Shelley: A Prophetic Novelist' on 22 February 1951. It was translated into German and published by Insel in 1992 as an Appendix to Muriel Spark's biography of Mary Shelley.

his situation; she deals with the disintegration, first of domestic life, then of civilised society, and lastly of the very concept of mankind. The novel may be taken as an essay on the futility of mankind when faced with universal disaster outside its own agency; it posits those very social and political problems which Godwinism had made perceptible, but in circumstances which made them unanswerable by *Political Justice*.

The scene of *The Last Man* is set in the future, about the year 2075. England has become a republic by the peaceful bloodless means that Godwin advocated; and the first part of the story tells of the domestic life under a Protectorate – of the loves, marriages, births and ambitions of an English family. A plague breaks out in Eastern Europe, but attracts little attention in Britain, until it spreads across Europe and westward to America – a swift, incurable and fatal disease.

Our attention is now focused away from the domestic to the social and political scene. Refugees from the plague crowd into Britain and the fortunes of the family are subordinated to a national emergency. Mary Shelley writes,

> When any whole nation becomes the victim of the destructive powers of exterior agents, then indeed man shrinks into insignificance, he feels his tenure of life insecure, his inheritance on earth cut off.

And she describes the emergency measures adopted by society, as it may seem with some foresight. Private parks, gardens, pleasure-grounds are ploughed up to grow food; it becomes fashionable to walk instead of ride and to generally behave as we now behave in wartime. Meanwhile the republican leaders are still giving out that nothing is happening.

But the plague reaches Britain and introduces, as the next phase, the complete breakdown of society. Hedonism takes hold of the decreasing population. Criminal gangs spring up here and there, till they, too, fall victims of the plague. A temporary tyranny is exerted by a fanatical leader of a quasi-religious sect; the strong exploit the weak; and whatever human virtues are individually displayed everywhere succumb to Mary Shelley's relentless pessimism.

At last the few survivors decide, hopelessly, to search Europe for a refuge. Politics are now ludicrous, the great cult of mankind has come to nothing. Mary Shelley reduces and reduces as she shows the struggling emigrants dying off. 'Man,' she says, 'existed by twos and threes; man, the individual who might sleep and wake, and perform the animal functions; but man, in himself weak, yet more powerful in congregated numbers than wind or ocean; man, the queller of the elements, the lord of created nature, the peer of demi-gods, existed no longer.' So, she depopulates the earth until only one man remains to say, 'A sense of degradation came over me. Did God create man, merely in the end to become dead earth in the midst of healthful vegetating nature? ... Were our proud dreams thus to fade? ... How reconcile this sad change to our past aspirations, to our apparent powers? Sudden[ly], an internal voice, articulate and clear, seemed to say: Thus, from eternity it was decreed ...' This was the matter of the argument Mary Shelley was instinctively moved to make against the rational-humanist doctrines in which she had been educated. But it was a negative argument – the argument of *vanitas vanitatum* without its religious corollary; she was impotent to arrive at that or any other positive precept.

But in both *Frankenstein* and *The Last Man* she did turn rationalism back upon itself; she demonstrated the flaw in a way of thought which was becoming a way of life. I have called these novels prophetic, because I think that within their fictional premises they show an extraordinary access of foresight: the divided individual whom Frankenstein represents is not unknown to us; and we are aware of the possibility, at least, of universal devastation and the consequence to civilisation, as expressed in *The Last Man*.

Mary Shelley died a hundred years ago, on 1 February 1851. She was never, herself, an integrated being. Her temperament was unsuited to her environment, for as the daughter of two libertarian Progressives and the widow of Shelley, she was expected to further their cause. But she lived to declare she had no 'passion for reforming the world' – a phrase associated with Shelley – and to say, 'I have no wish to ally myself to the Radicals – they are full of repulsion to me ...' It was an attitude that lost her many friends, nor did she find many new ones, because the doors of convention were closed against her.

Her claim to distinction lies in her macabre inventiveness and her strong rational turn of mind. She was not a great novelist, she was not artist enough to be considered one. But the Gothic-rational synthesis of *Frankenstein* and *The Last Man* establish her historical importance as a novelist; and their powerful speculative themes established her uniqueness.

[1951]

Shelley's Last House

The Casa Magni stands on the sea-front at San Terenzo, near Lerici, on the Ligurian Gulf of Spezia in Italy. It is a simple, elegant house with a portico of five arches at the front and one at each side, upholding a long, deep terrace. Above the main archway is a worn plaque, with the quaint words (here translated from the Italian):

> From this portico on which an oak tree cast its ancient shade; in July 1822 Mary Godwin and Jane Williams awaited with tearful anxiety
>
> PERCY BYSSHE SHELLEY
>
> who was brought from Livorno in a fragile sailing vessel by unexpected fortune to the oblivion of the Elysian Isles.
> O Blessed Shores where love, liberty, dreams, have no chains

By the time the poet Shelley came to his Casa Magni he had been married to his second wife, Mary Shelley, for six years. It was the end of April, 1822. He was not yet thirty; she not yet twenty-five. Their wanderings in Europe, especially in Italy, had occupied most of their life together. Shelley, the rebellious and estranged son of an English country gentleman and Mary the daughter of the progressive thinkers and writers William Godwin and Mary Wollstonecraft, formed that sort of literary couple who are a living myth, and they knew it. Shelley's most durable poetry was written during this union and Mary had written her famous novel, *Frankenstein*, six years before at the age of eighteen. Intellectually, they grew up together.

Their nomadic life in Italy, moving from house to house – Rome, Florence, Pisa, Lucca, Livorno – was still in course when they took the Casa Magni. They were the type of couple who attracted an ever-changing circle of friends. They seldom lived alone. Claire Clairmont, Mary's step-sister, had actually 'eloped' along with Mary when she and Shelley first ran away together; and Claire was almost constantly with them.

Byron, with his mistress Countess Giuccioli, was at Pisa, comparatively nearby. Leigh Hunt was to arrive from England to start a new magazine with Shelley and Byron. Shelley, always attracted to group living, had invited a young couple, not formally married, Edward and Jane Williams, with their two children to stay at Casa Magni. Mary, who had by this time had four children, only one of whom had survived, was now pregnant again. Claire's five-year-old daughter by

Byron had recently died of typhus, alone in a convent, but when Claire joined the group at Casa Magni she had not yet been told.

San Terenzo is no longer an isolated village, but in those days it was little more than a fishing base with a church, a ruined castle and, right on the sea-front, the Casa Magni.

It should be remembered that all five of the Casa Magni set – Shelley, Mary, Jane, Edward and Claire – were still in their twenties. They were very much like a group of unorthodox young people to-day who might take on a place of strange, wild, isolated, beauty for the summer. Shelley dominated the party with his restless genius.

But from the start there was a feeling of crisis in the house. They crowded into the Casa Magni in May. Claire was then told of the death of her daughter Allegra, and was stricken with passionate despair and hatred of Byron who had wilfully taken the child from her. Shelley had one of his eerie visions: while talking with Edward on the terrace by moonlight he 'saw' a naked child, with its hands clasped, rising out of the sea. At that time too, Mary, who was having a bad pregnancy, although sensitive to the loveliness, at the same time suffered from mysterious forebodings. She described years later, in a Note on Shelley's poems of that date how the local fisherfolk unnerved her: 'Many a night they passed on the beach, singing, or rather howling; the women dancing about among the waves that broke at their feet, the men leaning on the rocks and joining in their loud wild chorus.'

Beautiful Jane Williams enchanted Shelley; she sang and played the guitar. Edward and Shelley ordered a boat to be made. It arrived from Livorno, their plaything for the summer. Shelley was in high spirits. But Mary had a miscarriage of which she nearly died, being saved only by Shelley making her sit in a bucket of ice, against the protests of Jane and Claire. Shelley's was a febrile temperament. 'The fright my illness gave him,' Mary wrote, 'caused a return of nervous sensations and visions as bad as in his worst times.'

The Casa Magni seems to have become a personality, to be feared and awesomely lived in. The living quarters comprised one large room with three bedrooms leading off it; windows and doors led from here to the great terrace which spread the width of the room and the Shelleys' rooms. Mary describes in a letter the atmosphere of terror that followed her illness. One day Jane 'saw' Shelley pass by the window on the terrace twice in the same direction. She looked out, and seeing no one, imagined he must have leapt from the wall. In fact, he was out of the house at the time. Shelley had a screaming fit one night, and walked in his sleep. He had been frightened by a dream that Edward and Jane came to him with 'their bodies lacerated, their bones starting through their skins'. In Shelley's dream Edward said to him, 'Get up, Shelley, the sea is flooding the house and it is all coming down.' Shelley then dreamt he looked on the terrace and thought he saw the sea rushing in. This was followed by a dream where he saw himself strangling Mary.

Shelley had other 'visions' at this time: he had seen the figure of himself which met him as he walked on the terrace and said to him, 'How long do you mean to be content?'

Not long after this Shelley and Edward, both now in high spirits, sailed away on a trip to Livorno and Pisa, to establish Leigh Hunt, his wife and numerous children. Shelley and his friend arrived safely in the new boat, and saw to their business; but the return trip was fatal. The boat went down in a storm, with both men and their sailor-boy Charles Vivian, on 8th July 1822. It was not till 19th July that Mary, Jane and Claire gave up hope of their return: the bodies had been washed ashore.

When, in February 1985, I went to San Terenzo to look at Shelley's last house, I didn't expect to be able to see inside. It is in the private hands of Dr Arrigo, who now lives and has his medical practice there. However, I rang the bell and when I explained that I wasn't a patient, but an English writer who had written a book on Mary Shelley, Dr Arrigo very courteously agreed to break his rules of privacy.

To-day, a street runs in front of the house where the sea used to come up to the portico. The ground floor has been reclaimed for living space, but the large room upstairs and the long, handsome terrace are as unchanged as the dramatic expanse of the bay and the dark promontories facing it. That very terrace, the location of so many of those young people's psychic crises and infectious hysteria, in the days before the tragedy, is where Mary sat in her convalescence, listening to the howling ritual of the fisherfolks' nightly sea-dance, and where Shelley met his own image. It is where Mary, Jane and Claire anxiously watched for the sails of the doomed boat. The large room is where Shelley ran, screaming, crossing from his bedroom to Mary's in his frightful nightmares. There is indeed, on that terrace, a sense of the sea coming into the house. One does not see the road beneath. 'We almost fancied ourselves on board ship,' Mary said. Yes, one still does.

Behind the house, the garden rises up to thick woodland. Shortly after Shelley's death Mary wrote to a friend, 'The beauty of the woods made me weep and shudder.' A sense of misfortune hung like a thunder-cloud over Casa Magni that splendid summer of 1822.

I went back again to see the Casa Magni, in the September of 1985. This time, I didn't ask to go inside. There was a bustle of painters and workmen. The garden was being put in order for a happy family of our days. A brown workman's face looked out of an upper window. He waved and smiled as I took him on my Polaroid.

[1986]

The Essential Stevenson

[...]

The essential background of all Stevenson's work is Edinburgh, no matter by what name the streets and landscape of his fiction go by; and it is not merely Scottish speech that Stevenson reproduces, but an Edinburgh way of putting things.

An Edinburgh way, but an Edinburgh of Stevenson's youth, of the last half of the nineteenth century. It has been too easy for critics knowingly to place R.L.S. in an historical category, by Victorian reckonings. [...] The Industrial Revolution, no less the Romantic Revival, no less the Symbolist Movement, will not altogether explain the R.L.S. temperament. These may help to explain his voluptuous gestures, but not his meditative serenity of attitude (which was in no way a manifestation of 'apostasy' from a bohemian order of life); they may explain his imagination's twilight and sinister colourings, but not his scrupulous artistry.

[...]

Exactly what environment formed Stevenson? An environment in which the manners and modes of the eighteenth century still loitered; where Calvinism remained obdurate in the city's bloodstream, where the element of contrast, clear and unequivocal, was apparent in the whole civic design.

'Outwardly,' wrote Moray McLaren in his *Stevenson and Edinburgh*, 'the eighteenth century had gone, but it lingered on even now in the manners and mannerisms of the people just as, in the faintest possible way, it lingers today' [1950]. If the eighteenth century was dying hard in Stevenson's Edinburgh, it is not quite dead yet. There are 'fashionable' streets in Edinburgh within a few yards of the streets of the poor; but unlike most European cities, Edinburgh does not merge her grandeur into her squalor with impressionistic vagueness. You have to turn a definite corner to move out of Castle Street into Rose Street, just as an eighteenth-century writer 'turned' his phrase and swivelled his thought.

[...]

Edinburgh people were either sane, eccentric, or plain mad; they were not neurotic. That, too, is a mark of the eighteenth century – neuroticism springs from a nineteenth-century germ. Stevenson was eccentric, but he was not neurotic; he was his own man. His attachment to the strange, the sinful and the misplaced among humankind, was always strong in him; yet, while those choice plants of neuroticism, the Decadents of the 'nineties, were languishing in the feverish climate of exotic speculation, Stevenson was hurling forth his *Open Letter in Defence of Father Damien*.

If I seem to digress from McLaren, it is because I wish to formulate a point that he wisely only suggests. That is, Stevenson reflects in his life and work the classical and romantic synthesis of Edinburgh. McLaren is wise in avoiding these terms, since they perhaps mean too many things to mean precisely what he demonstrates when he so skilfully invokes the atmosphere of Heriot Row and Princes Street a hundred years ago, and pits them against the villainous aura of Stevenson's youthful night-haunts in Leith Walk.

[...]

What will impress those who are acquainted with most of Stevenson, is the variety of his achievement, the variety, not only of subject but of style. This is an aspect of Stevenson not fully realised until his work is seen in a miscellany.

Possibly the most neglected of his work remains his poems, more especially the poems of childhood. Despite the patience that has been lost over his anthology pieces, the most impatient critic must concede the evocative sweep and rhythm of 'To S. R. Crockett'; but the poems of childhood have been considered childish things. Yet they, I believe, show most saliently how careful and devoted a craftsman was Stevenson, even under the more exacting stress of verse. They are models of form and balance within their unpretentious limits:

> Spring and daisies come apace;
> Grasses hide my hiding-place;
> Grasses run like a green sea
> O'er the lawn up to my knee.

There is something here of a miniature Marvell. There is something in this group of poems which possesses both the classical and the romantic temper. True, it is classicism without intellectual persuasion, and romanticism without passion, but the accents of both are there.

[1950]

Robert Louis Stevenson

This is an occasion of great pleasure to me. I was born and lived all my early youth in Edinburgh. As a child I often used to go to play with my best friend Frances Niven at her parents' house at 10 Howard Place, which was exactly next door to No. 8, the birthplace of Robert Louis Stevenson, and in those days a Stevenson museum. Both Frances and I were ardent admirers of R.L.S. As we grew up we came to know all his works. But as children, it was our delight to slip through the hedge dividing the two gardens to Robert Louis Stevenson's territory, although in reality he had been little more than two years old when his parents moved house. Still, we felt he meant that spot when he wrote:

> ... it is but a child of air
> that lingers in the garden there.

Stevenson was superb at his craft. It had the particular persuasiveness of the just and haughty Edinburgh temper. How greatly the success of his novel, *The Master of Ballantrae*, depends on the narrative style: it is a story of wild scenes and high passions soberly and reasonably unfolded. Only a very subtle artist could combine these two ideas: that of a dramatic theme and that of a cool and limpid prose, to create such a rare and strange effect. That was the essence of R.L.S. No artist, no writer, who knows R.L.S can fail to have been influenced favourably by him.

He often made fun of monuments. But I think we all know how much he would have appreciated this simple and good memorial executed by Ian Hamilton Finlay, who has in all senses so appropriately described R.L.S., and who has placed our act of homage to our Man of Letters in so delightful and so leafy a corner of his city.

Robert Louis Stevenson wrote of his feelings as a native of his beloved Edinburgh: '... the place establishes an interest in people's hearts; go where they will, they find no city of the same distinction; go where they will, they take a pride in their old home'.

[1989]

Celebrating Scotland

Culture is something that grows and matures from its native soil. A great deal of culture arises from the idea of leaving it alone. 'Strategy' is anti-culture. A 'Scottish' culture would be the natural expressiveness of everyone to whom the land of Scotland has actually contributed. Scottish Italians, for instance; Scots of West Indian origin; Scots of English and Irish descent. These, if they are Scottish by formation, all make up the sources of Scottish culture. The 'Caledonian Society' view of culture is amusing, but not deep enough, and most unlikely to survive. It travels only as Scotch whisky and tartans travel, no more and no less.

In the field of literature with which I am mainly concerned I would like to see more, far more, writing about Scotland in general and Scottish domestic life in particular. I see no point in a dialect that the average intelligent reader in Essex or Worcestershire cannot understand. I see no point in offering Scots dialects (which in any case are not regionally constant) to the intelligent readers in the United States or in Australia. The object of art is to diffuse intellectual pleasure, which includes the appreciation of tragedy as well as comedy. (In the case of a work written naturally in Gaelic or a specifically Scottish tongue that is different: it should be offered for translation abroad.)

The main task in literary achievement is simple, expressive, atmospheric and yet precise writing. The Scots have always been among the finest English-speaking writers. Their best language is English. The practice of English by Scots cannot be too seriously promoted. As regards 'culture' itself, I recommend *Notes Towards the Definition of Culture* by T.S. Eliot. It is a golden book, irreplaceable.

[1999]

The Books I Re-Read and Why

The question I have been asked (which books do I re-read and why) makes me realise that the books I go back to are not necessarily those I admire the most. A great many books that have delighted me remain vividly in my memory; I don't feel any desire to re-read them. Then there is the category of books that I keep on the shelves for reference purposes – a quantity of poetry, the classics – Plato,

Machiavelli – I go to them when I want to check up – what was that passage, how did it go? When I'm away from home, staying with friends, I can always content myself with a volume of Henry James or Jane Austen, however familiar.

But at home, there are two works that I do re-read continually, neither of them belonging to English literature. When I want to relax and get into a thoughtful mood invariably I take down a volume of Proust's *A la Recherche du Temps Perdu*. Any volume, any page: the magic works, sinuous as a snake. Normally, what would one care about an old degenerate like Charlus, or Swann with his airs, or the Duchesse de Guermantes in her self-satisfied felicity? But Proust makes these people matter through the sheer force of his style, his extraordinary time-manipulations. It is his style that is the drug for the Proust-addict.

The other book which I re-read with unfailing pleasure is the Bible, especially the Old Testament. I don't read it so much for religious consolation, as I was brought up to think proper, as for sheer enjoyment of the literature. So much poetry, so many literary forms, such wonderful stories. And, from a novelist's point of view, what clearly delineated characters. God himself with his attitudes of I did this, and I made that, his Thou shalt perish, and his I repent, Thou shalt survive and prosper. Intrigues, thunderbolts, smiles... A character so true and yet so contradictory. He basks unashamed in his own glory, and in his anger is positively blasphemous. Few works of world literature contain so many great, wild and precise characters as appear in both the Old and the New Testament. Students of creative writing should study them.

There is one set of books that I never re-read: my own. They bother me; they put me right off my future literary plots and plans; they cloud my creative joy. I don't keep them on my bookshelves; I put them in a cupboard. It's not that they embarrass me intellectually; I just don't want to re-live those books at all.

[1983]

London Exotics

I could not actually say that I had seen them turning a somersault in the streets of South Kensington, but any night now they might do so. They sported the regalia and attitudes of the eternal acrobat. The other night I had seen one of them make a leap and a half-turn which surely was to prefigure the full cart-wheel to come. It was the spring of 1952. They were young boys and girls drifting in little bands of five or six, already forming themselves into a phenomenon.

There was a time, before our time, when they would be observed gliding through Chelsea only. Then 'exquisite' was the holiest and most advanced adjective. It was the time when Aubrey Beardsley, wizard-supreme of the Aesthetic Ideal, not content with the proper fame of his drawings, was moved to perpetrate some prose:

> The Abbé Fanfreluche, having lighted off his horse, stood doubtfully for a moment beneath the ombre gateway of the mysterious Hill, troubled with an exquisite fear lest a day's travel should have too cruelly undone the laboured niceness of his dress. His hand, slim and gracious as La Marquise du Deffand's in the drawing by Carmontelle, played nervously about the gold hair that fell upon his shoulders like a finely-curled peruke, and from point to point of a precise toilet the fingers wandered, quelling the little mutinies of cravat and ruffle.

Yes, but now in the early 'fifties there was a new autumnal tide, and these little bands of exotics had been overflowing from the river at Chelsea when evening fell. By the spring of 1952, they had seeped westward, and would turn up at midnight everywhere in the streets adjacent to the London parks. In Cromwell Road they capered by fours and fives. You would see them standing akimbo beneath the lamps of Old Brompton Road. And there, more or less, they have been ambling since, slender, contemptuous and very young, as far inland as Bayswater. It is a phenomenon to blend reality with memory, and merge the tenses of contemplation.

I doubt if they are professionals. They are too old-fashioned for television, and much too insolent to get jobs on the stage. Where they come from and where they go, it seems absurd to wonder, it is like contemplating the past and future of a flame. They arrive in their own portable environment, and likewise they depart, bearing their strange excitement away with them. And like a little flame, each one gives out a flickering nervous hilarity, expressed only by these giddy antics; for their faces are quite grave and they seldom speak to one another. Sometimes, while crossing a road, diagonally and at leisure, one of them might cast an obscure high fluting trisyllable at the traffic, but the real eloquence and hullabaloo comes in terms of motion, with a triumphant pirouette on the opposite pavement. They are dressed with ceremonial care and beauty. I may be, or may have been, touching them up a bit as I warm to the subject, but on my artistic word, these boys and girls have been wearing apple-green duffle coats, amethyst blouses, birettas of burnt-ochre since 1952. They wear tights of scarlet and black, in which their legs are forever carrying on like a pair of compasses which someone is absent-mindedly twiddling.

The fact is, that these apparitions of 1952 have become, in the London year of 1966, an established social reality. Everyone knows that English girls and boys in their teens and twenties are dressing up like elegant unsmiling pierrots and doing proud jerks in the streets. The fashion designers have got the whole idea under control. But those few of the early nineteen-fifties were more of a wonder.

One night of early summer, before the light had quite failed, I sat in a motor car in the Old Brompton Road waiting for a friend to emerge from a flat. A woman with a dog floated by. She was a woman of resignment to weary, lonely wealth and the dog was a dachshund. She floated – for already, at a short distance, I could see approaching a set of four or five of the new exotics, and the mere sight of them altered the behaviour of the environment. The woman was etiolated, like an El Greco painting. Her face was pale. I thought she was an elegy in a country churchyard all unto herself, and wondered what she was doing in London.

The group of boys and girls had come up to her. I looked through the windscreen. The street lights went up and the woman cast a sharp, long mauve shadow; her dachshund cast an awkward blur. The young people silently encircled her in their bright clothes, moving slowly like somnambulists hand-in-hand. They cast no shadows.

That is all. I have no corroborative evidence.

It was the absent-mindedness of one of these harlequinades that made me think of Rilke's acrobats, those of the Fifth Elegy, a compound of his beloved Parisian somersaulters and his beloved Picasso, *Les Saltimbanques*. Rilke was moved by them, as he would have been by these Kensington pernoctators. He observed unreality and pathos in their performance. Swinging and smiling with automatic precision, those equilibrists of the Fifth Elegy have got their facile tricks by heart; the first and real inspiration of their act, mastered with an effort of concentration and sacrifice, has been done for by habit. They do their turn with blank-eyed perfection; their performance is a 'fake fruit of boredom'.

Boredom. It insinuated itself into the clever contortions, the whirlwinds and arabesques, executed on the London pavements. It is 1952. All these delightful things are done in a daze. Why do the acrobats seem sadly affecting? They are jauntily pleased enough with themselves, they appear to have no cares. Why are their purple blouses so pathetic? Because boredom has got them young, and where Rilke's professionals degenerated into apathy, rehearsal by rehearsal, year by year, these lovely Bayswater fly-by-nights were born with the thing. It precipitates them forth to this desperate nightly ritual. Rilke's acrobats are bored because they perform, but ours perform because they are bored. Ours are in a worse predicament. What is boredom? It is the absence of curiosity, for one thing. In boredom, the world lacks possibility, and is pre-ordained.

Now, on the London streets, it is difficult for me not to see in the conscious practitioners, the half-submerged performers of my memory. It is when they appear hand-in-hand, that their plight seems keenest. These hectic tribes were united by isolation. While Picasso's *saltimbanques* are exclusive because of their common calling and purpose, these employ their skill in order to cultivate exclusiveness. Exclusiveness was really the tragic art they practised. For their weird and wayward talent lacked inspiration; and half-asleep, they embraced the choice aesthetics of the past.

In their capacity as mimics of the past, though, they were seen at their best. How like they were, in their defiant irresponsible prancings, to Proust's 'little band', his amoral darlings of the Balbec shore! And as Gide's 'little band' in his *Faux-monnayeurs*, they uphold the proper solemnity, the stylish antinomian confidence, and were quite the part.

To have taken them as they wanted to be taken, as original material, as a jubilant cult of inspired splendour: nothing doing. Even then, they had come too late, to me and my like. We regret to say, my captious like and myself, that we prefer the splendid originals in the books. But as curious imitations arriving late on the market, they were welcome indeed. For it was a kind of comedy and a kind of tragedy, and altogether a wonder, to watch this young scornful Priesthood of the Aesthetic Ideal advancing *in pontificalibus* up the Old Brompton Road.

[1953]

A Drink with Dame Edith

It was a summer day in 1957. I had published a novel, *The Comforters*, with some critical success. In the literary world of those days I had become the new young thing. In fact, I was not very young. I was in my late thirties. I had already published poems, stories and reviews, a critical biography of Mary Shelley and a work on the then poet laureate, John Masefield. But it was the novel *The Comforters* that established my name. It was greatly praised by reviewers, especially by Evelyn Waugh. It was immediately transformed into a radio play on the then prestigious Third Programme. I had been given a contract for the novel by Macmillan – a lousy contract in which they controlled radio and film rights. I was poor, very poor, with a dependent son. I had therefore to find myself an agent. I had also, during the crowded year prior to the publication of *The Comforters*, started my novel *Robinson*, to be published in 1958.

Well, I employed an agent, David Higham Associates (earlier, Pearn, Pollinger & Higham). David Higham himself ran the firm, an old wooffie behind moustaches. It fell to my lot to deal with one of their men, Paul Scott, later a well-known novelist and author of the *Raj Quartet*, celebrated as a television series. I subsequently became friendly with Paul Scott, but I never put him at the highest level of fiction writing. At the time, he knew of my literary success, but when he read *Robinson* (if, in fact, he did read it) he wasn't at all impressed. He asked me to come and see him about it. My clothes were old-fashioned but my best. He sat there pontifically with my manuscript in front of him on his desk, and said, after all, what was this novel about? A man and a girl on an island? It was, in fact, about a lot more than that. As he spoke, Paul flicked the typescript of my novel across the desk towards me with a contemptuous gesture of his third finger and thumb. I fairly loathed him for that. I said: 'Don't represent me if you don't want to.' 'Oh,' he condescended, 'I'll see what I can do.'

That afternoon, it so happened, I had been summoned to meet Edith Sitwell. I went round to the Sesame Club, where Edith held court. I was still fuming against that ghastly agent, especially his rude gesture. The very thought of his touching my typescript now offended my guts.

As soon as I caught sight of Edith Sitwell it brought a totally new dimension into my day. She was impressively grand, quite eccentric, but she had no doubt whatsoever of what the artist in literature was about. High priests and priestesses: that's what we all were. She wore her usual loose, dramatic robes, her high, Plantagenet headdress. Her lovely hands were covered with the most beautiful rings I had ever seen actually worn: they were deep, deep, coloured stones – aquamarines, blue agates, large and pool-like. A junior editor from Macmillan, an alcoholic who thought nobody knew, was fawning and 'hand-washing' and fussing around her, a performance which Edith, with half-closed eyes, magnificently and pointedly ignored. She asked me what I would drink, suggesting her own preference, gin and pineapple juice.

I had been in some trepidation lest Dame Edith should remember from seven years back an article I had written in *Poetry Quarterly* based on books by herself, Louis MacNeice and Kathleen Raine. In the course of the essay I had suggested something to the effect that W.B. Yeats was a 'greater' poet than Sitwell. This did not please her at all. She protested to the editor. I forget what happened next. The years pass ... I am sitting next to the wonderful woman herself in the Sesame Club and she is telling me how taken she is by the mysterious qualities she finds in my writing. Plainly she has not connected me with the impudent reviewer of yore. Let it stay that way.

With her was another equally splendid woman, about Dame Edith's age of seventy. She was introduced as a 'war heroine'. I fancy she was also a Dame. How I wish I could say who in fact she was. Another young editor from another publishing house had now joined the gin-and-pineapple party. I let my eyes rove among the Sesame Club attendants, wondering which of them was the one who was reputed to have 'converted' Dame Edith to Catholicism. I have put converted in inverted commas because I know that her actual entering the Catholic Church took place under the guidance of our mutual friend, Father Philip Caraman, SJ. The Sesame Club waiter, however, was no doubt the object of many conversations on the subject. I chose as a possibility an Italian-looking fellow with intelligent eyes.

While a great many of these impressions played on my mind like a left-hand accompaniment on the piano, the main topics came forth like those played decisively with the right hand. Dame Edith wanted to tell me an amusing story of her youth, already knowing from my writings that it would be dear to my merry heart. Her father, Sir George Sitwell, she said, had received an anonymous letter accusing him of having an affair with a well-known woman of the village. Incensed, he wanted to find the culprit, and to that end posted up the letter in the window of the village post office, offering a £5 reward. Edith said it was one of the joys of those days for her to go down to the post office with her brothers and read the salacious letter.

We found we had another friend in common, the poet Roy Campbell, whom I greatly admired, both as a person and as a poet. Edith told us with some relish how the critic Geoffrey Grigson had been accosted and slapped by Roy Campbell for having 'insulted' her in a review. Those were the days! (I felt, actually, that this was going a bit far, but when I looked up the review later on I saw that it was indeed decidedly and deliberately insulting.)

Inevitably, I came out with my experience that very afternoon with my agent, showing her how he had flicked my typescript at me with his thumb and third finger. She took an intense interest in the story. 'My dear,' she said, 'you must acquire a pair of lorgnettes, make an occasion to see that man again, focus the glasses on him and sit looking at him through them as if he was an insect. Just look and look.' She showed me with her own eyeglasses, which were hanging on one of the chains around her neck, how it was done.

I didn't have any lorgnettes, but the next time I had an appointment with Paul Scott I meant to slip into my bag a magnifying glass, fully intending to subject him to a scrutiny if necessary. I forgot to do so, and anyway it wasn't necessary. He had now read something else of mine. 'I didn't think you had it in you,' were his words. I still think they were strange words, neither one thing nor another. But I thought of Edith Sitwell's advice, and I simply didn't care.

[1997]

Pensée: *Miss Brodie* on the Stage

For any creative undertaking what you need is courage. It is the first requirement for an artist.

Courage to adapt. Jay Allen has not transferred the words of my book to the stage script, she has rather lived and absorbed the book, and transferred the ideas, for dramatic purposes. It is a very successful technique when in the right hands. I think the duration of the play – over thirty years – testifies to the adaptability of the book.

Every work of literature should make a world of its own. In my view this entails excluding all other worlds. The reader or the audience should not be aware of it, but actually this is achieved by isolating the girls from any family considerations. In real life they have mothers and fathers. In the play the parents do not appear. This provides an artistic concentration, and I think makes the production as a whole less diffused, more enjoyable.

[1998]

The Short Story

The short story has generally one commanding idea whereas the novel should have several interacting ideas – in my view as many as there are chapters.

It is not a bad system to write each chapter as if it were a short story. I did this once, in my novel *The Mandelbaum Gate*. It also allowed me to speak from the point of view of a different character in each chapter. This is also good from the commercial point of view. One can serialise or sell extracts more easily.

(Incidentally the commercial point of view is not necessarily the adversary of art. The commercial discipline is no different from any other discipline, it should not have undue influence on the artistic process. The only adversary of art is bad art.)

The short story does not bring the life-force of the characters to an end. If it is true as Aristotle said of tragedy that the story should have a beginning, a middle and an end, I would say that the short story deals mainly with the middle. The novel deals with all three, although there the middle is often the beginning, and it is possible to start with the end.

For a short story I have said that a single idea is best. That is my opinion. For that reason it is often good to start with merely a title, but with one that contains the whole of the idea, the theme of the story.

Finally, I would like to say that in my experience the short story is a more difficult form than the novel. To me, the more one writes the easier it is for the author, and sometimes for the reader the more boring.

The short story is to me a form of poem and for that reason alone, difficult though it is, it is the form from which I derive the most pleasure.

[1989]

Daughter of the Soil

Within six weeks of publication in America *Gone With the Wind* had sold 326,000 copies. The English sales to date are close on a million and the book has recently been revived in paperback. The American sales [to date] are something like five million. The book contains over 400,000 words. It took seven years to write. When the English edition appeared in 1936, already surrounded by glamorous statistics, the *Observer* reviewer cattily submitted that it was somewhere between two and three pounds in weight.

Perhaps because I read, and thoroughly enjoyed, *Gone with the Wind* in my teens I incline to think it appeals to the eternal teenager. It has an inspired (or at least unpremeditated) emotional immaturity, which is a requisite of every best-seller, and is sometimes a minor ingredient of great art. When I saw the film some years later on the quivering screen of a Central African bioscope I was less impressed. The passage of years, if it improves our taste, corrupts our joy. Reading those solemn pages again a few weeks ago I hardly recognised the book, and noted the repetitive tedium, the soporific padding, the callow ethic.

What I found most dreary was the fact that nothing whatsoever is left to the reader's dimmest intelligence. Every time a point of remote subtlety arises it is followed by a detailed explanation. Not a character opens his mouth to speak but a protracted gloss appears in the next paragraph. It is very disconcerting, when you have quite grasped a situation (and the situations are all simple), to find it being plugged home lest you should have made any mistake.

All the same, the book remains an impressive one because it sweeps on and on, over and above its defects. Large gestures have a fascination. On its appearance in 1936 the cautious critics of these shores were, on the whole, surprised that such a big and best-seller could be so entertaining. The book was awarded the Pulitzer Prize in 1937. The author, Miss Margaret Mitchell, was killed by a drunken motorist in 1949. *Gone with the Wind* was her only book.

***

There are two narrative streams in the book. One is Sherman's progress from Atlanta to the sea, and the other is Scarlett O'Hara's activities on the home front where she demonstrates without pause the life-force within her.

The author was well versed in the Civil War period, her bias being strongly Southern. She must have made volumes of notes and I suppose she put them all in the book. She could tell you that the hoops of ladies' dresses in those parts were worn narrower in 1866 than in 1865, jackets were shorter, bonnets out of style, curls worn at the back of the head. She knew how the Southern whites and blacks reacted to the war at its every stage. She knew the workings of the Ku-Klux, what the towns of Georgia looked like before, during and after the war. She had what you call a wide canvas and everything at her fingertips.

Miss Mitchell was *keen* on sociology. If she implies once that the book is about a world in transition she does it a hundred times. She never tires of reflecting, in the voice of some defeated Southerner, 'The old days had no glitter but they had a charm, a beauty, a slow-paced glamour.' And that, as has been remarked above, is never enough. There are page-long preliminaries to every such utterance, in which the slow-paced glamour of the old days is shown to be definitely superseded by the glitter of the new.

These discussions, representing the more 'serious' flavour of the book, continually interrupt the meaty human drama which centres round Scarlett O'Hara. The effect is the more incongruous in that Scarlett is by nature indifferent to the war and the Southern cause or any cause:

> She, Scarlett O'Hara Hamilton, alone had good hard-headed Irish sense. She wasn't going to make a fool out of herself about the Cause ...

And so you are always wondering whose story it is, Scarlett's or America's. And you have two books for the price of one. It is undoubtedly Scarlett, however, who has been selling the book these twenty-odd years and who will probably sell it for another twenty before it finally departs with the wind.

The moment Scarlett makes her entrance on the first page, in the cool shade of the porch at Tara, her father's plantation, you realise she is going to be a woman of mettle.

> The green eyes in the carefully sweet face were turbulent, wilful, lusty with life, distinctly at variance with her decorous demeanour.

In course of time you learn that she is ruthless, selfish, courageous, and one who permits passion to do nothing if not take its course:

> There was a curious low roaring sound in her ears as of sea-shells held against them and through the sound she dimly heard the swift thudding of her heart. Her body seemed to melt into his and, for a timeless time, they stood fused together as his lips took hers hungrily as if he could never have enough.

Few novelists would have ventured to take characters so patently out of stock, and few would have succeeded so well in enlivening at least two out of the four principal parts. Besides Scarlett, there is her male counterpart, Rhett Butler, darkly dangerous as Heathcliff, gruff as Mr Rochester, a cynic, a dandy, and a social outcast. But despite his exterior he has plenty of cold mush under the vest, as can be seen from his refusal to be parted from his child's coffin. The antitypes of Scarlett and Rhett are Ashley Wilkes and his wife Melanie. Melanie is so virtuous she is nearly a half-wit. As for Ashley, though he is your Southern dreamer, much given to 'book-learning', he is the unattainable object of Scarlett's desire.

> Ashley Wilkes – bah! [comments Rhett]. His breed is of no use or value in an upside-down world like ours. Whenever the world up-ends, his kind is the first to perish.

Scarlett is no fool, she comes round to these sentiments in the end.

***

She is essentially and consistently a daughter of the soil. That is what gives her character alone a certain memorable quality. Nothing at all really matters to her except the land, the physical soil, of her birth. Rather than give up her home for Yankee taxations she is prepared to sacrifice her status and reputation, to pick cotton with her former Negro slaves, to marry for money and march into business on her own account amidst the disapproval of a bereft Atlanta society. Whenever poverty threatens, the peasant in Scarlett emerges. 'The silly fools,' she fumes, 'don't seem to realize that you can't be a lady without money.' Not a noble character, only a sturdy and significant one, the survivor of the toughest, the indomitable New Woman of the West:

> I believe women could manage everything in the world without men's help – except having babies, and God knows, no woman in her right mind would have babies if she could help it.

To evaluate a mammoth labour like *Gone with the Wind*, whether it is a good book or a bad book, seems irrelevant. Of course it is bad art. But you cannot say fairer than that it is, like our Albert Memorial, impressive.

[1958]

Heinrich Böll

The contemporary German author I most admire is Heinrich Böll for the variety and steadiness of his vision and its extra-territorial dimensions; and for the stamina of his patient, almost documentary style. He portrays his characters indomitably proceeding with their lives within, against and in spite of the interference and imposed values of modern bureaucracies, and moulds with wit and intelligence these characters in their own sweet and sour uniqueness.

Böll does not try any 'magic' as a writer. Whatever pains he takes as an author, they do not show. Böll's narrative methods, especially where he uses the very data-building techniques of state machinery that he satirises, are wonderfully effective in filling the action with small cumulative surprises, items of information that would mean nothing to pinch-hearted bureaucrats or in computerised ministries. Böll is in charge of his own mind. In *Group Portrait with Lady* the state, whether it is operating the war machine or the peace machine, is expressed obliquely: it has the power and ignorance of the weather.

I always find Böll's novels warm, authentic and rich.

[1977]

Eyes and Noses

I was given to think about noses by being given to think about eyes for an essay competition. And the more I thought about eyes, the less I had to say about them, and the more did I ponder noses. Not that eyes lack scope: but for me there was too much scope: in particular, too many adjectives capable of being associated with eyes. Dry, ambiguous, blue, beastly, wee or haunting eyes are manageable, but after that, the deluge: the Arcturian eye, the strychnic and the televisionary eye, usher themselves to mind; and still to be embraced remain the United Provincial, the Jacobean, the extra-mural, the blunt and biting, eyes.

I am for noses, because they are frugal as to adjectives and constant in form. It is said that the eyes are the windows of the soul. A fallacy; they are the windows of moods and inclinings, alarums and excursions, which act only as a magnet to more adjectives. No one with a flighty imagination should touch upon a subject which is prone to adjectives.

It is not so with noses. For, incapable of deceit, noses express only themselves. But they mean much. In fact, the nose is the signpost of the soul. In the sweeping and general sense, that is. That anyone's nose can be interpreted to mean 'steady and cheerful' or 'homicidal and industrious', I, as an aphysiognomist, truly doubt. I note that the nose of an officious bus conductor is, from base to tip, altogether too officious. He lets his bus take me past my stop. I am sure he has put the Evil Nose on me. I have to walk all the way back to the National Portrait Gallery, where, on the bust of John Keats, I see an identical nose lending itself an air of the compassionate sublime.

The adjectives proper to noses can therefore be reduced to a few anthropological terms, so plain is the nose on your face. It is true that these peninsulas of the human landscape have their individual endearments. The people I admire most have noses which go off at all angles; they have nostrils like panniers, bellows, cabbage butterflies: in profile, they are cliff-edges, dromedaries, spouts of teapots and chianti-bottles. You can keep your tiny tip-tilts, which are for shop-window dummies. You can have your chiselled classicals, they are for a romantic taste. But what you prefer and what I fancy are beside the point, which is, that the nose has a function.

It has three functions: olfactory, respiratory, and proclamatory, but the first two are also beside the point. The transcendent function of the nose is to proclaim humankind. That the nose is our tether between spirit and substance, Heaven and Earth, is evident from Genesis, 'the Lord God formed man of the dust of the ground, and breathed into his nostrils the breath of life; and man became a living soul'. The first thing that happened to Adam happened to his nose. Therefore the nose is an emblem at once of our dusty origin and our divine.

Why else do infants reach out for our noses, except that they doubt whether we have got souls, like themselves? Remember that the newly born are, all unawares, deeply versed in the Book of Genesis. Thus counselled, our children clutch our emblematic noses, generously to give us the benefit of the doubt. Why do they consider a funny man with a false nose funny? Because, of course, they spot the heresy. He was quite a heretic, that Dong with a Luminous Nose of Edward Lear.

If neither the utterance of Genesis nor the pathetic fate of the Dong convinces you, hear what John Donne said about the nose. 'The worthiest member', he said. Regrettably, he did not actually say that noses stand for souls, but I take him to have meant it. Also in support of my proposition, Rostand provides his Cyrano. No spirit could be choicer than Cyrano's, no nose more monstrous. This dramatic issue between Cyrano's prominent nose and his prominent soul properly testifies to my nose-soul theme.

And I ask consideration of the case of the noses of Botticelli's nymphs and goddesses, because it confirms my conviction. These figures have colds in their noses suggested by a touch of pink at the tip. And not without reason. Botticelli wished to convey the supreme spirituality of the exalted females. He understood that they exist, by nature, in an element so purified and perfect that when they came into a natural framework they would find the atmosphere odd. Giving them human form, in their immortal poses, he gave them a human reaction to change of climate, a cold.

[1953]

Simenon: A Phenomenal Writer

[...]

Georges Simenon was born in 1903 at Liège, the elder of two brothers. His parents were of the petit bourgeoisie that Simenon's books depict so thoroughly. He was attached to his father, an insurance man, but he rightly didn't like his mother, a woman of narrow limitations who appears to have resented her elder son's luminous talent. He had a Catholic education.

In the First World War the Germans were in Liège until 1918. That year Simenon left school at the age of 15 and, after occupying himself with several jobs including that of pastry-cook, he joined the *Gazette de Liège* as a reporter. From then, at the age of 16, he was an undoubted success. He wrote articles and pulp novels for the *Gazette*, some of them of a vitriolic anti-semitic nature which he later repudiated as having been written under orders, although, as Pierre Assouline points out [in his book], they were written with apparent conviction.

Simenon moved to Paris in 1922 and [the following year] married his fiancée, Regine, an art student otherwise known as Tigy. In Paris Simenon, who now devoted all his time to literature, had a tumultuous affair with the star entertainer Josephine Baker, after which he set off with Tigy and her maid, 'Boule', on a tour of France by river and canal. In 1929 he travelled the waterways of northern Europe and developed a new fictional character, Commissaire Maigret.

In 1931 he arranged for a mammoth Parisian party, called the Anthropometric Ball, to be thrown to launch the Maigret novels. It went on all night, a wild and memorable success. (Maigret novels alone have since sold many millions of copies.) [The] next year, Simenon was saying, 'I'm already 29 and I've only published 277 books.' It is true that his travels in no way interfered with his astonishing output. Where other novelists of good quality take months, or years, to brood on the next novel, Simenon took one day to think about it, and roughly fourteen days to write a book. This also applies to his 'hard' novels, those masterpieces of psychology which caused André Gide to proclaim Simenon 'the greatest novelist we have had this century'.

In 1940 Simenon was once again caught in a German-occupied part of the world. Anyone who was making a living by writing in occupied countries during the two world wars could be said to be a collaborator. The questions are, how far and ardently did they collaborate, did they know exactly what they were collaborating with and did their political sympathies anyway affect or change their work? In Simenon's case, he wrote for money – it was either that or do some totally different job – and it is very unlikely he could have known the full miseries and horrors of the Nazi system. But the answer to the third question is more elusive. I would say yes, a political bent, involvement or acquiescence does affect the work of a writer for better or worse. In the case of Simenon, his Germanic methodology and his racial prejudices are lurkingly present throughout everything he wrote. This impedes the longevity of his books. It gives them at times too old-fashioned and dated a flavour, far more than does the stove in the corner of Maigret's office on the Quai des Orfèvres.

Towards the end of the Occupation in 1944, Simenon sensed the way the wind was blowing. He sent a pig and a cask of red wine to the Resistance. He had already been investigated as a Jew on the basis of his name, which it was falsely alleged was originally Simon. On that occasion he had scratched around for his grandparents' baptism certificates and eventually solved the problem by moving to a safer zone. Now, at the end of the war, he found himself blacklisted as a Nazi collaborator both in London and in France, where he was condemned by the purge committee at the Ministry of Arts and Letters. This was excessive. He lost no time in getting a visa for the United States, where he took his family in the autumn of 1945. There, in the peace of a form of democracy he had never before experienced, he met his second wife, Denise, and formed a second family with Tigy, his first wife, as part of it.

He wrote some of his best non-detective novels during his American years, starting notably with the terrifying *The Stain on the Snow* (1948), so much admired by such contemporaries as Gide and T.S. Eliot. In [this novel] he created a criminal Dostoyevskian type of character, known and recognised more and more as our [twentieth] century wears on – the perpetrator of the gratuitous act, the motiveless crime.

Here, the young anti-hero Frank, while under police interrogation, reflects to himself:

> *Because ... because.* All his life he had seen people being wrong with their *becauses* ... There was no *because* ... It was a word for fools.

Simenon's life and literary worth are not to be considered outside the amazing statistics attached to them. He is said to have limited his vocabulary to 2,000 words, to avoid a 'literary' tone; it is true that he is wonderfully translatable, marvellously readable – lucid, simple, absolutely in tune with that world he creates of run-down hotels, cold, dark, barges, quay-side canal-taverns, lurking prostitutes, pot-bellied burghers, taciturn youths, slippery barmen. The facility with which he wrote his newspaper columns in his boyhood remained with him to his last days. His self-discipline was formidable.

Simenon returned to Europe in 1955, first to the South of France and finally to Switzerland. Boule was now Simenon's mistress. His only daughter Marie-Jo, whom he adored, was born in 1953. She committed suicide in 1978 in her Paris apartment, mentally trapped by her hopeless love for her father. She had made six previous attempts at suicide. Simenon could not have prevented her act, but he and his writings were deeply affected by it.

Pierre Assouline tells us:

> André Gide died without ever figuring out how the Simenon factory worked, though it must be said that Simenon never gave him any help, lest he kill his secret by revealing it. 'How *sincerely* can I describe a novel's gestation? It's a form of self-deception, nothing more,' he said as early as 1939. But it was a methodical self-deception, a technique polished by decades of practice ... Eight or nine chapters in as many days.

Simenon drank wine as he wrote. He took long walks to immerse himself into the conditions of his novel. He worked himself into what he called 'a state of grace' or trance, before he could enter 'the novel mode'.

In the early stages of the 'trance' he would sometimes pick up his mail at the post office, just to have a destination for his long walk. The excursion would then become a ritual, repeated at the same time each day, by the same route, for as long as it took him to complete the novel.

Simenon left three sons. He died in Lausanne aged 86, a truly wonderful writer.

[1997]

The Book I Would Like to Have Written, and Why

The book I would like to have written, and why? – I think I must be soused to the core by the deadly sin of pride. There are scores of my 'favourite' books on my shelves. Years pass, and when I come back to them at least 50 per cent disappoint me. I remember only once reading a new book – Evelyn Waugh's *The Loved One* (it was before I started writing fiction) when I thought I'd like to have written that. I still admire it but would no longer like to have written it. The Book of Job enchants me above all other books in the Bible, but I would not want to have written it, or, if so, there are points of characterisation and philosophy on which I think I could improve.

I have reached a stage where I would not want to have written anyone's book – not the sonnets of Shakespeare, not the dialogues of Plato, not the notebooks of Kierkegaard, nor, to come nearer home, lovely stories like 'Daisy Miller' or T.F. Powys's *Mr Weston's Good Wine* – all old favourites. Nothing, even, by most most-admired contemporary novelist Heinrich Böll. In fact, I would not want to have written anything by anyone else, because they are 'them', and I am 'me'. And I do not want to be anybody else but myself with all the ideas I want to convey, the stories I want to tell, maybe lesser works, but my own.

[1981]

Pensée: The Supernatural

Some of my work can be described as gothic because it deals with the supernatural. I have often found that the supernatural is a good factor for intensifying the vision of a story. It gives an extra dimension. It also helps to increase the element of suspense by which the reader is induced to turn the pages.

[2003]

Part IV

Religion, Politics and Philosophy

*The demands of the Christian religion are exorbitant,
they are outrageous.*
The Comforters

The more religious people are, the more perplexing I find them.
Memento Mori

Myself, I have had to put up a psychological fight for my spiritual joy.
What Images Return

Testament of Faith

This anthology of extracts from the testaments and teachings of Eastern and Western masters of the spiritual life, is a personal one – N. Gangulee, the compiler, says he found these selections helpful in his own 'quest for self-realisation and peace', but they are arranged here to have a broad universal application.

The anthology shows, as T.S. Eliot who prefaces the book points out, 'how frequently contemplatives of religions and civilisations remote from each other are saying the same thing'. Thus, Western thinkers from Eckhart to Aldous Huxley are set beside Sufi mystics and Jewish, Hindu, Moslem and Buddhist religious writers. If we find this surprising it is because we are accustomed to cutting a sharp vertical distinction between Eastern and Western 'ways of thought' – though, if the world's thought is considered as a whole, distinguished only by different levels, then what is more surprising is the quite justified inclusion of Nietzsche, Whitman and Shelley in a book containing Fénelon and Pascal. Where these mystics, philosophers, devotional writers and poets meet, is on a plane transcending doctrine and orthodoxy. Eliot reminds the reader who discerns this common essence, that 'no man has ever climbed to the higher stages of the spiritual life who has not been a believer in a particular religion or at least a particular philosophy'.

There are, however, many conflicting statements to be found in this selection; but it would not do to use the book as a means of philosophical comparison, firstly because Mr Gangulee disclaims such a purpose – his extracts are there to be meditated upon; and because, secondly, each quotation is orphaned from its context, though representing a unique moment of illumination. But the fact that there are discrepancies in thought rather challenges the seriousness of the compiler's statement (concerning particularly those mystics he quotes), that 'the ardours of their spiritual experience reveal ... a positive proof of the immanence of the Divine Spirit within us'. It is merely the term 'positive proof' which may be questioned. The mystics have given their testament of faith; positive proof was not required by them, their evidence bears a non-scientific relation to Truth; nor is positive proof required for the conviction which their experiences may convey to others.

The mystics represented here, many of them, are practical teachers in the exercise of meditation; and perhaps one of the most rewarding features of the work is that it contains many pronouncements on how to go about meditation; most of us to-day can only brood, and then only when time permits. We need the implicit pragmatical instructions of a Fénelon. Both Gangulee and Eliot are concerned to say what meditation really means. To use the book properly, Eliot tells us, 'we have to abandon some of our usual motives for reading. We must surrender the Love of Power – whether over others, or over ourselves, or over the material world. We must abandon even the Love of Knowledge. We must not be distracted by interest in the personality of particular authors, or by delight in the phrases in which they have expressed their insights.' The latter is the first difficulty which faces the modern reader in approaching any devotional work which does not attempt equally to delight and improve the reader. Gangulee's instructional account of the directions for meditation in the *Upanishads*, likewise fulfils a profitable introductory purpose.

[1951]

Ailourophilia

If I were not a Christian I would worship the Cat. The ancient Egyptians did so with much success. But at least it seems evident to me that the domestic cat is the aristocrat of the animal kingdom, occupying a place of quality in the Great Chain of Being second only to our aspiring, agitated and ever-evolving selves.

The dog is known to possess a higher degree of intelligence than the cat. Cat addicts are inclined to challenge this fact. But I think the higher intelligence, as we commonly mean it, must be conceded to the dog, and the highest to ourselves. We need our intelligence more than we need anything, and so, for its purposes, does the dog. But with cats, as with all true aristocrats, intelligence is not the main thing; they do not need brains, since they have felicity.

Dogs are easily enslaved; they willingly regard their masters as gods and spend their lives proving their obedience, usefulness and devotion.

Cats prove nothing – they are above all that. They don't even catch a mouse unless it suits them to do so. No cat will pledge itself for life to its human provider, nor in any way sell its deep, sweet soul. When it forms an attachment, it is by way of gracious concession mixed with convenience. Very aristocratic. When a cat voluntarily disappears from home, it is not from want of intelligence or sense of its whereabouts, it is merely because the whim has seized it to look for something less boring elsewhere.

And, like aristocrats, they do not need stately homes. Whereas the bourgeois dog needs a kennel or a fireside in order to be a somebody, even the sleek alley cat retains the incomprehensible importance of its catness, and is silent unless tormented or raped to the fine point of anguish.

I cannot speak highly enough of the cat, its casual freedom of spirit, its aloof anarchism and its marvellous beauty. The Greeks, observing its fearful symmetry in motion, called the cat *ailouros* – a wave of the sea. Nothing restores the soul so much as the contemplation of a cat. In repose, it is like a lotus leaf. Its contentment is mystical; anatomists have still not discovered what or where the cat's purr-box is.

To my mind, the flower and consummation of the species was my late cat, Bluebell, short of whose perfection every other cat in history and literature inevitably falls.

[...]

Bluebell was given to me when she was a kitten. Her origins were of no particular account. She was partly blue-Persian, of exquisite miniature build. Her fur was fluffy and curiously luminous; but not too long, not bushy, like the fur of a vulgar Ritzy Persian. On the lawn, before rain or in the early morning, she shone with a blue, unearthly light, while her eyes took on the vivid green of the grass. Curled on a chair indoors, she glowed mulberry-coloured. She always seemed to radiate from her small body some inward, spiritual colour. When she sat in the window on sunny days, her eyes were pure amber as they stared intently at outer space. I am sure she saw objects in space that I could not see.

I never got used to Bluebell's loveliness. When I woke in the morning to see her sitting, a sheer Act of Praise, on my dressing-table, securely waiting for some life to happen, I would gaze at her with awe and with awe.

She was never exactly an ailourophobe but she grew to prefer human society to that of cats. At parties, she was gifted with the art of disappearing to nowhere from time to time. She was also greatly endowed with ESP. She would sit on my manuscripts if what I had written was any good, but if she stepped over the notebooks with her fastidious pads, I knew there was something wrong with the stuff. She came when called, but not invariably. Her sympathy, when she chose to exert it, was original and profound. She would brood comically over my wrongs, and, on occasions of rejoicing she quickly caught the spirit of the thing, sometimes taking a silly turn, leaping high, and landing with four legs outspread like a wonky new-born lamb. There was no end to Bluebell's virtues.

At the age of four she contracted a mysterious illness. She bore with numerous veterinary surgeons and many injections. Her eyes grew larger and her manners more delicate than ever. One day the vet said, 'We'll have to put her to sleep.' I said, 'You mean you want to put her to death.' The vet said, 'Oh, I wouldn't put it that way.' I said, 'You mean you want to kill my cat.' Next morning at nine o'clock the doorbell screamed. I clung to Bluebell, for I knew the Gestapo had come. They were sent up. In came the hired assassins, carrying between them a metal box, Bluebell's gas-chamber. The men asked me to leave the room. I said I wanted to stay with Bluebell. One of the men said, 'Sometimes they struggle.' I was then put out of the room, and was called back about four minutes later. The cat's body was lying stretched out on the table, longer than I had ever seen it before; the eyes were upturned, wildly staring, glazed amber. The men took Bluebell's carcass by the hind legs, dumped it in a sack and took it away.

Never again. Some friends tried to give me another cat. 'Enough,' I said. 'Never again.'

[1964]

All God's Creatures

The patriarch of Genesis, Noah – did he exist? If he didn't, someone else away back in the mists of time, equally imaginative, invented him, knowing that in any natural disaster from which the human race must be rescued, animals, too, must necessarily be saved. Noah and his family understood this dependency on other living creatures when they devised the ark and its immemorial zoo.

I have always been moved by the story of how, after the Flood, God sets a rainbow in the sky: 'This is the token of the covenant which I have established between me and all flesh that is upon the earth.'

It is not only in the Judeo-Christian religions that this imperative sense of oneness with the rest of creation is manifest. We know by ancient mythologies how former civilisations revered natural life. Birds, rivers, trees, fish and animals were frequently deified; and they did not poison their gods.

I have been induced to meditate on our own homely animals by the fact that the hunting sportsmen of Italy, where I live, find it acceptable to spread deadly portions of poison over our gardens and fields, on our walls and hedgerows, in order to kill our domestic cats and dogs. With sickening regularity they succeed in their aim. They say our animals spoil their game, although hardly any game is left to hunt in these recent years. Foxes are rare, but they are used as an excuse for bereaving practically every household of their faithful and beloved dogs, their lively, affectionate cats. I have been in Italy since 1968. In the country-side I know no-one whomsoever who has not lost an animal, generally more, to an average of three. I have lost five dogs and a number of cats through poison. I have already written of this grim experience and here I will only repeat that to watch helplessly while an animal agonises in poisoned death-throes is to encounter evil at first hand.

***

I dislike the word 'pets'. To me, it just doesn't suit the beasts with their special built-in instincts and intelligences, their intricate physical formations and in general the dignity and infinite care with which they appear to have been made. To me, dogs are dogs and cats are cats, and I call them by the name which seems most appealing and appropriate to me.

[...]

It often happens in countries like Italy where dogs are abandoned by owners who find them and their needs a nuisance, that they take to the hills and join wolf packs. Dogs and wolves mate. The wolf is in fact the early ancestor of the dog. It is believed that in primitive times the more adventurous wolves would approach the camp-fires of human beings, snatching the scraps and bones of a meal. In return, gradually, the wolf would make itself useful by warning of danger with its quick hearing. The dog thus came into being as a domestic follower, with smaller teeth than the wolf, and various mutated features. The wolf attaches itself faithfully to the chief of the pack; its descendant, the dog, adheres with the utmost devotion to its human owner.

According to their size and structure, and their hereditary training, dogs hunt, guard, herd, guide the blind, sniff out people buried under the snow of an avalanche or the rubble of an earthquake as we see so often on television. At the frontiers they sniff out cocaine, heroin and other dire drugs that are being smuggled in.

Dogs can be very comical and amusing if left to their own spontaneity, but to me, dogs that have been taught fancy tricks, either at home or, in the extreme case, for the circus, are really in a pathetic plight. I particularly abhor performing animals. There is nothing more insulting to our glorious world-creation than to make a great elephant stand on a tiny box; this is something that positively makes me ill. I won't frequent a circus where they make use of animals. It makes me positively choke with indignation to see a tiger jumping through a fiery hoop. I think I would rather watch the tiger eat the trainer.

How far from the stifling and sordid circus ring is William Blake's vision of the mighty beast:

> Tyger! tyger! burning bright
> In the forest of the night,
> What immortal hand or eye
> Could frame thy fearful symmetry?
>
> [...]
>
> What the hammer? What the chain?
> In what furnace was thy brain?
> What the anvil? What dread grasp
> Dare its deadly terrors clasp?

***

The domestic dog in all the varieties that we know was probably bred as such by our primitive ancestors. Many zoologists claim that some artificial selection of animals that were finer-toothed, smaller-framed, more manageable than the wolf must have taken place in the first eras of civilisation.

The dog was then apparently received with enthusiasm all over the world. Primitive tribes in America had no need to be introduced to the dog. There flourished a very wolf-like breed, the stout husky, reined in as it is to provide human transport by hauling sledges across the frozen tundra.

If you keep a dog it is a good thing to buy a dog-book which provides information about its maintenance and health. There is no need to take the dog to the vet for simple advice. Dogs thrive on preventive inoculations which only the vet can measure and prescribe according to the type of animal, but generally the dog will 'tell' you itself if it is ailing. Unlike cats and horses, dogs are extremely anxious to communicate. Horses like to feel secure, to know where they stand with human beings, and cats, splendidly, couldn't care less. But with dogs you get to know what they are thinking.

Tales of canine heroism and self-sacrifice abound in literature. What I think is so remarkable about these stories is that we can so very easily believe them. We don't have to stretch our imagination or suspend our capacity for belief, to recognise, for instance, the adventures of Lassie. Those movies could almost be documentaries. Lassie does just what any dog might do in the service of the people it loves.

***

Elizabeth Barrett Browning's dog, Flush, was the subject of one of her eloquent poems. Flush had kept watch by her bedside throughout a long illness and would not be coaxed or commanded away from her room so long as she remained in bed. Both Emily and Anne Brontë had faithful dogs which they adored. After their death, Charlotte Brontë described Emily's dog Keeper visiting her room every morning, and Flossie, Anne's spaniel, looking about for her in vain. Sir Walter Scott's Maida followed him everywhere and lay constantly at his feet while he sat writing his novels far into the night. Henry James had a series of dogs. One of the sadnesses of keeping a dog is that one usually outlives them. In the garden of Lamb House, Rye, where Henry James spent his latter years, there is a small dog cemetery where his animal friends are buried. It is a shock to part with a much-loved animal, however old it is, however expected the death. I remember many years ago when Gore Vidal and his friend Howard Austen lost their blind old dog through an accident, they were so upset that they took a trip round the world to help them get over their distress.

In Homer's *Odyssey*, when Ulysses returns from his long years of travel, he notices a poor dying dog on a rubbish heap. The dog, on hearing his voice, pricks up his ears. He is Argus, the favourite hunting hound of Ulysses in their young days.

I have often seen the beneficial effect of a domestic dog on the remaining member of a bereaved couple. The comfort of such an animal at such a time is enormous. And the very fact of the dog's needing to be cared for is a sort of grip on sanity.

From the earliest records of visual art, animals have been prominent. Those wonderful creatures of the hunt painted and engraved on the walls of the Lascaux and other caves are vital proof of how greatly our ancestors esteemed them over fifteen thousand years ago. Cows, bulls, oxen, bison, horses and reindeer are among the depicted treasures. From x-ray pictures of the hand-prints on these walls it seems evident that these animal pictures were a source of ardent pilgrimage among the primitives. To them, their animals were life itself.

And nearer our times, but still long ago, the fascinating historic tapestry of Bayeux depicting the Norman Conquest of England is decidedly humanised by the supporting dogs, horses and cattle. They are wonderfully arranged to give movement and a sort of gloating victorious buoyancy to the various episodes and scenes the tapestry portrays.

Strangely, there is nothing like an animal in a figurative painting to humanise the work. In the London National Gallery's *Jan Arnolfini and his Wife*, by Jan Van Eyck, the fifteenth-century Flemish painter, for instance, we see husband and wife touching hands modestly and formally; but it would all be a little too stiff were it not for a congenial little dog in the foreground; it is in fact the dog that humanises and imbues the scene with intimate loving contentment.

And also, in the famous painting of Velázquez, *Las Meniñas* in the Prado Museum, Madrid, the huge strong brown hound in the foreground provides a serene, still, contrast to the mercurial energy of a variety of people who are trying to persuade the Spanish princess to stand still for her portrait.

***

Cats in the home are quite different, although after some initial hesitation, the domestic dogs and cats generally get along together fairly well. In fact, cats are not very keen on each other after the kittens have grown up. They like themselves and their comfort, which frequently includes and coincides with the satisfaction of their owner.

The cat is a much older race than the dog, going back, some say, seven million years. It would seem that our domestic cat is a diminutive mutation from the tiger and the lynx of the jungle.

Cats were revered by the Egyptians. On Cleopatra's state visit to Rome she brought a considerable following of her court cats, most of them no doubt forebears of Rome's prodigious feline population. Cats were gods in Egypt. They were often mummified and sometimes mice were mummified and entombed with the cats to keep them well-fed on their metaphorical journey to the next world.

Cats have been known in literature and in literary biographies, as the inspirational muse of the writer. Personally, I always choose to have a cat in the room when I write. They are so agile when they move, thanks to their abundance of elastic muscles. Their grace is inimitable. For creative work, cats are excellent to contemplate when they are in repose.

Poems and stories about cats abound. Christopher Smart, Baudelaire, Kipling, T.S. Eliot, Stevie Smith among many others were all cat-admirers.

Smart's poem (of the eighteenth century) is often quoted:

For I will consider my Cat Jeoffrey.
For he is the servant of the Living God, duly and daily serving him.
For at the first glance of the glory of God in the East he worships in his way.
For is this done by wreathing his body seven times round with elegant quickness.

I feel it to be a pity that T.S. Eliot did not live to see his famous *Practical Cats* performed as a world-stirring musical. It was probably the last thing he would have envisaged. But the musical should not be allowed to eclipse its grand original in verses such as:

Mungojerrie and Rumpelteazer were a very notorious
    couple of cats.
As knockabout clowns, quick-change comedians,
    tight-rope walkers and acrobats
They had an extensive reputation. They made their home
    in Victoria Grove –
That was merely their centre of operation, for they were
    incurably given to rove.
They were very well known in Cornwall Gardens, in
    Launceston Place and in Kensington Square –
They had really a little more reputation than a couple of
    cats can very well bear.

Cats are affectionate when it suits their convenience. They like to snuggle up to their human owners in winter, and wander off in summer. They have an uncanny sense of time and so are very punctual for meals. A house cat should be castrated or spayed if it is allowed to wander. They can otherwise have as many as twenty kittens a year and the male cat will spray a very strong-smelling advertisement for a female; all of which is not hygienic for ourselves nor manageable. But to be unsexed, for the cat, does not impair their sense of fun or their capacity for enjoyment; on the contrary, the fixed male cat does not often get injured in fights; he lives longer and seldom gets lost.

I have often envied the cat its ability to purr when I want to express supreme contentment. It is a beautiful sound. But quite recently I read in an edition of the *Encyclopaedia Britannica* that 'purring manifests itself in extremes of both pain and pleasure'. I find this surprising, and indeed, I don't remember any time when a cat of mine purred in pain. I wonder if other cat owners have had any such experience?

Purring is mysterious. It has no connection with the cat's vocal cords. Nobody, in fact, quite knows where the cat's purr-box is situated.

In case a cat has kittens, it is useless to prepare a basket or box for this purpose, for the very fact that you have done so precludes the acceptance of your plan. Cats make their own arrangements. They prefer the top shelves of wardrobes which they arrive at by clawing their way up your clothes. Their births are not very messy, however, as the mother scrupulously recycles the placenta.

With cats, as with dogs, a cat-book is helpful after the initial inoculations have been administered.

***

Throughout the Middle Ages and the Renaissance the civilised worlds of Byzantium and Europe expressed their love for animals and their symbolic feeling for the beasts of the earth, known by their ancestors as 'The Great Chain of Being'. This Chain pronounced a remarkably knowing ecological system. Insects depended on plants, birds and fish on insect life, mammals on the existence of everything under the sea and in the air. We know now that these early nature lovers were very far advanced in ecology.

There was a religious fervour in their feeling for animals. The great mosaics of Istanbul and Ravenna are the best examples. In Ravenna, too, at the Archbishopric Museum, is a famous animal pulpit covered with tiers of marble-carvings; sheep, goats, birds and fish, with an inscription reminding us that God created them. I wonder if sermons to that effect were ever preached from that pulpit? I have yet to hear a sermon in any church of any denomination reminding us of our duties towards animals who partake of the gift of life along with us, and who ennoble us with their coexistence on the earth.

PART IV. RELIGION, POLITICS AND PHILOSOPHY

It is in Ravenna that the earliest mosaics are preserved, in temple after temple, in museums, presbyteries, baptisteries and churches. The animal kingdom is always there, superbly executed, quietly waiting in its impervious stone for succeeding generations of worshippers. Religion and nature were closely co-ordinated between the sixth and sixteenth centuries. These mosaics make it easier for us to penetrate the minds of those early Christians who apparently thought and felt in symbols.

The seventh-century Basilica of S. Vitale contains magnificent animal portraits in ceramics: a bullock, symbol of St Luke, a sixth-century eagle; a lion, the symbol of St Mark. Lambs symbolise Christ, and elsewhere in the treasure-box of Ravenna's mosaics, lambs represent the Apostles. Doves, standing for peace, abound in all depicted allegories.

Portraits of animals are to be found in all ancient cultures. In the British Museum we find the owl of the goddess of wisdom, Athena, in 440 BC. In the Louvre of Paris an Egyptian sculpture of 685 BC shows a small King Taharqa in bronze making a humble offering of wine to a large golden god-falcon.

A painting of St Francis, the notable patron of the animal creation, is also in the Louvre. (This is a formal version of the marvellous mural in the upper church of St Francis at Assisi.) It has a gold background. A congregation of swallows* are lined up in front of the Saint who preaches gratitude for the divine providence that feeds them.

We come back to the promise that God made after the Flood, that rainbow in the sky pledging God's solidarity with every living thing. Centuries later, in the biblical Book of Job there is an even more prominent intervention of God in the context of animal creation.

Job has undergone a great many losses and personal sufferings. He has been warned by a series of friends, 'the comforters', that he must have done some wrong to deserve his fate. 'No,' says Job, 'I haven't done anything wrong in God's sight.' It is not till God answers Job out of a whirlwind that the hero of that magnificent poem is finally comforted. God takes Job's mind right out of himself; he speaks proudly of his own creation, the special features of nature, and finally his animals in all their respective glories:

> Gavest thou the goodly wings unto the peacocks? or wings and feathers unto the ostrich?

---

*Could Muriel Spark have meant 'sparrows'? Swallows don't sit on the ground, as they appear to be doing in the fresco with St Francis, since they apparently can't fly from that position and must drop off from something – a wall, a tree. See *St Francis Preaching to the Birds* at Assisi, etc.

> Which leaveth her eggs in the earth, and warmeth them in the dust ...
>
> Hast thou given the horse his strength? Hast thou clothed his neck with thunder? ...
>
> He saith among the trumpets, Ha, ha; and he smelleth the battle afar off, the thunder of the captains; and the shouting ...

God points to the eagle; he specifies his mighty creature behemoth:

> Behold now behemoth, which I made with thee: he eateth grass as an ox ...
>
> His bones are as strong pieces of brass; his bones are like bars of iron ...
>
> Behold, he drinketh up a river, and hasteth not: he trusteth that he can draw up Jordan into his mouth.

Next comes a sea-monster:

> Canst thou draw out leviathan with a hook? or his tongue with a cord which thou lettest down? ...
>
> Will he make many supplications unto thee? Will he speak soft words unto thee? ...
>
> I will not conceal his parts, nor his power, nor his comely proportions.

And it is truly a healthy thing to sometimes meditate, as Job was obliged to do, on the wealth of created life around us. The animal creation ennobles us; we cannot survive without it; it makes us whole.

[1999/2000]

The Sermons of Newman

Over the past twelve years, at times when I have felt my mind becoming congested from hearing too many voices, including my own, I have turned to the sermons which Newman delivered to the undergraduates of Oxford when he was Vicar of St Mary's. His voice from the pulpit was, by all accounts, something very special indeed. I am sure nothing has been lost in the past hundred and twenty years, only gained; for if there is one comprehensive thing that can be said about Newman's writings, it is that he has a 'voice'; it is his own and no one else's. To me, at least, it is a voice that never fails to start up, radioactive from the page, however musty the physical book.

If I can help it, I never read books for information only. I don't like books that are designed for spiritual improvement unless they are well written. I wouldn't touch the Bible if it wasn't interesting in historical, literary, and other ways besides its content. I read Newman's sermons because they are Newman's, not because they are sermons. He was as sincere as light. 'Every thought I think is thought, and every word I write is writing,' he said.

His reasoning is so pure that it is revolutionary in form. He does not go forward from point to point; he leads the mind inward, probing the secret places of the subject in hand. You can never anticipate, with Newman, what he is leading up to. Occupied entirely with the penetrable truths of his subject, he turns his argument with simple freedom, regardless of the moral direction it seems to be taking. He was out for the psychological penetration of moral character, and he achieved it.

I take as an example his sermon, 'Obedience without Love, as instanced in the character of Balaam', because I think it shows not only his typical habits of thought and expression, but more noticeably than in any other sermon, the theme of the love of God, which I think can be called Newman's basic one. It is, indeed, basic to the Christian religion that from the love of God all other movements of charity proceed. But Newman, who at an early age, conceived the thought 'of two and two only supreme and luminously self-evident beings, myself and my Creator', seems to me to have had an immediate relation to that one idea, the love of God, throughout his life and work.

This is the idea that he is directly investigating in the Sermon of Balaam. Balaam, he points out, is

> a high-principled, honourable, conscientious man. He obeys as well as talks about religion; and this being the case, we shall feel more intimately the value of the following noble sentiments which he lets drop from time to time, and which, if he had shown less firmness in his conduct, might have passed for mere words, the words of a maker of speeches, a sophist, moralist, or orator. 'Let me die the death of the righteous, and let my last end be like his' ... and so on.

It is not an ironic portrait. It is true there is a fine hair's breadth of irony in the phrase 'the following noble sentiments which he lets drop from time to time', but that is by the way. It is Newman's manner always to praise the good in what he is bound to depart from. He goes on to elaborate and establish the delightful and noble aspects of Balaam, with as much sincerity as he employed in portraying the English Gentleman in his *Idea of a University*. And with as much sincerity, too, as he gave to the lovely outlines of his Oxford years in his *Apologia*. The *Apologia Pro Vita Sua* is the saddest love story in the world; it tells of his love for a beautiful idea of the spirit, the Anglican tradition in the setting of Oxford, and of his parting with this spiritual creature for the love of God. Balaam, he goes on to show, citing verse after verse in every perplexity of meaning, was a marvel of gracious, upright, pious living, lacking only the vital thing for the prosperity of his soul: the love of God. It was Newman's conviction that the nature of God was vastly misunderstood by his fellow countrymen when they assumed divine approval for the outward standards that they themselves approved. There was a moral movement in Newman's day, there is a moral outcry in our own times, there is worse to come: ethical, germ-free citizens will be springing up all over the place to prosper more and more visibly in public reward for their virtues. Newman declares:

> But if Scripture is to be our guide, it is quite plain that the most conscientious, religious, high-principled, honourable men (I use the words in their ordinary, not in their Scripture sense) may be on the side of evil, may be Satan's instruments in cursing, if that were possible, and at least in seducing and enfeebling the people of God.

Charles Kingsley's famous cry, 'What then does Dr Newman mean?' was typical of the Christian moralists of the time. It is the doctrine of all Christians that without charity we are as sounding brass and a tinkling cymbal. But Newman points out some of the alarming implications of this nice poetry. What did he mean? He meant that God had not been educated at Rugby; that is more or less what he meant. Serious-minded people still call, from time to time, for a 'return to the moral standards of Christianity', by which they mean those codes of decency which have evolved in the chivalrous West from the Christian faith. Many hold that it is the morals that count; Christianity can go. I am not an expert in such matters, but I always sense, underlying these moralistic appeals and urges, a demand for something showy. Let us show the spirit of service, people say, let us have some austerity, work harder, clean up our streets; morality must not only be done, it must be seen to be done; let us return to the hypocrisy of our forefathers – God used to like it so much when everyone went to church and didn't commit adultery.

Newman's contribution to this field of study is to say that conscientious people of high moral principle may be on the side of evil. He says that, however inspired, however honourable, they may be Satan's instruments in seducing and enfeebling the people of God. Moreover, those who are genuinely pleasing in God's sight, only God knows. The disposition of every soul is a secret matter, not easily discernible.

I spend most of my reading time with Newman's books. I find every Life of Newman irresistible, even if it is the same story over and over again. When I am not reading Newman, the books stand in peaceful reflection on the shelves, reading and revising themselves, so to speak, for the essays, lectures, sermons and letters all give out something new at each reading.

I have noticed that to those who have been attracted by Newman his personality continues very much alive. It is one of his gifts. He is far less dead, to me, than many of my contemporaries; and less dead, even, than Socrates, for whom, in the day-dreams of my young youth, I thought it would be lovely to lay down my life. Socrates, too, had the love of God at heart; like him, Newman was said to be a 'corrupter of youth'. It was by way of Newman that I turned Roman Catholic. Not all the beheaded martyrs of Christendom, the ecstatic nuns of Europe, the five proofs of Aquinas, or the pamphlets of my Catholic acquaintance provided anything like the answers that Newman did.

In his own time his persuasive power was greatly feared. But what did it consist of? Simplicity of intellect and speech. Simplicity is the most suspect of qualities; it upsets people a great deal. I think it was this, more than his actual doctrine, that caused suspicion to gather round the Vicar of St Mary's. James Anthony Froude, an undergraduate at the time, has left one of the least ecstatic accounts of Newman's pulpit manner, and so I will quote him:

> I attended his church and heard him preach Sunday after Sunday; he is supposed to have been insidious, to have led his disciples on to conclusions to which he designed to bring them, while his purpose was carefully veiled. He was, on the contrary, the most transparent of men. He told us what he believed to be true. He did not know where it would carry him.

[1964]

Newman's Journals

Portions of Newman's autobiographical papers have already appeared in various bulky 'Lives and Letters'. They have been carefully arranged and introduced by Newman's late executor, Fr Henry Tristram, whose successor, Fr Stephen Dessain, now gives the collection in its entirety. It is an enlightening contribution towards any attempt to understand Newman.

Among the various miscellania stand the *Journals* from 1816 to 1876, a record of misgiving, introspection, scruple, tortured pride, fear of God, and other manifestations of Newman's unique and touchy inwardness. At the end of his last *Journals* he wrote, 'I am dissatisfied with the whole of this book. It is more or less a complaint from one end to the other.' So it is. 'But it represents,' he continues, 'what has been the real state of my mind, and what my Cross has been.' Newman's Cross was a sort of capacity for misunderstanding: in the Anglican period of his life, his failure to understand others; as a Catholic, his failure to make himself understood.

Strangely scarce among his reflections are references to the great popularity he enjoyed in the Victorian world at large after the appearance of the *Apologia*. He dwells rather on his immediate environment with which he was perpetually at odds, exiled by his superior intellect and exacting ethical standards. From this distance of time his enemies appear as a set of cranks and mediocrities, memorable only in that they opposed Newman.

His personal development took such an agile form that no phase recorded in these writings represents the total man. They are not in the category of 'wisdom' journals; one does not get from them, as from Kierkegaard or even Simone Weil, a consummate spiritual utterance, or chance aphoristic glory, though in his critical mentality Newman resembles both. His *Journals* are applicable only to himself, to his fluent and fascinating personality.

[1956]

An Exile's Path

About the middle of his life, John Henry Newman remarked: 'Even those who think highly of me have the vaguest, most shadowy and fantastic notions attached to their idea of me, and feel a respect, not for me, but for some imagination of their own which bears my name.' Already the myth was rife, which associates Newman with gentle, monastic sweetness, and holds him to be the writer of beautiful prose. This is true, but incomplete. The myth has not, on the whole, been put about by Newman's biographers; his friends, and, later, superficial readers of the *Apologia*, were at fault.

Newman's Way deals with the first, the Anglican, half of Newman's life. Sanity, eloquence, humour, informed judgment, are amongst what Newman would have called its 'notes'. The Newman family are traced back and forth in their pedigrees, followed in their flittings from house to house, and richly described. The father, first a banker, later a brewer, last a bankrupt, is at his prime as a member of the 'Beefsteak Club', bearing the motto 'Beef and Liberty'. The second son, Charles, was reputed mad, being an atheist, a socialist, an unemployable, and a lifelong nuisance. Francis Newman was of the stuff which precipitates itself to Persia, hoping to convert the adherents of Mahomet to the Plymouth Brotherhood. The three girls were girlish; and the mother the general mediator and upholder of tone.

Sean O'Faolain has fun with them all, and skilfully extricates from this scene of budding heterodoxy the eldest son, John Henry, who lived to become a Cardinal.* Engaged from boyhood in a specialised and unique interest in himself, Newman was, from the start, an exile on earth, speculating whether 'life might be a dream, or I an Angel, and all this world a deception, my fellow-angels by a playful device concealing themselves from me'. Throughout his life he personified the type and condition of the Romantic exile, with the controlling difference that he was never exiled from God, of whose existence he was as certain as of his own. Time and again he disengaged himself from the people and places he most loved. He withdrew from his family. He forced his break with Oxford at the height of his influence. Passionately as he valued friendship, he tore himself from his dearest intimates. He left the Church of England. And in the Church of Rome, too, he was exiled as only a greatly advanced mind, and a greatly misunderstood

---

*Pope Benedict XVI beatified Cardinal Newman in 2010.

man, can be; for it was the vast obtuseness of his critics from all factions – liberal, Roman, Anglican – which finally confirmed him in his isolation from the ways of nineteenth-century thought. And yet he was a monolith.

O'Faolain gives rewarding attention to Newman's growth at Oxford. As a new Fellow of Oriel, Newman heard, with trepidation, that the Common Room stank of logic; in the end he presented the Common Room with something to exercise logic upon thereafter. And he elevated logic; he distinguished the faculty from rationalism. He reinstated its alliance with language, for the celebrated grace and light of his prose is nothing but the beauty and power of his logic, which he never ceased to perfect to the end of his long life, and of which *The Grammar of Assent*, one of his last works, is perhaps his most luminous example.

As Sean O'Faolain shows, Newman's writings were a means of self-development. But their influence extends beyond his own purpose and time. His thought, denounced by his contemporaries as narrow, seems to broaden as time proceeds, yielding fresh aspects of his far-sighted spiritual discernment. Sean O'Faolain, with characteristic light malice, does not spare Newman's foibles, but leaves his essential nobility intact.

[1952]

A Sleep of Prisoners

This new play by Christopher Fry was written with more than one special purpose: it was written for the Religious Drama Society who are promoting religious plays for the Festival of Britain. And Fry has used the opportunity to experiment in some new directions. His meaning is conveyed more firmly than ever before, probably because his dialogue is less exuberant and his reliance on action more confident.

At St Mary's Church, Oxford it was not easy to grasp all the underlying allusiveness of the work. The acoustics of St Mary's are notoriously weak for dramatic purposes. But it was clear that within the self-imposed limits of a church play, Fry succeeded in gripping his audience.

To judge the play from standards of the theatre would be to miss a great deal of its force. *A Sleep of Prisoners* is not theatre drama. The time has not yet arrived when religious festival plays can be properly synthesised with modern stage requirements, and so, to those who look for the swift dovetailing of events which the stage demands, the play is certain to appear awkwardly constructed. It is arranged in one long act without interval, and carries only four characters, all male. The action occupies one night, during which four prisoners-of-war are confined in a church in a foreign country. The theme rests on a succession of four biblical incidents, occurring in the dreams of one of the men; the other three prisoners are the protagonists of these dream-flashes.

First the story of Cain's murder of Abel is presented. (It seems to be Fry's intention to date the Fall of Man from that act.) Next comes the story of Absalom's treachery and death; then, Abraham's reprieve from the sacrifice of Isaac; lastly, Jonah and the whale. Each story is approached in a highly original manner with emphasis on its present-day significance. The Pilgrim Players – Denholm Elliott as Pte Peter Able was particularly good – succeeded in interpreting the piece as a modern miracle play. Their miming, where the austerity of stage-scenery required it, was excellent.

[1951]

Psychic Searchlight

People are more apt to be haunted by spiritual theories than by spirits. An extra-normal happening may be proved an illusion or a fraud, but susceptible minds cling obstinately to those ideas which might have been valid had the thing been true. Real spooks are easier to exorcise than hypothetical ones. In *Psychical Research To-day* Dr D.J. West brings due respect and decent scepticism to the lores of clairvoyance, telepathy, elevation, mediumship, stigmatisation, haunting, rappings and all manner of divinings. Special attention is given to the department of psychical phenomena known as ESP.

ESP experiments have yielded the most acceptable and fruitful results so far. But Dr West warns the theorist that the basic facts are few. The book is enlivened by illustrations which include fake spirit-photographs and other trophies testifying to the vigilance of the Society for Psychical Research.

[1954]

A Pardon for the Guy

According to Julius Caesar, the Druids of Celtic Gaul used to burn a huge wicker cage in the shape of a man, crammed full of living people. Anthropologists have told us much about world-wide ancient practices of human sacrifice, and the ritual burning of human effigies in place of the real thing.

Who has not felt a passing clutch of sorrow for the guy amidst the fun and frights and startles of bonfire night? Guy Fawkes, his beady-eyed head awry on his neck, his battered hat, his painted leer; the limbs of a well-constructed guy swing wherever they are put; he resembles a scarecrow in a harvest field, evoking an inexplicable and fleeting grief.

The original Guy Fawkes was born at York in 1570. During his boyhood he converted from Protestantism to ardent Catholicism. Later, he went to the Continent where he enlisted on the Spanish side in the current wars, became well thought of for his adventurous spirit and fine bearing; he was tall, with a brown beard and auburn hair.

By 1604 the Gunpowder Plot had already started to take shape amongst some Catholic zealots in England. The plan was to blow up the Houses of Parliament, with a full assembly including the King. James, Sixth of Scotland and First of England, had lately united the two Kingdoms. He was first inclined to be lenient to Catholics, permitting them to worship quietly as they chose, and requiring only loyalty to himself and the country. But a small set of tiresome Catholic gentry dreamed of creating the conditions for a Catholic coup, which could scarcely have taken place even if the plot had succeeded.

Everything went surprisingly well with the conspiracy over a period of two years. Guy Fawkes, cool and courageous, filled with pious enthusiasm, was enlisted in Flanders to put the plan into action.

A house adjoining Parliament House was taken in the name of one of the plotters, Thomas Percy, in 1604. They began to burrow into the walls next door. Over the following year in the guise of Percy's servant Guy Fawkes, acting as a look-out, helped to direct the operations. They had got half-way through the wall by the following March, when they found that a cellar immediately under the House of Lords was in any case available for rent. Thomas Percy rented it. They brought in 1 ton 12 cwt of gunpowder, 36 barrels in all, and stacked these under a pile of coal and wood. By May everything was ready for the holocaust. Guy Fawkes was sent back to Flanders to gain support. Rome was informed of the plans to take over the country if the plot succeeded in

November, on the date of the Opening of Parliament. Fawkes returned to his explosive cellar.

But as the human reality of the thing came closer, various intriguers started to bethink themselves of their own cousins and uncles, the Catholic peers who were bound to be blown to bits along with the King and the Protestant lords. They enquired of their leaders if there might not be a way to warn their doomed kith and kin, but any such notion was firmly rejected. A counter-intrigue within the conspiracy now seems to have arisen. A supper was staged on 26th October in which an anonymous letter was brought in, warning the host, a Romanist supporter of the new King, to keep away from the forthcoming Opening of Parliament, since on that day 'God and man hath concurred to punish the wickedness of this time', and prophesying a 'terrible blow'. The host caused this spectacular letter to be read aloud at the table.

An investigation was started. The conspirators were alerted, but they were too far gone in euphoria to take any notice. Fawkes was arrested in the fatal cellar, where a fresh supply of gunpowder had been added to the pile. The other conspirators fled, soon to be hunted down, killed or captured for execution.

Guy Fawkes took up a defiant attitude. He withstood torture for four days, then on the King's orders, he was subjected to the most rigorous possible torture, a ghastly form which was, even for those days, illegal. This brought the names of his fellow plotters out of him, and a confession which is signed imperfectly by a hand trembling from the ordeal.

He was tried on the 27th January of the following year, and having been dragged through the streets of London on hurdles to Parliament House, he was helped up to the scaffold, too weak to walk. He declared his repentance. Certainly, he and other surviving conspirators who were executed with him realised that they had set back terribly the Catholic cause in England.

So we come back to our familiar Guy Fawkes on top of the bonfire. November the Fifth was declared by King James's Parliament to be a day of public celebration in perpetuity. Perpetuity is a long time and a grim concept. Eternity, the mind can only barely boggle with; but perpetuity – on and on and on, in time – is loaded with intolerable predestination.

Since 1605 there has been time for controversy; the official story has been ransacked for variations of it, but the cult of Guy Fawkes flourishes perpetually. His name is a household word in households where the origins of the story are unknown. The American popular 'guy' meaning a 'fellow', is derived from Guy Fawkes, as is our own phrase of humorous contempt 'looking a guy'.

I suggest we have had enough of parliament-imposed glee in perpetuity; the whole thing is inhuman. November the Fifth has become a day of rejoicing more dangerous to life than was the original plot; and at least the plot failed. What never fails is the annual sacrifice of the innocents: excited children burnt, maimed, disfigured and killed by fireworks. We might well spare the hospital beds and the ambulances, and remember the Fifth of November with a shudder. An old and picturesque custom however barbaric might be difficult to stamp out. But certainly an official Pardon for Guy Fawkes would dampen his inflamed annual orgy.

As for a Pardon on its own merits for the failed adventurer, who can doubt that he has earned it? He not only suffered frightfully for his treason, but has been made to atone for it ever since. For an economical convergence of reasons, it would surely be desirable to let him off.

'A penny for the guy': like everything else the present-day guys are not as carefully made as they once were, and are subject to inflation. Guy Fawkes, who, although greatly misguided, was never a depraved man, has been turned into a commercial menace; fireworks manufacturers do better out of him to-day than did the gunpowder suppliers of the seventeenth century.

Besides, the Ecumenical movement deserves a magnanimous gesture. Guilty as he was, plainly Guy Fawkes did not get a legally sound trial, even by the laws of his time. Alas poor Guy! – Procure him a Royal Pardon and let him go.

[1977]

The Religion of an Agnostic

A Sacramental View of the World in the Writings of Proust

Since the death in 1922 of Marcel Proust, his labyrinthine work which is published in twelve volumes under the English title *Remembrance of Things Past* has been regarded increasingly as the greatest novel of the twentieth century; its fame is celebrated even by those who doubt whether it is a novel at all. The reasons are worth examining, why a work of this length, one which demands a specially attentive approach, should enjoy so strong a response from a modern reading public.

For, in Proust, everything occurs on a slow-motion scale. In prose which exerts a drug-like charm, he takes a page to describe for example, a momentary gesture made by an aristocratic friend, and a further four pages to reflect on its meaning; in subsequent volumes Proust continues to re-interpret the gesture in fresh circumstances, until the whole nature of his friend is revealed and a theory of aristocracy constructed on a single gesture remembered from time past. This example represents only one thread in the vast tapestry on which Proust depicts the theme of Time. To an intelligent reader who has not read Proust, it may sound a tedious proceeding. And yet it is the intelligent and especially the sensitive reader who most rapidly becomes addicted to Proust, for reasons which I do not think are entirely due to a right conception of his work.

In Proust can be detected all the attributes of a deeply religious writer, except the two attributes indispensable in a religious writer, a moral sense and a faith. The irreligious environment of modern Europe embraces large numbers of intelligent aspiring souls who are nevertheless looking for a 'religion' which offers all things beautiful and demands nothing practical. These, I think, form the majority of Proust's public.

Proust writes always with the insight of a gifted religious and the fidelity of one devoted to a spiritual cause. He has the introspective enlightenment of a later St Augustine: one who, in his thirty-sixth year, withdrew from a flourishing life in society in order to contemplate its inner decadence, and to whom those very symbols of decay yielded their permanent essence, restored in eternity. It will be clear to the Christian reader who knows Proust's work that his thought repeatedly suggests, but does not coincide with Christian doctrine. Proust was not a Christian, nor was the intention of his work religious. It is necessary to be clear, in reading Proust, that his work is based on a pagan aesthetic.

In spite of which, my purpose is not to denigrate the name of Proust to the Christian reader but to canvass it. For in this truly pagan writer we find something of a tremendous value to the Christian imagination, a sacramental view of life which is nothing more than a balanced regard for matter and spirit. The sacramental dispensation of Providence – the idea that the visible world is an active economy of outward signs embodying each an inward grace – is nothing new to the Church. What has been lost to the European grasp since the seventeenth century is a sacramental conception of matter which is hierarchical* (all material forms possessing an ultimate eternal light) and not evolutionary (one form replacing or usurping another eternally as in the temporal laws of change). The most 'naïve' early cosmologists at least did not hold the notion that once they had looked at an object from all angles they have seen the whole of it, and when they had seen it perish, the last of it. Only a materialistic conception of Time – a strictly chronological one – could have obliterated that understanding of matter which acknowledges outward and changing forms to be invisibly and peculiarly 'possessed', each after its own kind in a spiritual embodiment.

It could be abundantly demonstrated that present-day Christian creative writing, that which is most involved in an attempt to combat materialism, reflects a materialism of its own; this takes the form of a dualistic attitude towards matter and spirit. They are seen too much in a moral conflict, where spirit triumphs by virtue of disembodiment. This is really an amoral conception of spirit. For a corrective to this situation, for a representation of life which, by its very lack of moral concern, escapes the tendency to equate matter with evil, and for an acceptance of that deep irony in which we are presented with the most unlikely people, places and things as repositories of invisible grace, we have to turn to a most unlikely source – Marcel Proust, agnostic, hedonist, self-centred neurotic, exotic darling of the aristocratic salons, sexual pervert, columnist of *Figaro*, the hypochondriac turned chronic invalid, the insufferable hot-house plant.

> I understood that all the material of a literary work was in my past life, I understood that I had acquired it in the midst of frivolous amusements, in idleness, in tenderness and in pain, stored up by me without my divining its destination or even its survival, as the seed has in reserve all the ingredients that will nourish the plant.

This was the literary work which Proust, inscribing a volume to a friend, described as the 'memories of the heart' of which the volume itself was the 'outward and visible form'. To write it, he enshrined himself absurdly in a cork-lined room, excluding the sounds of Paris in the present tense. 'Time, as it flows,' he wrote, 'is so much time wasted and nothing can even be truly possessed save under that aspect

---

*As conceived, for example, in the Elizabethan 'Chain of Being'.

PART IV. RELIGION, POLITICS AND PHILOSOPHY

of eternity which is also the aspect of art.' Lacking a redemptive faith, Proust's attempt was to save himself through art. And in refreshing our vision from a writer like Proust, we are following the tradition whereby a great amount of the most fruitful thought of the Church is derived from the efforts of inspired pagans to save themselves.

Many years after the world of his childhood has passed into oblivion except for certain incidents fixed in his mind, Proust (or the 'Marcel' of the novel) sipped a spoonful of tea, which he did not normally take, in which he had idly dipped a piece of madeleine cake.

> No sooner had the warm liquid, and the crumbs with it, touched my palate, than a shudder ran through my whole body ... An exquisite pleasure had invaded my senses, but individual, detached, with no suggestion of its origin ... I was conscious that it was connected with the taste of tea and cake, but that it infinitely transcended those savours ...
> And suddenly the memory returns. The taste was that of the little crumb of madeleine which on Sunday mornings at Combray (because on those mornings I did not go out before church-time), when I went to say good-day to her in her bedroom, my aunt Leonie used to give me, dipping it first in her own cup of real or of lime-flower tea.

Proust is no casual symbolist. Pursuing this isolated experience whereby he came upon the eternal essence of a mere crumb soaked in tea, and by contemplating the involuntary effects of this, and similar sensations – as when he heard the tinkle of a spoon, or stumbled on an uneven paving-stone – he found 'in the tiny and almost impalpable drop of their essence, the vast structure of recollection'. Most of us will recognise the experience. Suddenly the taste, smell or texture of something evokes the past in a special and meaningful way. Proust used this sensation as a point of contemplation. From it he recovered his past life – the Combray of his childhood, the Paris of his youth, the long Normandy summers, not in their fragmentary 'actual' guise, but in the artistic pattern of eternity. These places, their petty societies, the failing hierarchies of Dukedoms, fruitless love affairs, trivial gossip, vicious men and women, were so many 'monsters immersed in Time'; Proust satirises them in the flesh, by the same method that he exalts their essence, under that 'aspect of eternity which is also the aspect of art'.

Proust in many ways anticipated a revised notion of Time which is still in process of formulation. He regarded Time subjectively, and realised that the whole of eternity is present 'now'. Of the span of his life recollected in its eternal aspect, Proust writes 'I had at every moment to keep it attached to myself ... I could not move without taking it with me.' Proust fixes in our minds that when we use words like 'forever', 'eternal', phrases like 'everlasting life', 'world without end', we refer to an existence here and now, to which we cannot normally approximate. He reminds us that there is a method of apprehending eternity through our senses, analogous to our sacramental understanding of eternity by faith. We get from Proust's definitions a richer conception of the verities we hold by faith, he releases them from their sentimental or habitual connotations. An involuntary act of remembrance, to Proust, is a suggestive shadow of what a voluntary act of remembrance is to a Christian. This is what Proust meant by remembrance:

> Let a sound, a scent already heard and breathed in the past be heard and breathed anew, simultaneously in the present and in the past, real without being actual, ideal without being abstract, then instantly the permanent and characteristic essence hidden in things is freed and our true being which has for so long seemed dead but was not so in other ways awakens and revives, thanks to this celestial nourishment. An instant liberated from the order of time has recreated in us man liberated from the same order, so that he should be conscious of it. And indeed we understand his faith in his happiness even if the mere taste of a madeleine does not logically seem to justify it; we understand that the name of death is meaningless to him ...

Proust, who never once, so far as I recall, used the word 'sacrament' in his novel, is enabled by the persuasive beauty of his language to convey to the world more about the nature of a sacrament than any modern treatise on the subject could hope to teach. In support of which I offer, for comparison with Proust, the definition of the seventeenth-century Anglican Divine, Edward Reynolds:

> The nature of a Sacrament is to be the representative of a substance, the sign of a covenant, the seal of a purchase, the figure of a body, the witness of our faith, the earnest of our hope, the presence of things distant, the sight of things absent, the taste of things inconceivable, and the knowledge of things that are past knowledge.

Which saying about a Sacrament is one to keep in mind when we read *Remembrance of Things Past*.

[1953]

The Only Problem

Before I became a novelist I was a poet and literary critic. I know that the practice of poetry and criticism contributed to my work in the novel form, and that both faculties are to some extent articulated within the fabric of my novels. This is more especially the case in *The Only Problem* than in any other novel I have written.

Years ago I started to study the Book of Job, which is surely one of the loveliest, most intricate and most ambiguous books of the Bible. Uncountable works have been written on Job, and although textual and interpretive scholarship has progressively helped us with the details, it remains unmanageable as a rational narrative, and yet hypnotic as a poem. I intended to write a critical book. In 1954 I wrote a few essays and many notes on the Book of Job, and put away the subject to get on with my life.

But I could never quite leave the Book of Job alone, and it would not leave me alone. Over the years I have begun to think more and more in terms of fiction, of myth. In that context I see life both poetically and critically. I conceived a character of our times, Harvey Gotham, a very rich man, like Job himself, who, also like Job, is a studious type. Harvey Gotham is studying the Book of Job. *The Only Problem* is not in any sense based on the Book of Job but rather, Job is the myth from which my novel proceeds, and there is no literal and exact analogy. The biblical poem is only reflected in my book like a shadow reflected on water.

The Book of Job deals with the problem of suffering – Job cannot understand why God has afflicted him with a series of misfortunes. While he suffers he is visited by three friends, known as his Comforters, who variously represent the then established view that suffering is the result of sin. Job rejects this explanation, insisting on his personal innocence. The Comforters turn into Accusers. To me, there is a touch of a modern police-interrogation about these nerve-wracking dialogues between Job and his friends thousands of years ago. This, too, is reflected in *The Only Problem*.

But above all, I was inspired by the beautiful painting *Job Visited by his Wife* by Georges de La Tour which hangs in the art museum at Epinal in the Vosges district of France. It is a mysterious fact that I had already started the novel and conceived the characters Effie and Ruth, before I had actually seen this picture of Job's magnificent wife. After seeing it myself I naturally 'sent' my hero Harvey Gotham to see it.

The story of Job was a starting point but my story is my own. The problem of suffering is indivisible from life itself. It is insoluble, a mystery. It is a reality, both soft and harsh, and I have sought to convey it.

The American critic, the late Allen Tate, made a claim, in a broadcast discussion, to the effect that a good novel should be a poem. He meant this in a very special sense; he was not thinking of ornate language or of the prose-poem; he meant the intrinsic construction, the conception, the vision. I would wish all my novels, and particularly *The Only Problem*, to be judged under this deep and haunting light.

[1984]

The Mystery of Job's Suffering

For the reader acquainted with the Book of Job but not with Dr Jung's writings, the major difficulty about this book is the idiom, which is largely allegorical. Terms like 'God' and 'Wisdom' are employed, not in their usual theological connotation, but as symbols for psychic concepts.

That Dr Jung does not hesitate to draw theological conclusions is a different question which may be considered in the light of his Preface. There, Dr Jung writes,

> I shall not give a cool and carefully considered exegesis that tries to be fair to every detail, but a purely subjective reaction ... I shall answer injustice with injustice, that I may learn to know why and to what purpose Job was wounded, and what consequences have grown out of this for Yahweh as well as for man.

The Book of Job, according to Dr Jung's thesis, represents a decisive point in human and divine development. (He conceives God and man developing together, dependent one on the other.) It was in the figure of Job that the capricious Yahweh of the Old Testament met his match. Job is subdued to silence only by the thundering of superior brute force; morally, he emerges superior to his Creator. Job, moreover,

> has seen God's face and the unconscious split in his nature. God was now known, and this knowledge went on working not only in Yahweh

but in man too. Thus it was the men of the last few centuries before Christ who, at the gentle touch of the pre-existent Sophia, compensate Yahweh and his attitude, and at the same time complete the anamnesis of Wisdom.

God, having failed to consult with his own omniscience, has revealed to Job a savage, unconscious side of the divine nature. It does not dawn on God until later that Job's submission was insincere, a reply intended to humour and placate the deity rather than express Job's true feelings. The realisation at a later date of Job's moral victory forces God to honour His own attribute of justice. 'Yahweh must become man precisely because he has done man a wrong.'

The cult of Wisdom, occurring about the time of the composition of Job, is cited with emphasis on the typological identification of Wisdom with the Blessed Virgin. God, preparing for the Incarnation, calls Wisdom to mind. Eventually, 'Yahweh's intention to become man, which resulted from his collision with Job, is fulfilled in Christ's life and suffering'.

So far as the Book of Job is concerned, the thesis ends here. As theology, it is far too anthropomorphic to be satisfying; as a history of the development of Hebrew conceptions of God, there is nothing very new. But Dr Jung allows himself the next half of his book in which to speculate seriously on the theological implications of his reading of Job. It is not, therefore, good enough for Dr Jung to plead a 'purely subjective reaction'; his conclusions are didactic, dogmatic, presented in the guise of facts.

A psychological rendering of the post-exilic saga of Israel may be pretty enough, but theology has to do with objective reality; and though Dr Jung's method of 'answering injustice with injustice' produces an intensely real theory as it concerns the experience of Dr Jung himself, we ourselves who also possess souls have to test his reality against our own experience of Job, and our own beliefs.

In Dr Jung's belief, God is an irrational union of opposites containing both good and evil. Although this belief is argued here from the Book of Job, it is well known that a lifetime's study of the human psyche has gone to form the author's opinions. Dr Jung emphasises that to him, God is a 'psychic reality', and that this reality is very real indeed.

The psyche is a natural phenomenon. Dr Jung, as an empiricist, admittedly does not deal with things supernatural. 'It is only through the psyche that we can establish that God acts upon us, but we are unable to distinguish whether these actions emanate from God or from the unconscious. We cannot tell whether God and the unconscious are two different entities.'

That is where his findings differ from those of Christian theology. His further tenet, that God 'continually incarnates through the Holy Ghost in the temporal sphere', is in line with Christian belief, but allied with a dualistic conception of deity, it throws on mankind the tremendous task of bringing to light 'the dark side of God'.

We are at present concerned with these doctrines as they derive from Dr Jung's study of the Book of Job, his rationale.

The Book of Job is a magnificent dramatic poem. It is fictional, not historical; that is clear to the common intelligence and the fact also enjoys the approval of the strictest orthodox. In it a character called 'Job' is ruinously beset by a character called 'Satan' by permission of a character called 'God'. The anonymous poet arranges for Job to engage in a circuitous dialogue with three predatory characters, his Comforters, to whom a fourth is later added.

The poet has conceived Job's character as one which provokes suffering. Job, by his punctilious uprightness, has, in a sense, tempted Satan. When, bereft of his family and property, he sits nursing his boils on an ash-heap while his friends wait silently by him, it is Job who bursts forth with an eloquent curse, the sort of holy blasphemy that is inevitably misunderstood. The Comforters respond, they develop into tormentors. Job's tribulations increase as the poem proceeds. He not only argues the problem of suffering, he suffers the problem of argument.

The harm Satan did to Job seems trivial in comparison with the crushing afflictions which we actually see in progress. He appears surrounded by a conspiracy of mediocrity, obsessed with a raging need to shock them and at the same time to communicate his feelings. The zealous patriarchs are no less exasperated. The appearance of the fourth Comforter, Elihu (whether inserted by a later hand or not), merely aggravates the situation; the dialogue makes no rational progress, and Elihu is in every sense the last straw.

At this point God speaks from the whirlwind; the characters cannot understand each other, but this is something they can all understand. To distinguish God's speech from those of the previous cycles, a close study of the imagery would be necessary; the imagery follows a poetic 'rationale' and indeed it is only by this means that the poet conveys the deeper import of the speeches underlying their apparently inconsequential rhetoric.

In tone, God's first speeches do not differ from what has gone before, in fact he speaks of Himself in terms which appear to support the Comforters rather than Job; the effect is of a grandiloquent display of power. There follows an epilogue, in which God addresses Job and his first three Comforters. Job is commended for what he has spoken, and instructed to pray for his friends, while they, who have not spoken rightly of God, are to offer burnt sacrifices for themselves. Job's property is restored double-fold, and he is blessed with a new family.

The stumbling-block for most intelligent readers of Job is the epilogue. The poet has elevated his hero in our eyes by subjecting him to a purgatorial inquisition; having survived this, Job must, we feel, emerge in a different, more highly spiritualised form. What, then, are we to make of his reward? – 14,000 sheep, 6,000 camels, oxen, asses; seven sons, unnamed; three daughters respectively and frivolously entitled by names which, translated, are 'Turtle Dove', 'Cassia' (a perfume), and 'Box of Eye-Paint'. Can we really imagine our hero enjoying his actual reward? The tendency of commentators to ignore the epilogue is understandable.

The construction of the Book of Job is commonly understood to be as follows: prologue and epilogue, written in prose, are derived from a traditional story, current at the time of composition and representing a pre-exilic, patriarchal point of view. We have here the beginning and the end of the older story (of which a Babylonian version is known), presented by a later hand but preserving the traditional situation. The dialogue, written in verse, makes up the body of the book.

Anyone interested in the literary form of the work will notice the almost Aeschyllian twist which the dialogue gives to the ancient narrative, an observation which is not at odds with modern textual research. It is as if the poet employed the fable in order to question, though not necessarily to refute, its tenets, reflecting as they do the complacent sentiments by which the Comforters take their several stands.

On textual grounds there is no justification for absolutely ignoring the prologue and epilogue. They appear in all texts of Job as we know it. For purposes of exegesis some commentators prefer to regard both prologue and epilogue as decorative, background material, concentrating on the import of the dialogue. It is difficult to suspend consideration of these passages, since they include indispensable information, without which the poem loses all dramatic significance.

Without the prologue, we cannot begin to understand Job's first outburst; and in the epilogue we find the only rational words which God is represented to speak in his answer to Job; that is where Job is instructed to pray for his friends and they to offer sacrifices for themselves. (This is, in fact, the only intelligible answer to the problem of suffering, from a literal reading, which the Book of Job has to offer; the importance of retaining the epilogue should be evident from this fact alone.)

None the less, if commentators make their method sufficiently clear, it is possible to treat the dialogue separately. But there is no logical foundation for the practice of accepting the prologue and rejecting the epilogue. That is what Dr Jung does. He chooses to cut the work short at Job's final speech of submission. He even congratulates the poet on doing so! He actually writes:

> The poet of this drama showed a masterly discretion in ringing down the curtain at the very moment when his hero, by prostrating himself at the feet of God's majesty, gives unqualified recognition to the *apophasis megale* of the demiurge – his 'great declaration' of himself. No other impression was permitted to remain.

Yet the epilogue remains, giving quite a different impression from what Dr Jung asserts of the poem. It is true that the literary sense of Western humanism would be better satisfied without the epilogue, but one cannot edit the writings of the ancients if true knowledge is desired of what went on in their psyche. If Dr Jung wants the prologue (and his whole theory hangs upon it) he must have the epilogue, no less than his hero Job had apparently to suffer his reward.

A sense of horror at God's indulgence of Satan, as it is presented in the prologue, is Dr Jung's predominant motif; himself a compassionate man who has presumably seen much suffering, he is angry with God for permitting evil. Christians accept this fact, and call it a mystery. They mean by this to recognise a situation which cannot be explained by human analogy. At the point where human reason cannot reconcile the fact of evil with the goodness of God, an anthropomorphic conception of God breaks down. Is this not the main point of the Book of Job?

Dr Jung does appear to see that the poem marks a critical stage in the development of Israel; knowledge of God could not be calculated from human standards, that is what the poem teaches. But Dr Jung, if he sees this, does not apply it to his speculative reckonings. By human standards he calculates a God in whom good and evil are together contained. The epilogue of Job reveals, perhaps, too good a God to be true in Dr Jung's conception of what is true. Or is the epilogue too 'goody-goody' to be convincing?

The question turns on the epilogue. And it is, after all, a question of common sense. We are dealing with a work of art; it is susceptible to many interpretations throughout; and then we do not apply the same quality of interpretation to every part. That the prologue and epilogue are to be read in a different sense from the dialogue is obvious; the former are prose writings, the latter verse. The prologue and epilogue belong to the childhood of the race. They are fabulous and suggestive; the dialogue is immediate and particular.

If we read only the prologue and the dialogue, the effect is extremely ironical; add the epilogue and we are given that type of anagogical humour which transcends irony, and which is infinitely mysterious. Read aright, the epilogue is not merely a conventional happy ending; it represents something beyond the reach of discourse which Job, for all he was an upright man, really had to come to terms with in order to gain his peace; some wisdom which combines heavenly ideas with earthly things not the least of which, perhaps, are symbolised by Eye-Paint and her sisters.

[1955]

An Unknown Author

'The Patience of Job' is a popular nineteenth-century concept. I know of no serious or studious reader of Job since, and including, the poet Shelley who ever thought of Job as a patient man. Professor Scheindlin attacks the concept without need. That apart, he has given us a beautiful new translation and a profound commentary which should last a long time in the field of Job studies.

If the Book of Job were a true story, one might be struck by the number of times Job asserts God's innocence, refusing ever to attribute to God any blame for his agonies. Is this because he is being overheard by God? One wonders what Job might have said had he been assured of complete privacy. With God we have none of us any privacy, in itself an almost intolerable burden. If we did not set God aside in our minds for most of the time, we would be semi-paralysed. We could never get anything done, never be ourselves.

The Book of Job is one of the most magnificent narrative dialogue-poems ever written. The original myth sprang from a source or sources known as 'the Babylonian Job', but the Book of Job as we know it belongs to a single author of the fifth or fourth century BC.

It is the one book of the Bible that we are not invited to take literally. There was no real Job in the sense that there was a Moses, an Abraham. Job, like a character in the parables (say, the Good Samaritan), is an idea, not a person of history.

Job is afflicted with great suffering. Some say it was an attack of shingles, which, as anyone who has suffered from the affliction knows, is extremely painful. He is shown sitting alone outside the city, visited by a series of friends who are commonly known as the Comforters. They do little to comfort him. They keep telling him: 'Job, this is a punishment from God. You must have *done* something.' But Job answers emphatically that he has done nothing to deserve this fate. Suffering falls on the worthy and the unworthy alike. 'But Job, you *must* have sinned', they say. 'No,' says Job, 'God is not like that.'

I feel that Job's friends the 'comforters', who come to question and counsel him, and occasionally gloat as he sits outside the city among the ashes, are very much alike. There is a bureaucratic duplication of what they say, and nothing of it really applies to Job's condition. They resemble interrogators sent in one after the other to question a suspected prisoner and try to trip him up.

At this point in Hebrew development the moment was ripe for a Prometheus-like figure to challenge the all-mighty powers of creation. Job challenged God to come out like a man and reason with him.

[…]

What resolves the situation is a whirlwind, and God himself speaking out of it. And from here we come to the finest poetry of all time. God points to his creation of the world.

Professor Scheindlin observes:

> Job's poetry achieves the book's purpose of consolation partly by providing its own vigour as an antidote to its pessimism, by changing the level of the discussion from a meditation on life's injustice to a parade of life's sheer multitudinousness. The poetry is in part a vehicle for steering us away from the suffering with which life burdens us towards the delight at what life has to offer. This is not a quantitative argument. The author does not make the simplistic claim that life's delights are commensurate with or compensation for life's sorrows. He does not make any argument at all. All arguments have been rendered nil by the book's premise. Since the narrative presents Job's complaint as rational and correct, there is no room left for a rational solution. Rather, poetry is used to shift the ground from reason, where life must lose, to emotion, where it at least has a chance.

The construction of the Book of Job is a poetic joy. There was an author, the one who perfected the final Hebrew version. Who was he? How one would like to know.

[1998]

Man's Estate

In *The Phenomenon of Man* Father Teilhard de Chardin applied himself to reconciling Christian theology with natural science. With the same grandeur of vision *Le Milieu Divin* is set in a more specific field to reconcile personal aspirations, the religious and the natural, and to define their ultimate single purpose.

What puts people off Christianity, he says, has nothing to do with historical or theological difficulties. It is a fear that their possible levels of attainment may be diminished if they follow the Gospel teaching. Even among Christians, he says, nine out of ten feel that man's work is always at the level of a 'spiritual encumbrance', worldly success makes them feel guilty. And this is a false idea of Christianity.

We live in a divine milieu or context. God is everywhere and fills all things whether we know it or not; but it is better to know it so that we can act with confidence and detachment. Man must give himself to God but he must first exist, that is develop and fulfil himself; he must possess the world before he can transfigure it by his detachment. There should be no tension in the Christian between God and the world; the two are inseparable. 'The man with a passionate sense of the divine *milieu* cannot bear to find things about him obscure, tepid and empty which should be full and vibrant with God.' Lacking this sense, we have lost our sense of the Second Coming. The Christian affirms it, but 'in reality we should have to admit, if we were sincere, that we no longer expect anything. The flame must be revived at all costs.'

This will probably be opposed by theologians, not for what it says but for what it omits. An Anglican bishop, reviewing the book, has already asked, 'What about Original Sin?' My own first reading gave rise to the speculation that some of the worst tyrants and arch-criminals of history have done their deeds in the belief that they were acting in a 'divine context'. But, says Father Teilhard, your *intentions* must be pure. Yes, we know, all their intentions were pure. A dualistic conception of God and the World (of which the Devil is the Prince) at least ensures that we are never quite certain which side our actions fall on; this way of looking at things is a normal safeguard that we are born with, it somewhat deters the strong from oppressing the weak, and is a natural defect of vision which has perhaps assisted our survival as much as our having eyes only in the front of our heads. Too much range and unity of vision in an imperfect world, and only the Supermen would be left standing.

Which objections, of course, are altogether irrelevant to *Le Milieu Divin*. It is not a moral treatise, nor a theological one. It is a meditation on the psychological development of the Christian. The first parts of the book, which reaffirm the more neglected Christian doctrines, predominantly that of Immanence, are comparatively simple in that they refer to man as he is at present, and only in relation to what he is destined to be. Part III, which deals with the Divine Milieu and its attributes, describes a more ideal state of being, an advanced spiritual condition. To me, the difficulties here are not rational ones, it is all clearly reasoned; they are imaginative difficulties. My mind understands, indeed believes, the proposition: 'The only subject ultimately capable of mystical transfiguration is the whole group of mankind forming a single body and a single soul in charity', but my imagination pictures a revolting great monster. The author insists that personal individuality is retained in a state of completion within this mystical union. It is difficult to imagine. These last pages are for readers more conceptually advanced and less pictorially beset.

Father Teilhard has not, in fact, overlooked the problem of evil, nor the possible objections to his book on this charge. But he is interested in the psychological development of the soul, he speaks of 'growth' and 'diminishment' instead of good and evil. 'Passivities of growth and diminishment' are the universal forces outside our control and knowledge which make for our fulfilment or failure. Sin 'only interests us here in so far as it is a weakening, a deviation caused by our personal faults'; it comes under the same heading as suffering. In diminishment as well as growth, God is to be found.

One is left with the impression that this is an intensely personal book. More than it is, as he claims, addressed to waverers it is the history of the soul of Pierre Teilhard de Chardin, scientist and Jesuit, gifted with a foretaste of eternity and a vast curiosity about the universe.

[1960]

Kierkegaard

Few scholars have done better service to Kierkegaard than Dr T.H. Croxall, who is one of the minority of writers on the subject with a knowledge of both the Danish language and the philosophical environment to which Kierkegaard's Christianity was a corrective. In *Meditations from Kierkegaard* Dr Croxall assembles from his vast writings a number of meditations on the Scriptures and Scriptural personalities. Most of this material is translated by Dr Croxall into English for the first time. As was Kierkegaard's way, partly his intention, these meditations provoke resistance, reservations, qualifications, as well as assent or mere admiration; the main thing is that they do not leave the reader indifferent unless he is indifferent to religion. It is to establish Kierkegaard's religious, and especially Christian, thought as the central factor in his life and writings that Dr Croxall presents his admirable Kierkegaard Commentary, covering the whole of Kierkegaard's work. It is questionable whether Kierkegaard in his entirety – i.e., the sum total of his 'message' – is as relevant to the present day as are certain isolated but luminous fragments. Nevertheless, this is a serviceable summary and exegesis for students of Kierkegaard and of Christian existential philosophy.

[1956]

Karl Heim: Two Important Works

There has been a remarkably wide area of response to the recently translated works of the Lutheran theologian, Professor Heim; the intellectual interior of these islands is rarely penetrated by continental thought within the space of months, and that this has happened in the case of Dr Heim is a testimony to the success of his intentions. Perceiving that most of the modern evangelistic literature which addresses the unbelieving public does not reach any but the believing public, on however popular, distinguished or learned a level it is pitched, Dr Heim starts from the recognition that all such discussion 'is not a dialogue between the Church and the World. It is never more than a monologue of the Church within itself.' The word 'Church' in this connection is used in a sense which includes 'all those who are still within the field of force of any sort of belief'. (One senses behind his mature benign style, Dr Heim's tactful reluctance to use the suggestively pharisaical phrase 'Church and World' at all.)

To reach the unbelieving world, Dr Heim suggests, it is no use theologians proclaiming the Sacraments, the Episcopacy, the Bible, ritual, morals and so on, as the centre of the Faith. God is the point at issue. Furthermore, he observes that the question of God's existence no longer oppresses the majority of intelligent agnostics; the nineteenth-century atheist was a profoundly troubled man, he was essentially religious, and was infinitely vexed by a sense of God's absence from the universal scheme. The modern agnostic has acquired an empirical view of the world, takes life as he finds it, and is content to observe the phenomena of life without the need of positing even so remote a concept as a First Cause. Dr Heim, supporting his assertion with examples from modern writings, and facing the situation without deprecation or moralising, traces its source in a scientific world-view. The top levels of scientific thought have perforce relinquished the Cause principle, and are devoted entirely to Effect.

True missionary fashion, Dr Heim deals with this problem by himself entering the 'scientific' world – the world, that is, which embraces the sciences, literature, and every kind of human creativity within the folds of that empirical attitude to life, that happy indifference to the supernatural (though with the unhappy tendencies of modern neuroses) which he sees stemming from the justifiable methods of physical science. It is the purpose of the present books, as well as further promised works in the series, to expound the Faith to this entire area, in its own terms. Learned in natural science and in modern agnostic literature, in the psychological writings and the philosophies which inform our age, Dr Heim possesses the rare twin merits of a far-ranging vision and a grasp of his single appointed task of introducing God into the scheme of things before him. Many writers in recent years have attempted to tie up this or that scientific discovery or philosophy with this or that doctrine. St Thomas Aquinas may have anticipated Jung, St Augustine may have been ahead of Bergson; but this is no compelling idea to the modern unbeliever. Dr Heim, surveying the landscape of the 'scientific world view', demonstrates that science has now reached a point at which it is necessary, for practical purposes, to presuppose a perpetually unknowable factor; before it can pursue its aim of discovering the unknown, physical science needs must acknowledge a factor which it is incapable of knowing. This is supported by abundant quotation from authoritative scientific sources, and Dr Heim, in St Paul's fashion, locates the unknown God in the vacant 'unknowable' of the scientific world.

For the reader who is neither scientist nor theologian, Dr Heim is not easy reading, but that is only to say he makes slow reading. The language, where it is technical, is not beyond the lay reader, for its framework is essentially humane. Drawing upon a vast field of scholarship and creative literature, the books constitute what our forbears were wont to call 'an education in themselves'.

[1954]

Letter from Rome: The Elder Statesmen

'It was an historic occasion,' said Mrs Golda Meir, and this, too, was the definition given to the encounter by Pope Paul VI when he received her in audience on 15th January 1973. It was a moment of history surrounded with historic misunderstandings, informed by a rather atavistic echo of ancestral voices and unaccountably not what it was intended to be. 'It was an application of Murphy's Law,' said one Vatican dignitary in a resigned voice. What was Murphy's Law? 'Murphy's Law,' said the dignitary, 'is that everything that can possibly go wrong will go wrong.' The main reason for the meeting between the Pope and the Prime Minister of Israel, was of course to take a step towards peace in the Middle East. But no sooner had Mrs Meir driven away from the Vatican than a different kind of question took over: what is the Church's present attitude to the Jews?

The Pope was seventy-five, some months older than Golda Meir. He was born into a pious Catholic professional family in a provincial town north of Milan. She was born in Kiev at the south-west of Tsarist Russia into a family of poor Jews and was taken on an immigrant ship to the United States. At the age of twenty-three Golda Meir, already an active Zionist, went to Palestine. At the same age young Montini in Italy was ordained priest. The confrontation at the Vatican was between two tenacious characters, each thoroughly formed by a long lifetime's dedication to causes and cultures vastly different and yet somehow akin: basically, both the Vatican State and the State of Israel owe their conception and territorial existence to the doctrine that God says so. It is always an unarguable claim: you have to take it or leave it.

In Rome, the announcement late on 14th January that Golda Meir was to visit the Pope the next day was not treated with much comment or any special surprise. Every celebrity who makes a progress through Europe, from Yugoslavian pop singers to the daughters of United States Presidents, stops off to see the Pope. Nobody expected the material for a Verdi opera that in fact came out of it.

What happened was only to be pieced together two weeks later after the Vatican spokesmen, pestered tenderly day by day by the press and other nosey-parkers, finally came round to admitting all the points of the Israeli version. 'You see,' remarked the Israeli Ambassador to Italy, 'our form of Machiavellianism is to speak the truth.'

The Italians took exceptional security precautions for Golda Meir's visit to Rome from 14th to 16th January. It was only a few weeks after the terrorist attempt on the Israeli Embassy at Bangkok. Her plan to visit the Pope on the 15th had evidently not been made known to any of the Arab states who have diplomatic relations with the Vatican and it was not until late on Sunday, 14th, that the Arabs heard of it. Israel, who has no diplomatic ground in the Vatican, had prepared the visit through its Ambassador to Italy, Amiel Najar. The Vatican had left the Israelis free to announce the forthcoming meeting at their own time. For security reasons the Israelis chose to hold over the announcement until the preceding day.

Informal talks between Israel and Vatican representatives have been going on since 1967. Abba Eban, the Israeli Foreign Minister, was received by the Pope in 1969. A former Governor of Jerusalem, Dr Chaim Herzog, had an audience with the Pope in 1971. The Israeli Ambassador to Italy was present on both occasions. The idea of arranging a meeting between Mrs Meir and the Pope at some opportune moment had often been discussed and was well prepared for. When Golda Meir's visit to Paris in January of 1973 was known, the Ambassador ascertained that a request for an audience would receive a positive reply. (This is the rule of protocol: one always formally applies for an audience with the Pope, although, says the Vatican, a certain amount of diplomatic 'ascertaining' and 'indicating' on one or the other side usually precedes a papal audience with a head of government.) Anyway, as Golda Meir pointed out later, there's no shame involved in asking the Pope to receive the Prime Minister of Israel any more than there's a loss of honour in asking to meet President Nixon or any other political personality.

As it happened, the Ambassador took the opportunity of asking, first Mrs Meir if she was agreeable to the meeting, then his friends in the Vatican. He was told by telephone on 10th January that the

Pope would be agreeable. Then the day and the hour were arranged. A statement intended for release after the audience by the Vatican Press Office was negotiated first in draft then finally agreed between Najar for the Israeli government and the appropriate Vatican office.

On 12th January an official invitation to Mrs Golda Meir arrived at the Israeli Embassy, from the Prefecture of the Vatican. So far, every step of the ceremonial dance, in perfect order.

This agreed statement, later headed Bulletin No. 12, reads as follows (translated from the Italian):

A communiqué on Mrs Golda Meir's visit

This morning, 15th January 1973, at 12.15, His Holiness, Pope Paul VI received in audience Her Excellency, Mrs Golda Meir, Prime Minister of Israel, who was accompanied by the Israeli Ambassador to Italy, His Excellency, Mr Amiel E. Najar.

The themes of the talk, which lasted about an hour, were the Middle East situation and the particular problems concerning the Holy Land.

His Holiness, after recalling the history and the sufferings of the Jewish people, put forward the Holy See's point of view on matters which primarily have close connections with its humanitarian mission, such as the problem of the refugees and the situation of the various communities living in the Holy Land, and those matters concerning more specifically its religious mission, so far as that concerns the Holy Places and the sacred and universal character of the city of Jerusalem.

The Prime Minister emphasized Israel's will for peace and amply explained the Israeli position on the possibility of reaching a peaceful solution of the Middle East conflict through negotiations between the parties concerned; and on the above-mentioned topics she touched not only on the phenomenon of terrorism but also on particular situations concerning Jewish communities in certain parts of the world.

His Holiness ended by expressing his fervent wishes that justice and right should establish peace and coexistence amongst all the peoples of the Middle East, and he once again expressed the Holy See's intention to do everything it possibly could to achieve this end.

Mrs Meir arrived for the audience at 12.15 p.m. Full preparation had been made; the courtyards were clear; the guards of honour lined the way.

Mrs Meir left the Vatican at 1.30. The Pope had presented her with a silver dove, suitably inscribed. As she drove away under heavy escort the reporters rushed to the press room for the hand-out.

Here, the Vatican Press Officer, Federico Alessandrini, a lay man, read a statement which was then handed out to the world press. It goes as follows (translated from the Italian):

Verbal Statement by the Director of the Press Office on the Audience of Mrs Golda Meir

Concerning the visit of Mrs Golda Meir, Prime Minister of Israel, to the Holy Father, I want to point out that it is not an exclusive or preferential gesture. In fact Paul VI has received King Hussein of Jordan and other high officials of the world and of the Arab countries; and the Holy See, as is known, has cordial relations with Egypt, Lebanon and Syria, in the same way that it has diplomatic relations with various other Arab countries, such as Tunisia, Algeria, Kuwait and Iraq.

The audience was requested by Mrs Golda Meir, taking advantage of her trip to Paris, and it was not the object of prior agreements or 'programizations' [previous talks or 'programmes'].

This audience neither signifies nor implies the least change – and in fact there has been no change, nor, moreover, are there any grounds for one – in the attitude of the Holy See concerning the problems of the Holy Land; an attitude that was confirmed by His Holiness in his address to the Cardinals on 22nd December, 1972 [an unprovocative and not widely publicised plea for the rights of Palestinians in the Middle East to be realised in harmony with the rights of other peoples there]. Even with regard to Israel this attitude is unchanged.

The Pope granted Mrs Golda Meir's request because he believes it to be his duty not to miss any opportunity to act in favour of peace, in defence of the rights of the human individual and of communities, in defence of the religious interests of all and especially in aid of the weakest and most defenceless, primarily the Palestinian refugees. As for the defence and protection of religious interests, one need not mention that in this specific case it is a question of the native and inalienable rights of the three monotheistic religions, connected with the universal and pluralistic character special to Jerusalem.

The previously negotiated bulletin was later put out in Italian, only over Radio Vatican and in the *Osservatore Romano*.

Golda Meir had an appointment that afternoon with Mr Andreotti, Prime Minister of Italy. During her visit to Italy she was treated in the best possible manner by the Italian State and Government; although her visit was a private one she was given the facilities of a state visit. It was not until her arrival at the Israeli Embassy, just before a press conference, that she was told about the Alessandrini version. During the conference she diplomatically stuck to the negotiated version of her papal audience. 'Mrs Meir,' asked a journalist, 'have you seen or heard about the statement that the Vatican issued following your meeting with the Pope? At least some people are describing it as a diplomatic slap in the face...' This was understating the case. People were describing it as a stab in the back, Borgia-style, and the Italian papers for the most part protested strongly on the subject. 'I'm very appreciative that the Pope found it possible to receive me and very happy that the audience took place,' Mrs Meir told this conference.

Next day, the Pope saw fit to send Mrs Meir further presents: a two-volume rare edition of the Bible splendidly bound with his coat of arms and a Vatican Library catalogue.

Two days later, Alessandrini gave an interview to a Jewish correspondent of the English-language *Daily American*, published in Rome. He gave it as his personal opinion that Israel over-played their Prime Minister's visit, 'irritating the Holy See and forcing it to issue the second statement'. He denied that the statement was all his own work: 'anyone who knows how the Vatican works also knows I could hardly have thought up that statement myself'. He said his statement was meant to contradict an Israeli announcement that the meeting was held at the Pope's initiative.

Thereafter Mr Alessandrini was unobtainable on the subject. His assistant explained: 'A verbal declaration is not an official declaration.' – 'What's the difference?' – 'One is verbal and the other is not.' – 'I'm afraid I don't understand the distinction and I'd like an appointment with Mr Alessandrini.' – 'Mr Alessandrini *wrote the statement himself.* Mr Alessandrini can't say any more.'

Is it possible, we onlookers in Rome asked ourselves, that the Church has changed its scapegoat overnight? – It is no longer the Jews, it is Alessandrini.

Another voice from the Vatican, this time of an archiepiscopal timbre: 'Alessandrini didn't do it. He was only obeying orders. The tone and the timing were deplorable, especially the tone.' – 'Well, it was ordered by someone in the Secretariat?' – 'Nobody will ever know.'

Still, everyone did want to know what was going on back there in the Vatican. The lack of any public relations system adequate to modern times only serves to increase the zeal of the lay-inquisition. In the Vatican, that strong octopus, none of the right hands of which knows what the left are doing, there are other communications-offices besides the press office. 'What happened,' another personage of communications explained, 'is that the audience was to have been kept secret until afterwards, but the news was leaked to the Israeli cabinet and it got in the press too soon.' – 'Is this official?' – 'No, I believe I read it somewhere in the newspapers.'

Next, in reply to some pages of written questions submitted at the suggestion of another good-hearted Vatican personality came the note: 'That [Archbishop Giovanni] Benelli [of the Secretariat of State] was party to the statement is I should say certain. Whether he vetted the final version, much less so. That the Pope saw it in advance is extremely unlikely.'

Yes, but the most important question was why the second statement was substituted for the first, at the last moment behind the Israelis' back.

'Arab pressure,' was the general answer.

Meantime, on her return to Israel, Mrs Meir had a heart-to-heart interview with the Hebrew newspaper *Ma'ariv* about her visit to the Pope. She confirmed: 'Our Ambassador in Rome was told, "If you request a meeting with the Pope there will be a positive response."' Mrs Meir then dropped some amazing news about the audience itself: 'Right at the start I didn't like it at all. Right at the start the Pope told me he found it difficult to understand how the Jewish people, who should conduct themselves mercifully, should react, in their country, so harshly. I can't stand it,' said Mrs Meir, 'when they talk like that ... So I said to the Pope "Your Holiness," (that's how I addressed him all during the conversation, and he called me "Your Excellency"), "do you know the first memory of my life? The Pogrom of Kiev! When we were merciful, and didn't have a country and were weak, then they took us to the gas chamber."'

The important thing, Mrs Meir was at pains to stress, was that the meeting took place. But the idea that a modern Pope could be so far out of touch with reality as to start weighing in to a modern Prime Minister (the first woman head of government to be received in the Vatican) on the level of the old-time Renaissance moral admonishment of the Jews, rather gave the outsider to blink.

The audience did not literally start in quite so abrupt a manner. Certainly, there was an exchange of courtesies. The Pope declared himself honoured on this historic occasion and Golda Meir expressed herself honoured on the historic occasion. The talk proceeded, according to Mrs Meir, in an atmosphere of tranquil solemnity.

It is clear, now, that late on the night of January 14th, having heard the news of Golda Meir's visit planned for the following day, the representatives of the Arab States with whom the Vatican has formal diplomatic relations, put a concerted pressure on the Pope's Secretariat of State to make a counter-statement.

The Secretary of State is Cardinal Jean Villot, and there is no need at all to go into all the creepy demonology of what personality cited by which 'source close to the Vatican' is responsible for foreign diplomacy, because Cardinal Villot is responsible for his department, as in real life. Of the two under-Secretaries of State, Archbishop Benelli was plainly put in charge of the Arab countries' complaints. The Arabs had not been consulted. They felt aggrieved. In a panic, late at night Vatican time, at least after 9 p.m., the bulletin was drafted. And if the Pope did not see the actual wording, then he is not exercising his authority enough. He must have been told of the new statement, and his moralising approach to the Prime Minister of Israel was very probably a reaction to the embarrassment he felt. 'The whole affair was harsh, it was not Christian,' said a Catholic Priest in Rome whose entire job is Christian–Jewish relationships. 'Do you think the Vatican's hand-out suggests that the Israelis alone are responsible for the plight of the Palestinian Arabs?' – 'Yes, coming at that moment, the statement can't mean anything else. We have to stop blaming the Jews for everything and look into ourselves. It was not *Christian*.'

Estimates of the number of Roman Catholics in the world put the number at probably between 500 and 600 million. The Reformation never took hold in Italy, and although the Ecumenical Council indicated to Italian Churchmen the existence in the world of another estimated 500 million Christians who don't acknowledge the Pope as their leader, the notion that the Pope is not the spokesman for the whole of Christendom has not yet sunk in.

'It may be,' said an official of the World Council of Churches (which represents 400 million non-Roman Catholics), 'that the Pope sometimes says something of such spirituality that the whole world says "Amen". But it can never be said that the Pope speaks for the whole of Christianity.'

In her interview with *Ma'ariv* Golda Meir spoke happily of the Pope's gratitude for the Israelis' care of the holy places in Jerusalem. 'He said thank you three times: thank you, thank you, thank you.' That is delightful, but it does not mean that the Christian shrines in Jerusalem and other parts of Israel are largely under control of the Catholic Church. The Greek Orthodox Church is the title-holder to vastly more of the holy places on Israeli territory than any other church. Strong interests in the Holy Land by way of hospices, study centres, schools and shrines are held by numerous other non-Catholic bodies, not all of whom share the Pope's anxiety for the internationalisation of Jerusalem.

None of them, so far as one can gather, shares the view that the Vatican's diplomacy on the visit of Mrs Golda Meir is much of a contribution towards resolving the conflict in the Middle East.

The British Methodist, Lord Soper, who is Secretary of the Society for Christian–Jewish Relations, said forcefully, 'You can quote me as saying that the Pope's treatment of Golda Meir was gratuitous and uncalled-for. The Christians should be the last to preach the virtue of mercy to the Jews.' Lord Soper said, with some reason, that we might all have sympathy with the Palestinian Arabs and see their point of view, but the occasion of the Prime Minister of Israel's visit was not the moment to express it. 'Mrs Meir,' he said, 'behaved with great dignity under the circumstances.'

At the Church of England communications office, a spokesman said they frequently went along with the Pope. But he knew very well from his dealings with Jews that they did not know very much about the development of the Christian church, just as he supposed the Christians knew too little about them. It would be easily assumed by the young Israelis that the Pope spoke for the whole of Christianity.

'Back to the Middle Ages,' was the comment of a young Greek Orthodox priest. 'When the Jews are in question the Pope speaks when he shouldn't and fails to speak when he should. For us, the days of hatred and contempt between Christians and Jews are past. Our relations with the Jewish people in Israel are good: on both sides, respectful indifference, tolerance. Our dialogue with the Jews is mainly concerned with interpretations of the Old Testament.' On the question of the Pope's stated efforts towards conciliation he said, 'It's out of date.'

From another official of the World Council of Churches: 'Mrs Golda Meir might well come and visit us in Geneva. She might very well do so.'

Then, from the Presbyterian spokesman of the Church of Scotland: 'I don't think that in any way anyone could say that the poverty and defencelessness of the Palestinian refugees solely rests with the Israeli Government. One would obviously ask what about the use to which Jordan has put UNESCO aid.' It was probably unnecessary to ask, once more, if he thought the Pope had spoken for the whole of Christianity. However, this Scottish Churchman drily replied, 'The Pope speaks only for the Roman Catholics.'

And not always for the Roman Catholics. In Rome the people like to do things in style. The natural Italian sense of hospitality was afflicted by what went on behind the high sheltering walls of the

Vatican. Whatever their feelings about the Middle East, Italians felt the incident set a poor example in ethics and taste. 'She would never have been treated like that if she had gone to visit King Hussein,' was one of their more memorable remarks.

[1973]

Ritual and Recipe

One learns with surprise that *Cannibalism and Human Sacrifice*, by Garry Hogg, is the first book devoted entirely to this subject to be published in England. It is intended for the general reader who, accustomed to coming across scattered references to cannibalism in anthropological studies, will probably find the more concentrated effect of this work rather alarming.

Garry Hogg has made intelligent use of Missionary Society transactions and missionary letters, as well as the best anthropological works. It appears that the motives for cannibalism are sometimes more simple than is popularly thought. Though the custom can often be attributed to primitive religious rituals, magic and tribal revenge, some cannibals – notably those of the Fiji Islands up to at least the end of the nineteenth century – ate human flesh because they liked it. Moreover, the author tells us, once the taste for human flesh has been indulged it has been widely found to develop into 'a fierce and eventually unappeasable lust for flesh which no mere animal flesh can satisfy'.

Cannibalism was fairly universal in ancient times. The Irish ate their dead; the Scots ate their enemies. Hogg's researches cover the cannibal habits, rituals and gruesome recipes of several continents, and his work ends with a brief outline of the Mau Mau's more politically deliberate man-eating activities.

[1958]

The Next World and Back

Never has so much been written about a place of which nobody knows a thing. When religious Victorians put about that the Hereafter was not a place but a State of Being, the sublime Cardinal Newman opined that the idea of place was inherent in that of the after-life.

It is a place where I would like to go and come back to write a book about. But to the most sophisticated of travellers it is Hamlet's 'Undiscovered country from whose bourn / No traveller returns'. I must say most of the Christian ideas of Heaven are fascinating as a visitor's project but no place to settle. I would love to see the Heaven predicted by the anonymous medieval singer of England:

> Thy walls are made of precious stones,
>   Thy bulwarks diamonds square;
> Thy gates are of right orient pearl,
>   Exceeding rich and rare.

But it would be uncomfortable, as is Ezekiel's vision of the firmament, noisy with the wings of massive angels. Dante's *Paradiso* is to me a fireworks show.

Nor would I be content in a general place where all good souls are supposed to go. Oh God, imagine finding yourself seated in a celestial omnibus next to Billy Graham! Far rather would I reside in the shady groves of the pagan outsiders, Aristotle, Virgil, Socrates.

As for Hell, there is no visiting that place. To my mind it is the essential void. 'Hell is empty,' cries Ferdinand in *The Tempest*, 'and all the devils are here'. With that, few would disagree.

[1990]

Publishing History

Part I. Art and Poetry

The Golden Fleece
Apart from the Poetry Society editorials, this was one of Muriel Spark's earliest known essays, published March 1948 in *Argentor, The Journal of the National Jewellers' Association* (London).

The First Christmas Eve
Essay on the *Madonna del Parto* fresco by Piero della Francesca, Monterchi, commissioned by and published in *Vanity Fair*, December 1984, under their title 'Spirit and Substance'.

Love
Commissioned by *Mademoiselle*, but first published in *Partisan Review*, 1984. (A mangled version, with unauthorised insertions, changes and abridgements, was also published in the *London Daily News*, February 1987.) Published in volume form in *The Norton Book of Love*, 1998.

Ravenna: City of Mosaics
Commissioned by and published in *The New York Times* magazine *Sophisticated Traveler*, Part 2, 'Legendary Cities', 4 October 1987, under their title 'Ravenna's Jeweled Churches'. Reprinted by *Antique and New Art*, Winter 1990, under their title 'The Ravenna Mosaics'.

The Art of Verse
Broadcast 13 February 1999 on the BBC Radio 4 *Today* programme and subsequently published in *The Scotsman*, 1999 and in the *Literary Review*, December 2000/January 2001.

Ruskin and Read
Review of Peter Quennell's *Selected Writings of John Ruskin* (Falcon Press, 1952) and Herbert Read's *The Philosophy of Modern Art* (London: Faber & Faber, 1952), published 1952.

Robert Burns
Reviews of *Dirt and Deity* by Ian McIntyre (London: Harper Collins, 1995), published in the *Daily Mail*, Saturday 21 October 1995, under their title 'Auld Acquaintance, Not Forgot'; and of *The Tinder Heart* by Hugh Douglas (Alan Sutton Publishing Ltd, 1996), published in *The Sunday Times* Books, 23 June 1996, under their title 'Highland Flings'.

Andrew Young
Extract from 'What You Say and How You Say It', review of *Andrew Young – Collected Poems* (London: Jonathan Cape, 1950) with wood engravings by Joan Hassall, published in *Poetry Quarterly*, Winter 1950/51.

Giacomo Manzù
Interview with the sculptor, commissioned by and published in *Architectural Digest*, May 1988 and republished on the death of Manzù in *Scotland on Sunday*, February 1991.

The Desegregation of Art
The Blashfield Foundation Address to the American Academy and Institute of Arts and Letters, New York, 1970, published in *Proceedings of The American Academy of Arts and Letters*, 1971 (New York: Spiral Press). Reprinted in *The Month*, 1972.

The Wisdom of Mr T.S. Eliot
Review of *The Confidential Clerk* at its opening at the Edinburgh Festival, published in the 'Edinburgh Festival Diary' of the *Church of England Newspaper*, Friday 11 September 1953.

Ingersoll Foundation – T.S. Eliot Award (1992)
Speech of acceptance of the Award, given at the Drake Hotel, Chicago, 12 November 1992.

Pensée: T.S. Eliot
Extract from 'A New Voice on an Old Theme', review of Michael Mason's poem *The Legacy* (Sheed & Ward), published in the *Journal of the Scottish Secondary Teachers' Association*, October 1953.

The Complete Frost
Review of *The Complete Poems of Robert Frost* (London: Jonathan Cape, 1951), published in *Public Opinion* No. 4662, Friday 30 March 1951.

John Masefield
Introduction to Muriel Spark's biography of the poet (London: Peter Nevill, 1953 and New York: Coward, McCann, 1966; reissued London: Macmillan, 1962), with a note to the new Hutchinson edition (1991) and Pimlico reprint (1992). Also published in *The New Yorker* magazine, 26 August 1991, under the title 'Personal History: Visiting the Laureate'. (Original text taken from Muriel Spark holograph manuscript 'Gutch Memorandum', National Library of Scotland, Edinburgh.)

Decorative Art
Review of 'Professor' George Burchett's *Memoirs of a Tattooist*, edited and compiled by Peter Leighton (Oldbourne Press), published in the *Observer*, Sunday 4 May 1958.

Poetry and Politics
Essay published in *Parliamentary Affairs*, Journal of the Hansard Society, Vol. I No. 4, Autumn 1948.

Emily Brontë
Introduction to *Selected Poems of Emily Brontë*, selected and edited by Muriel Spark (London: Grey Walls Press, 'Crown Classics', 1952).

Part II. Autobiography and Travel

My Most Memorable New Year's Eve
Commissioned by and published in the *New York Times Book Review* in Enid Nemi's article of 21 December 1982.

When I Was Ten
Published in the *Daily Telegraph*, London, 15 March 2003.

Pensée: Scottish Education
Taken from answers to questions from *Il Messaggero* newspaper, Rome, July 2003.

My Book of Life
Published in the *Sunday Telegraph*, London, 18 March 2001, under the title 'Guide to Life'.

Note on My Story 'The Gentile Jewesses'
Extract from BBC Third Programme broadcast talk, 1963.

The Celestial Garden Party
Essay published in the *Telegraph Magazine*, London, Autumn/Winter fashion special, 14 September 2002, under the title 'Addicted to Hats'.

What Images Return
First published in the *New Statesman*, 10 August 1962, under the title 'Edinburgh Born'. Reprinted in *Memoirs of a Modern Scotland*, edited by Karl Miller (London: Faber & Faber, 1970).

The Poet's House and Comment on 'The Poet's House'
Both published in *Encounter*, XXX, No. 5, 5 May 1968. First broadcast on BBC Home Service, 7 July 1960.

Footnote to 'The Poet's House'
Published in *Architectural Digest*, November 1985. Reprinted in the *Independent Magazine*, 5 November 1988.

My Madeleine
First published in *The New Yorker* magazine, 25 December 2000 and 1 January 2001. Published in London in *Tatler*, November 2001, as 'The One that Got Away'. Reprinted in *QPB Calendar of Days, 2004*, USA.

How I Became a Novelist
Originally a BBC radio broadcast talk called 'Two of a Kind', 26 April 1960. Published in *John O'London's Weekly*, III, No. 61, 1 December 1960 and in *Books and Bookmen*, November 1961.

The Writing Life
First published in the *Washington Post* Book World, 11 March 2001; reprinted by the *Washington Post* in *The Writing Life: Writers on How They Think and Work. A Collection from the Washington Post Book World*, edited with an introduction by Marie Arana (New York: Public Affairs, 2003).

Living in Rome
Commissioned by and first published in *The New York Times* magazine *Sophisticated Traveler*, 13 March 1983, under their title 'My Rome', and in volume form in *The Sophisticated Traveler: Beloved Cities Europe* (New York: Villard Books, 1984). Reprinted in the *London Weekend Telegraph*, Saturday 2 April 1988 under the title 'There's No Place Like Rome'. Subsequently published in Italian and English in the anthology

Italy: The Best Travel Writing from The New York Times (Istituto Geografico De Agostini, 2004).

Venice
Commissioned by and first published in *The New York Times* magazine *Sophisticated Traveler*, 25 October 1981, under the title 'Venice in Fall and Winter'. Reprinted in Italian and English in the anthology *Italy: The Best Travel Writing from The New York Times* (Istituto Geografico De Agostini, 2004). Reprinted in *Desiring Italy*, ed. Susan Cahill (New York: Fawcett Columbine, 1997). (Muriel Spark's original title: 'Venice Out of Season'.)

Istanbul
Written October 1988. Commissioned by *The Sunday Times*, London, and published by them in their 'Travel and Leisure' section, 24 September 1989, under the title 'A Living Museum'. (Muriel Spark's original title: 'Sailing to Byzantium'.)

Tuscany By Chance
Commissioned by and published in *The New York Times* magazine *Sophisticated Traveler*, 7 October 1984, under the title 'Side Roads of Tuscany'.

The Sitter's Tale
Commissioned by and published in the *Independent on Sunday*, 22 August 1999.

Italian Days
Replies to questions from *Il Messaggero* newspaper, Rome, July 2003. Published in Italian under the title 'Quell'indulgenza che conquista', 14 August 2003. Unpublished in English.

The David Cohen British Literature Prize, 1997
Speech of acceptance given 19 March 1997 at Coutts Bank, Piccadilly, London, for the David Cohen British Literature Prize 'For a Lifetime's Achievement'. Published in *The Times*, London, 20 March 1997, under the title 'The Best Part of a Lifetime: Muriel Spark on her Place in English Letters'.

Part III. Literature

How to Write a Letter
First published in the *Independent Magazine*, 18 August 1990. Reprinted in *The Melbourne Age*.

Our Dearest Emma
Review of Lozania Prole, *Our Dearest Emma* (London: Museum Press Ltd, 1949).

Passionate Humbugs
Review of *Queens of the Circulating Library*, ed. Alan Walbank (London: Evans Brothers, 1950) and *Ouida* by Eileen Bigland (London: Jarrolds Ltd, 1950), published in *Public Opinion* No. 4657, Friday 23 February 1951.

Pensée: Biography
Extract from review 'Pageantry and Realism', published in *Public Opinion* No. 4638, Friday 13 October 1950.

Fuzzy Young Person
Review of *Bettina: A Portrait* by Arthur Helps and Elizabeth Jane Howard (London: Chatto, 1957), published in the *Observer*, Sunday 29 September 1957, under the title 'Romantic'.

The Brontës as Teachers
Essay published in *The New Yorker* magazine, 22 January 1966. Reprinted in Muriel Spark's *The Essence of the Brontës* (London: Peter Owen, 1993; Manchester: Carcanet, 2014). The essay has been translated and published in France, Germany and Italy.

My Favourite Villain: Heathcliff
Originally broadcast on the BBC's Light Programme, *Woman's Hour*, 12 October 1960. Reprinted in Muriel Spark's *The Essence of the Brontës* (London: Peter Owen, 1993; Manchester: Carcanet, 2014).

Mrs Gaskell
Review of *Elizabeth Gaskell: Her Life and Work* by Annette Brown Hopkins (London: John Lehmann, 1952), published in *The Contemporary Review*, vol. 186 (1954), edited by A. Strachan, p. 124, 'Muriel Spark on Mrs Gaskell, 1954'.

Mary Shelley
'Author's Note' written 2006; 'Proposal', written 1950. Muriel Spark's critical biography of Mary Shelley was first published as *Child of Light: A Reassessment of Mary Wollstonecraft Shelley* (Hadleigh, Essex: Tower Bridge Publications, 1951), revised as *Mary Shelley* (New York: Dutton, 1987; London: Constable, 1988); reissued in 2013 by Carcanet Press, Manchester, including the 'Author's Note' and 'Proposal'.

Mary Shelley: Wife to a Genius
Published in *Public Opinion*, 2 February 1951.

Frankenstein and *The Last Man*
Originally broadcast on the BBC Light Programme, Thursday 1 February and Friday 2 February 1951 (recorded). Published in *The Listener*, 22 February 1951, under the title 'Mary Shelley, a Prophetic Novelist'.

Shelley's Last House
Commissioned by and published in *Architectural Digest*, June 1986, under the title 'Echoes of Shelley in Italy'. Reprinted in the *Independent Magazine*, 29 July 1989 and *Ulysse 2000* in Italy, September 1989, under the title 'La Casa dei Presagi'.

The Essential Stevenson
Extracts from review published in *Public Opinion*, 10 November 1950, of *Stevenson and Edinburgh* by Moray McLaren (London: Chapman & Hall, 1950), *The Tales and Essays of Robert Louis Stevenson*, edited by G.B. Stern (London: The Falcon Press, 1950) and *Selected Poems of Robert Louis Stevenson*, edited by G.B. Stern (London: Grey Walls Press, 1950).

Robert Louis Stevenson
Address given on the occasion of Muriel Spark's unveiling a stone memorial dedicated to R.L.S. by Ian Hamilton Finlay in Princes Street Gardens, Edinburgh, 14 July 1989.

Celebrating Scotland
Opinion sent to the Royal Society of Edinburgh regarding *Celebrating Scotland: A National Cultural Strategy*. Unpublished letter, August 1999.

The Books I Re-Read and Why
Answer to question from *The New York Times Book Review*, published summer 1983.

London Exotics
Originally published in June 1953 in the *Scottish Secondary Teachers' Association Magazine*. Reprinted in *The New Yorker* magazine, 28 January 1967, under the title 'Exotic Departures'.

A Drink with Dame Edith
Memoir published by the *Literary Review*, London, February 1997. Muriel Spark's original title: 'Drinks with Edith Sitwell: A Memoir'.

Pensée: *Miss Brodie* on the Stage
Unpublished note written in response to the stage version of *The Prime of Miss Jean Brodie* at the National Theatre, London, 1998.

The Short Story
Address given at an international conference on the short story at Angers University, France, 21 January 1989.

Daughter of the Soil
Essay published in the *Observer*, Sunday 12 January 1958, under their title 'Best-Sellers of the Century – 9' (*Gone with the Wind* by Margaret Mitchell).

Heinrich Böll
Response to the brief 'The Living Author I Most Admire', commissioned by and published in *The New York Times Book Review*, 4 December 1977.

Eyes and Noses
Essay published in the *Observer*, Sunday 18 January 1953.

Simenon: A Phenomenal Writer
Review of Pierre Assouline, *Simenon: A Biography* (London: Chatto & Windus, 1997), translated from the French by Jon Rothschild, published in *The Sunday Times*, 17 August 1997.

The Book I Would Like to Have Written – and Why
Reply to question from *The New York Times Book Review*, published December 1981.

Pensée: The Supernatural
Answer to a question published in the newspaper *Il Messaggero* (Rome), July 2003.

Part IV. Religion, Politics and Philosophy

Testament of Faith
Review of *Thoughts for Meditation*, selected by N. Gangulee with a Foreword by T.S. Eliot (London: Faber & Faber, 1951), published in *Public Opinion* No. 4671, Friday 1 June 1951.

Ailourophilia
Essay published in *Book Week*, 27 December 1964, under the pseudonym 'Evelyn Cavallo'. (Muriel Spark wrote a review of cat books with this title which was published in the *Observer*, 15 December 1957.)

All God's Creatures
Abbreviated essay published in *Seven Days*, the magazine of the *Glasgow Herald*, 9 January 2000. Muriel Spark's original title: 'Dogs, Cats and Others'.

The Sermons of Newman
First published in *The Critic* (USA), Vol. XXII, No. 6, June–July 1964. Taken from Muriel Spark's introduction to *Cardinal Newman's Best Plain Sermons* (New York: Herder and Herder, 1964); published in the UK as the foreword to *Realizations: Newman's Own Selection of His Sermons* (London: Darton, Longman and Todd, 1964).

Newman's Journals
Review of *John Henry Newman: Autobiographical Writings* (London: Sheed & Ward, 1956), published in the *Observer*, 1956.

An Exile's Path
Review of Sean O'Faolain, *Newman's Way* (London: Longmans), published in the *Observer*, Sunday 30 November 1952.

A Sleep of Prisoners
Review of play by Christopher Fry for the Religious Drama Society, written especially for the Festival of Britain and performed at St Mary's Church, Oxford, 1951. Published in the *Spectator*, 27 April 1951.

Psychic Searchlight
Review of D.J. West, *Psychical Research To-day* (London: Gerald Duckworth, 1954), published in the *Observer* ('Shorter Notices'), Sunday 1 August 1954, signed 'M.S.'.

A Pardon for the Guy
Essay on Guy Fawkes, forgiveness and a plea for a royal pardon. Published in the *Observer*, London, 6 November 1977 (abridged and edited by the *Observer*).

The Religion of an Agnostic: A Sacramental View of the World in the Writings of Proust
Essay published in *The Church of England Newspaper* on Friday 27 November 1953.

The Only Problem
Preface to the novel *The Only Problem* by Muriel Spark, published as a signed and limited first edition by the Franklin Library (Pennsylvania, 1984).

The Mystery of Job's Suffering
Review of C.G. Jung, *Answer to Job* (London: Routledge & Kegan Paul, 1954), translated by R.F.C. Hull, published in *The Church of England Newspaper*, 15 April 1955.

An Unknown Author
Review of *The Book of Job*, translated and introduced by Raymond P. Scheindlin (New York: W.W. Norton & Co., 1998), published under 'Meditation' in the *Literary Review*, London, October 1998.

Man's Estate
Review of Pierre Teilhard de Chardin, *Le Milieu Divin* (Paris: Seuil, 1957, and London: Collins, 1960), published in the *Observer*, 18 December 1960, under their title 'A Foretaste of Eternity'.

Kierkegaard
Review of T.H. Croxall, *Meditations from Kierkegaard* (London: Nisbet, 1956) and *Kierkegaard Commentary* (London: Nisbet / New York: Harper & Brothers, 1956), published in the *Observer*, Sunday 29 July 1956.

Karl Heim: Two Important Works
Review of Karl Heim, *The Transformation of the Scientific World View* (London: SCM Press, 1953) and *Christian Faith and Natural Science* (London: SCM Press, 1954) published in *Journal of the Scottish Secondary Teachers' Association*, February 1954.

Letter from Rome: The Elder Statesmen
Letter from Rome to *The New Yorker* magazine. Published (in an abridged version) in *The Tablet*, 24 March 1973, under the title 'When Israel went to the Vatican'.

Ritual and Recipe
Review of Garry Hogg, *Cannibalism and Human Sacrifice* (London: Robert Hale, 1958), published in the *Observer*, Sunday 27 July 1958.

The Next World and Back
Response to the brief 'A place I have never been to but would like to go', commissioned by and published in *The New York Times, Sophisticated Traveler*, 4 March 1990, under their title 'A Peek Through the Pearly Gates'.

Index of Names

Alexander, Sir Kenneth 102
Allen, Jay Presson 150
Atatürk, Kemal 89, 92
Auden, W.H. 17, 67, 79
Austen, Howard 171
Austen, Jane 111, 144

Baudelaire, Charles 73, 173
Beardsley, Aubrey 145
Beerbohm, Max 107
Belloc, Hilaire 57
Bellow, Saul 103
Blackwood, Algernon 57
Boccaccio, Giovanni 16
Böll, Heinrich 155, 160
Bonaparte, Napoleon 113
Brentano, Bettina 113–14
Brontë, Anne 49, 50, 71, 75, 114–20, 171
Brontë, Branwell 49, 114–20
Brontë, Charlotte 46, 48–49, 71, 75, 114–20, 171
Brontë, Emily 46–53, 71, 75, 114–20, 171
   Wuthering Heights 121–23
Browning, Elizabeth Barrett 171
Browning, Robert 80, 102
Burchett, George 44
Burne-Jones, Edward 40
Burns, Robert 18–21, 46, 50, 51
Byron, George Gordon (6th Baron Byron) 11–12, 16, 46, 129, 132, 137

Caballé, Montserrat 82
Campbell, Roy 149
Carlyle, Jane 124
Carroll, Lewis 16
Cecil, Lord David 47, 51
Chardin, Teilhard de 199–200
Chekhov, Anton 22, 103
Chesterton, G.K. 57
Clairmont, Claire 137–40
Clare, John 22, 50, 51
Clough, Arthur Hugh 17, 80
Coleridge, Samuel Taylor 16–17
Conrad, Joseph 103
Cowper, William 46, 52

Dante Alighieri 11, 16
Day Lewis, Cecil 67
de la Mare, Walter 22, 57
de La Tour, Georges 79, 191
Dickinson, Emily 36
Dryden, John 45

Eliot, George (Mary Anne Evans) 123
Eliot, T.S. 31–32, 33–34, 35–36, 103, 143, 159, 165–66, 173
Elliott, Denholm 32, 183
Emerson, Ralph Waldo 36

Fauré, Felix 5
Fawkes, Guy 184–86
Finlay, Ian Hamilton 142
FitzGerald, Edward 40–41
Forster, E.M. 103

INDEX OF NAMES

Francesca, Piero della 6–8, 95
Fry, Christopher 182–83
Frost, Robert 22, 36–38
Froude, James Anthony 179

Gaskell, Elizabeth 123–24
Gide, André 158, 159
Godwin, William 40, 126, 130, 131
Goethe, Johann Wolfgang von 113
Greene, Graham x, 76, 78, 103

Hamilton, Emma 110
Heim, Karl 201–203
Hitler, Adolf 29
Homer 171
Housman, Laurence 57
Hunt, Leigh 133, 133

Irving, Washington 129

James, Henry 13, 71, 86, 88, 144, 160, 171
John XXIII (Pope) 23
Josipovici, Gabriel 103
Jung, C.G. 192–97

Kermode, Frank ix, xiii, 103
Kierkegaard, Søren 34, 160, 180, 201
Kingsley, Charles 178
Kipling, Rudyard 173
Kundera, Milan 103

Lear, Edward 16
Leighton, Margaret 32
Loti, Pierre 93

Macdonald, Dwight 34
Machiavelli, Niccolò 144
Mackenzie, Compton 57
MacNeice, Louis 66, 67, 72, 149
Manzù, Giacomo 23–26
Márquez, Gabriel García 103
Marvell, Andrew 45
Masefeld, Constance 40–41
Masefield, John 12, 38–43, 75, 77, 148
Mee, Arthur 57

Meir, Golda 203–11
Merimée, Prosper 128
Milne, A.A. 57
Milton, John 45, 97
Mitchell, Margaret
 Gone with the Wind 151–54
Moffat, Sandy 99
Moore, Marianne 36
Moro, Aldo 100–101
Morris, William 40
Murdoch, Iris 61, 103
Mussolini, Benito 29

Nabokov, Vladimir xiii
Newman, Cardinal John Henry 101, 102, 176–82

O'Faolain, Sean 181–82
Ouida (Maria Louise Ramé) 112
Özal, Turgut 93

Paul VI (Pope) 203–11
Patroni-Griffi, Giuseppe 100
Peniakoff, Vladimir 15
Picasso, Pablo 23
Pirandello, Luigi 103
Plato 143, 160
Poe, Edgar Allan 36
Pope, Alexander 45
Powys, T.F. 160
Praz, Mario 82–83
Proust, Marcel 9, 61–62, 73, 103, 144, 147
 Remembrance of Things Past 186–90

Radcliffe, Ann 111
Raine, Kathleen 149
Ransom, John Crowe 22, 36
Read, Herbert 18, 103
Rilke, Rainer Maria 146, 147
Rogers, Paul 31
Rossetti, Dante Gabriel 40, 121
Ruskin, John 18

Schiller, Friedrich 113
Sciascia, Leonardo 78, 103

Scott, Paul 148
Scott, Sir Walter 21, 46, 51, 52, 58, 111, 129, 171
Shakespeare, William 9, 17, 45, 160
Shelley, Mary 71, 75, 78, 124–30, 137–40, 148
   Frankenstein 129, 130–36
   The Last Man 129, 130–36
Shelley, Percy Bysshe 40, 52, 71, 126–30, 133–34, 137–40
Simenon, Georges 157–60
Sitwell, Edith 57, 147–50
Smart, Christopher 173
Smith, Stevie 173
Spender, Stephen 67
Stevenson, Robert Louis 74, 103, 140–42
Strachey, Lytton 103
Swinburne, Algernon Charles 40, 41, 46
Symons, Arthur 48

Tate, Allen 103, 192
Taylor, Elizabeth 100
Thackeray, William Makepeace 111
Thomas, Dylan 17, 20
Trilling, Lionel 103
Tynan, Katharine 57

Updike, John 103

Van Eyck, Jan 172
Velázquez, Diego 172
Vidal, Gore 171
Visconti, Luchino 82, 100

Waugh, Evelyn 79, 148, 160
Weil, Simone 180
Wellesley, Arthur (1st Duke of Wellington) 6
Wells, H.G. 130–31
Wharton, Edith 71
Whitman, Walt 36
Williams, Edward 137–40
Williams, Jane 137–40
Wollstonecraft, Mary 126, 130
Woolf, Virginia 103
Wordsworth, William 22, 46

Yeats, W.B. 149
Young, Andrew 22–23